# Towards a Federal Europe?

This book deals with federalism and the EU. Much has been said – separately – on both topics. However, combining federalism with European integration and investigating their mutual impact is a rather recent endeavour. While there is little doubt that the majority of contemporary observers ascribe to the EU certain federal qualities, detecting processes of federalization here and there, scholars of comparative politics increasingly include the EU among their cases when investigating the impact of federalism on, for instance, policy making. The last decade saw a new wave of scholarly publications hit the shores where research on federalism and on the EU comes together. These emerging strands of research genuinely enrich our understanding of the EU and its politics.

This volume contributes to the debate on the federalisation of the federalisation of the EU at a moment in time when it is undergoing profound changes. The book is structured around four interrelated dimensions:

1) the constitutional/theoretical dimension;
2) the institutional vision;
3) the party/citizens dimension and
4) the policy dimension.

This structure allows the reader to consecutively "funnel down" from the more theoretical and abstract levels to the more concrete, policy oriented level.

This book was previously published as a special issue of the Journal of European Public Policy.

**Alexander H. Trechsel** is professor of political science and holder of the Swiss Chair on Federalism and Democracy at the European University Institute (EUI) in Florence. He is also co-director of the Research and Documentation Centre on Direct Democracy (c2d) and direct of the e-Democracy Center (e-DC), both located at the University of Geneva.

## Journal of European Public Policy Series

**Series Editor:** Jeremy Richardson is a Professor at Nuffield College, Oxford University

This series seeks to bring together some of the finest edited works on European Public Policy. Reprinting from Special Issues of the 'Journal of European Public Policy,' the focus is on using a wide range of social sciences approaches, both qualitative and quantitative, to gain a comprehensive and definitive understanding of Public Policy in Europe.

Towards a Federal Europe
*Edited by Alexander H. Trechsel*

The Disparity of European Integration
*Edited by Tanja A. Börzel*

# Towards a Federal Europe?

Edited by Alexander H. Trechsel

Routledge
Taylor & Francis Group

LONDON AND NEW YORK

First published 2006 by Routledge
2 Park Square, Milton Park, Abingdon, Oxon, OX14 4RN

Simultaneously published in the USA and Canada
by Routledge
270 Madison Ave, New York NY 10016

*Routledge is an imprint of the Taylor & Francis Group*

Transferred to Digital Printing 2008

Typeset in Agaramond by Techset Composition Limited

*British Library Cataloguing in Publication Data*
A catalogue record for this book is available from the British Library

*Library of Congress Cataloging in Publication Data*
A catalog record for this title has been requested

ISBN10: 0-415-37586-X (hbk)
ISBN10: 0-415-46388-2 (pbk)

ISBN13: 978-0-415-37586-3 (hbk)
ISBN13: 978-0-415-46388-1 (pbk)

# Contents

# Introduction

Alexander H. Trechsel

The present volume developed from the proceedings of an international conference inaugurating the 'Swiss Chair on Federalism and Democracy' at the European University Institute (Florence) in the summer of 2003.[1] The selected contributions have been revisited in relation to key issues that emerged during the conference, including discussions of the most recent political events related to the topic. This volume is structured around four interrelated dimensions: (1) the constitutional/theoretical dimension; (2) the institutional vision; (3) the party/citizens dimension; and (4) the policy dimension. This structure allows the reader to consecutively 'funnel down' from the more theoretical and abstract levels to the more concrete, policy-oriented level.

The guest editor's introductory contribution focuses on one possible avenue, hitherto much neglected, for further federalization of the European Union (EU). The piece compares the EU's efforts to give itself a Constitution with the federalization processes in Switzerland and the US. In doing so, it is argued that the unanimity principle for adopting the EU Constitution – and maybe even more importantly for its future amendments – may lead to a situation of deadlock. Such a risk is enhanced by the combination of the enlargement-induced increase in the number of veto-players, the extensive form the European Convention has given the EU Constitutional Treaty and the referendum procedure for ratification that has become fashionable in several member states. As a result of this constellation, the EU's 'federalist deficit' may come to play a role even more prominent than that played by the famous democratic deficit. Overcoming the federalist deficit may even become a prerequisite for a fundamental reduction of the democratic deficit.

Following this introductory piece, the *constitutional/theoretical dimension* contains two contributions that use the analytical tools provided by theories of federalism to understand and illuminate recent developments in the construction of Europe. Relying on a comparative approach, this section of the volume identifies fundamental principles and current trends in the field of federalism and the EU. The contribution by *Andreas Auer* focuses on the linkages between the institutions of federalism and constitutional law. Starting off with a reflection on the contribution of federalism to modern constitutionalism, the author defines federalism on the basis of three main principles, which necessarily have a constitutional impact. Building on these principles, Auer shows that federal constitutions are different from non-federal constitutions, as they have some specific functions to perform. As a result, federalism can be seen as a main factor for fostering the legal, as opposed to the political, nature of the constitution. Finally, Auer – somewhat provocatively – contends that in terms of constitutional theory, a federal Europe has already become reality.

*Klaus von Beyme* addresses the questions 'whose Europe?' and 'who speaks for the Europeans?' which involve a basic contradiction in European constitutional engineering: federalist autonomy developed against democratic representation on the basis of popular sovereignty of equal citizens. Working on a European constitution includes the search for a fair balance of the modes of representation. Von Beyme shows, however, that the balance remains precarious. Asymmetries in *de iure* institutional settings and in *de facto* social and economic developments permanently reshuffle the balance. Europe – more heterogeneous than any of the existing federations or decentralized states in Europe – will suffer from this contradiction and has to be prepared for these dynamics.

The second dimension focuses on *institutional visions*. Whereas the first dimension looks at the development of federal principles, theories, constitutional engineering and their respective current problems, this second dimension provides a set of provocative visions about the institutional future of the EU. In this section, *Yannis Papadopoulos* stresses the tendency for comparisons of the 'European federation' to be made with the US or Germany. Yet, the Swiss model of federalism is in several respects the one that is closer to the EU model. In view of the many similarities between the two models there is much to learn from the Swiss experience. In particular, and as this contribution shows, some forms of participatory decision-making may be added to the European federalist framework. By conceptually simulating this potential addendum, Papadopoulos concludes that not only gains in legitimacy, but a significant contribution to the formation of a common European identity could well result from such an evolution.

The third – *party/citizens* – dimension concentrates on the impact of federalism on political actors and the frameworks in which they evolve. To this end, the contributions focus on the European party system, on electoral competition, on citizens' attitudes towards the multi-layered sharing of political competencies that exists within the EU. *Lori Thorlakson* draws upon research in comparative federalism to find insights into how institutions affect party systems and party organization in multi-level systems. These insights are then applied to the EU in order to identify how its institutional structure, and proposals for its reform under the European Constitution, will affect party competition. Applying the lessons from federalism as to how institutions structure politics is also very useful for addressing broader questions such as possible future paths of development for the representative linkages between the citizens and the governing institutions of the EU, and debates on the development of a European 'demos'.

*Thomas Christin, Simon Hug and Tobias Schulz* emphasize that, as a federal system, the EU has to deal one way or another with the distribution of competencies. While conflicting views about this thorny issue are proffered in the literature, their contribution highlights the implications for political accountability. At the present time, most authors would concur that political accountability flowing from the institutional structure and decision-making in the EU is, at best, mixed. Thus, the authors propose to explore the ways in which the distribution of competencies is viewed from below, namely by the EU citizens. As one might expect, a considerable element in this view from below is its blurring.

Finally, the last dimension addresses the concrete level of *policy*. How do federalist arrangements affect policy outcomes in the EU? The emergence of regulatory policies at the EU level as well as the development of European monetary union (EMU) can be understood by adopting a comparative perspective that links federal theory with the ongoing debate on public policy in the EU. First, *Fernando Mendez* delves into an internet-related policy domain. In doing so, he traces the EU's growing involvement in this emerging policy field with particular reference to cybercrime. Using a comparative federalism framework he compares developments in the EU with two other federal polities, Switzerland and the US. Mendez identifies similarities with regard to the mobilization of actors and the interactions between different levels of government in all three cases. However, when it comes to the specificity of policy outcomes and, in particular, some of the co-ordination mechanisms that have developed, he argues that the EU comes closest to the Swiss case.

In his contribution, *David McKay* claims that there is a growing consensus among economists that certain aspects of the ways in which EMU operates are in need of reform. The purpose of this contribution is to place the findings and the implications of the economists' recommendations for reform in the context of federal theory and in particular to establish a link between policy choices that are deemed to be economically sustainable and those that may be politically sustainable. To this end, McKay applies the nascent rational choice and comparative politics literature on the self-sustainability of federal systems to EMU. The contribution first makes the claim that EMU effectively established the federal credentials of the EU before summarizing the findings and political implications of recent economics research on EMU. EMU is then placed in the context of federal theory. Finally, the author draws conclusions for the sustainability of the EMU federal project.

*Herbert Obinger, Stephan Leibfried and Francis Castles'* contribution builds upon their work on the link between federalism and welfare state consolidation in six federations. They show that federalism tends to slow down welfare state consolidation. At the same time, their research shows that welfare progress in federations was enabled by different forms of bypass mechanisms. By applying their framework to the EU, they suggest that European regulatory mechanisms, the role played by the European Court of Justice as well as 'the open method of co-ordination' could well constitute equivalents of such bypass mechanisms on the EU level.

The last word of this volume is given to political philosophy. *Andreas Follesdal* elaborates on the EU Constitutional Treaty's federal features from a political theory perspective. He discusses the balancing of stability and legitimacy in the EU federal polity, arguing that the Constitutional Treaty facilitates trust and merit as well as trustworthiness among Europeans. This is, according to the author, of utmost importance for the development and future deepening of citizens' and political élites' 'dual loyalty' towards their respective member states and the EU.

## NOTE

1 I would like to express my thanks to all conference participants for their contributions: Anneli Albi, Stefano Bartolini, Carina Bischoff, Beniamino Caravita di Torrito, Colin Crouch, Bertus de Villiers, Rory Domm, Jean-Claude Eeckhout, Navraj Ghaleigh, Peter Haldén, Joachim Jens Hesse, Michael Keating, Raphaël Kies, Charles Kleiber, Arnold Koller, Jan-Erik Lane, Alexis Lautenberg, Mario Mendez, Yves Mény, Kalypso Nicolaidis, Jean-Claude Piris, Wojciech Sadurski, Philippe C. Schmitter, Jürg Steiner, Ute Wachendorfer-Schmidt and Neil Walker. Numerous colleagues have greatly helped me in this project, either administratively or academically, among whom I would like to particularly thank Marko Bandler, Donatella della Porta, Bruno de Witte, Isabelle Engeli, Matteo Gianni, Adrienne Héritier, Peter Mair, Roberto Noccentini, Lawrence Pratchett, Josef Renggli, Carsten Schneider and Claudius Wagemann. My thanks also go to Sandra Brière and Caroline Chaix for their outstanding secretarial assistance in Florence and Geneva. The success of the conference owes a very great deal to the dedication and professionalism of Gabriella Unger – I cannot thank her enough for all she has done. In the process of producing this volume, Jeremy Richardson's expertise, helpfulness, flexibility and kindness were invaluable to me. Last but not least, my warmest thanks go to our formerly anonymous but now uncovered reviewer, Andreas Follesdal, whose insightful comments and perceptive suggestions improved the quality of all our contributions.

# How to federalize the European Union ... and why bother

Alexander H. Trechsel

> Europe has charted its own brand of constitutional federalism. It works. Why fix it?
>
> J.H.H. Weiler (2001: 70)

## 1. INTRODUCTION

The present volume deals with federalism and the European Union (EU). Much has been said −separately − on both topics. However, combining federalism with European integration and investigating their mutual impact is a rather recent endeavour in political science. While there is little doubt that the majority of contemporary observers ascribe to the EU certain federal qualities, detecting processes of federalization here and there, scholars of comparative politics increasingly include the EU among their cases when investigating the impact of federalism on, for instance, policy-making. The last decade saw a new wave of scholarly publications hit the shores where research on federalism and on the EU come together (for those explicitly seeking this linkage see, for example, Hesse and Wright 1996; Bednar *et al.* 1996; Follesdal 1997; McKay 1999, 2001, 2004; Burgess 2000; Kelemen 2000, 2003; Nicolaidis and Howse 2001; Abromeit 2002; Börzel and Hösli 2003; Dobson and Follesdal 2004; Swenden 2004; Filippov *et al.* 2004; Schmitter 2004). These emerging strands of research genuinely enrich our understanding of the EU and its politics. At the same time these contributions further develop the discipline of comparative politics – which is to say the discipline where the emphasis is put on comparison (Mair 1998: 309).

Despite this recent wave the topic of federalism and the EU is not washed out, yet. Indeed, quite to the contrary. In this volume, the authors seek to contribute to the debate on the federalization of the EU at a moment when it is undergoing profound changes. It is worth recalling a few very recent developments of major magnitude to the whole European integration process: the establishment of the euro as a strong and stable currency shared by over 300 million Europeans in the euro area; the grave crisis in transatlantic relations over the Iraq war that both provoked calls for a common European foreign policy and exposed profound differences in foreign policies among governments of EU member states. At the same time, we witnessed a truly unprecedented coherence of public opinion in the EU, with an overwhelming majority of Europeans opposing the war. With the 2004 enlargement the EU grew from a fifteen-member state construct to a polity encompassing twenty-five member states. When the next two states join, in 2007, the EU will have nearly half a billion citizens. Finally, the EU is currently in the process of creating a new constitutional settlement. This process started with the Laeken Declaration in 2001, followed by the establishment of the European Convention (2002–2003) that elaborated the Treaty establishing a Constitution, signed by all twenty-five member states on 29 October 2004 in Rome. All of the above cited developments provide high-octane fuel for the debate and topic of 'federalism and the EU'.

The authors of this volume address a large variety of issues, problems and possible solutions surrounding the initial question and title of this volume: 'Towards a federal Europe?' We have been guided by a comparative perspective. Every contribution explicitly tries to shed some further light on federal, or 'federalistic', features of the EU by using *flambeaux* provided by the experiences and trajectories of federal polities in Europe and elsewhere. We have all been stunned by a particularly enlightening *flambeau* that has remained mostly unlit in the comparative literature: the Swiss case. Let me briefly make an additional use of the latter and focus on its ability to shed some further light on the EU's ongoing federalization process. In particular, three fundamental structural and institutional developments that the EU is facing will be discussed which, in combination, may severely hinder the EU's capacity to adapt its constitutional order. By looking in particular at the Swiss but also at the American trajectories of federalization three options will be proposed for the EU to overcome – what one might call – its 'federalist deficit'.

## 2. PUTTING THE SWISS CASE INTO A EU PERSPECTIVE

Despite its small size, the Swiss political system is in many respects one of the most complex and fascinating among contemporary Western democracies. Not only does it build upon historical developments that were initiated centuries ago but, furthermore, the unique structure of today's society, the richness of its political institutions, the refined political arrangements and the multifaceted pressure for reforms constitute a laboratory for any scholar in the various disciplines of the social sciences. Often presented as the paradigmatic case of political integration (Deutsch 1976), consensual democracy (Lijphart 1984), multinationalism (Kymlicka 1995), or direct democratic decision-making (Butler and Ranney 1994), the Swiss political system has become a benchmark case for analyses in comparative politics.

When it comes to the study of the EU, references to the Swiss political system have become more frequent especially for the discussion surrounding the 'democratic deficit' of the EU, a term first coined by David Marquand in 1979 (see, for example, Moravcsik 2002; Zweifel 2002; Mény 2003). Also, scholars nowadays refer to similarities between the EU and Switzerland with regard to their respective decision- and policy-making procedures, fiscal arrangements, etc. Various contributions in this volume show that, when discussing the federalization process of the EU, the Swiss case is particularly insightful.

Nobody would challenge the statement that Switzerland is a federal state. However, the literature does not universally describe the EU as a federation or as constituting a federal arrangement. Some authors see the EU as a confederation, some as an international or supranational organization, others as a federation and yet others see it as a half-way house between a confederation and a federation, between a *Staatenbund* and a *Bundesstaat*. To be sure, these considerations are based on different definitions, yardsticks, conditions and interpretations of the minimal requirements for a governmental arrangement to be considered as 'federal'.

It is not the intention of this contribution to elaborate on these fine distinctions, which, in any case, have arguably overly preoccupied scholars of comparative federalism. Rather, it proposes a comparison between the federalization process, with an emphasis on 'process', of Switzerland and the EU. In doing so, it relies on a 'pot-pourri' of constitutional, institutional and political elements that are highlighted by the theory of comparative federalism.

### Similarities

First, in both multi-tier systems we find activities of government that are divided between central governments and sub-units in such a way that each level of government has some activities in which it makes final decisions (Riker 1975). Changes to this division cannot be arbitrarily made, as formal rules of the agreement and how such an agreement can be changed exist in both cases. In both systems, the sub-units have a certain autonomy that is guaranteed and, at the

same time, restricted by a central government. For example, the form of cantonal governments cannot be simply altered by the federal level just as the form of
EU member state governments cannot be altered by the EU (Auer 2005).

Second, both the EU and the Swiss process of federalization correspond to
what is known in the literature as the 'coming together' rather than the
'holding together' type (Linz and Stepan 1996; Stepan 1999; Swenden 2004;
Kriesi and Trechsel 2005 – contra: Benz 2003). Also, the process follows a
pattern that could be best described as *federalization by aggregation* rather
than by *devolution* (Friedrich 1968; Watts 1994). The Swiss constitution contains an extensive list of competencies – known in the German literature as
a *Kompetenzkatalog* – assigned to the various levels of the federal state. The
EU Treaties do not include such a detailed competence catalogue. However,
the European Constitution is a very detailed and extensive text that contains
no less than eight articles (Articles I-9 to I-17) concerning the – partly new –
division of competences. In Switzerland and in the EU, competences have
been given to the central state with the residue or the 'residual power' staying
at the cantonal and member state level respectively. For example, a certain
competence to act in a new policy domain first needs to be handed over by
the sub-units to the central level before the latter can take legislative action in
the particular domain.

Third, the legislative process on the EU and Swiss federal level contains
complex consultation procedures allowing the sub-units, and even the sub-
sub-units, to effectively participate in this process. Decision-making processes
in both systems are highly negotiable rather than competitive, reflecting a consociational style (Papadopoulos 2005). For example, similar to the EU, the
cantons are widely consulted before and during a federal legislative process.

Fourth, once policies are agreed upon, their implementation procedures place
both systems into the category of administrative rather than legislative federalism. In both systems co-operative arrangements prevail. In domains where the
centre is either solely competent or jointly so with the sub-units, the centre
relies on the sub-units to implement its policies. As a consequence one finds
in both systems a high degree of variation in the implementation of public policies (Papadopoulos 2005; Mendez 2005). One could even speak of *asymmetrical implementation outcomes*. For example, when the federal measures in the
domain of energy saving were adopted, their implementation differed quite
strongly from one canton to the other, with some cantons revealing a very
passive attitude while others interpreted the federal measures by drastically accel-
erating the implementation of energy saving policies (Delley and Mader 1986).
The same holds true, for example, for the liberalization in the EU energy sector
(Schmidt 2002) where similar variations could be observed.

This is, of course, directly related to a fifth similarity among the two systems:
both have a rather weak centre. Brussels and Bern have to rely on very limited
budgetary resources with a very limited administrative apparatus. Large parts of
both central budgets are primarily assigned to redistributive policies (Donahue
and Pollack 2001: 109; Kriesi 1998: 64f.) and in both cases a high degree of

vertical fiscal autonomy prevails (McKay 2001, 2005). For example, the levels of taxation and the taxation mechanisms vary considerably from one canton to the other. In other words, the taxes one pays vary quite significantly from one canton to the other. The same applies, of course, for the EU.

Finally, one should note that asymmetries are also produced through horizontal co-operation at the sub-unit level. For example, there are inter-cantonal agreements involving a limited number of cantons in various domains, such as education, health care or security. This is not dissimilar from the asymmetric arrangements that occur in the EU. For example, Schengen and EMU gave rise to sub-sets of member states willing to co-ordinate their policies. There are also a number of central dissimilarities in the federalization processes of the EU and of Switzerland.

## Dissimilarities

First, nation-states, including Switzerland, rely on a common defence policy that is lacking in the EU. However, with the development of a common foreign and security policy, the strengthening of the European security and defence policy is to be envisaged. The EU Constitution, if ratified, would make a significant step in this direction. In the long run, this could therefore become more of a similarity than a dissimilarity.

Second, the EU fundamentally differs from other federal orders with regard to its lack of a common *demos*. Usually, the supreme sovereignty over a state is exercised by the people. For some authors, the EU is unique in the sense that it does not presuppose the supreme authority and sovereignty of a federal *demos* (Weiler 2001: 57). This would lead one to believe that, in this regard, the EU and Switzerland fundamentally differ. On closer inspection, such a view can be challenged by an empirical observation: in Switzerland, the supreme authority of the federal state is not only embedded in the people, but also in the cantons. For amending the Swiss constitution, a mandatory and binding referendum has to take place and a double majority – the majority of the people and the majority of the cantons – must be reached. One could add that in Switzerland institutional procedures have emerged – and this could be of value for the EU – allowing for the co-existence of a number of sub-national *demoi* (Nicolaidis 2004), speaking different languages, belonging to different religious and cultural groups, in the absence of a real federal *demos*. Therefore, this point could well serve as an example of similarity rather than dissimilarity.

This leaves us with two central differences between the two federalization processes under consideration. First, the EU treaties allow – in theory – for unilateral secession of a member state from the Union. The EU Constitution, while adding a procedural complication to this possibility in the sense that a withdrawal procedure should be negotiated, does not fundamentally change this state of affairs. Even under the EU Constitution unilateral secession would be technically possible. In this regard, and when excluding the non-democratic federal arrangement of the late USSR as well as the Ethiopian Constitution of 1994 (article 39), no other federal state allows for such a possibility. While this unilateral secession possibility might be an almost unique feature of the EU, it is worth reiterating that to implement such a move politically would be extremely difficult.

The second fundamental difference between the Swiss and the EU federal arrangement is, however, of utmost importance. What could be looked upon as the equivalent of a constitutional order, the European Treaties, can only be altered through unanimous consent of the member states. With the exception of Canada (and then only for a very limited set of articles) no Federal Constitution contains a unanimity requirement among the sub-units for its amendments. In general, supermajorities of various kinds are required. The EU, however, must rely on the unanimity principle for changes to its fundamental order.

The unanimity requirement's democratic value could be questioned. Most of classic democratic thought relies on the existence of majorities, with minorities accepting the majorities' will. Such minorities must develop a form of trust in the majority not to abuse power (see Follesdal 2005). Unanimity, however, is not simply a 'super-super-qualified-majority' – in fact, it is not a majority at all, as the very concept of majority implies the potential existence of a minority, the emergence of which, by definition, is not possible in procedures that require unanimity.

## 3. DOES THE EU SUFFER FROM A 'FEDERALIST DEFICIT'?

To be sure, the principle of unanimity in the EU has been greatly reduced by the generalization of qualified majority voting mechanisms, introduced by the Single Act of 1986 and extended thereafter. And if ratified the EU Constitution would expand majority voting even further (Follesdal 2005). However, for Treaty amendments, unanimity prevails. Therefore, and as the EU Constitution remains a Treaty, it can only be adopted by unanimity among all member states, ratifying the Constitution in accordance with their respective constitutional requirements. Also, supposing the ratification process would be unanimous, future amendments to the Constitution would have to follow, in principle, the same logic (Art. IV-443 EU Constitution). Of course, it would be possible to change this very rule through an amendment that, however, would have to be submitted to the unanimity-based procedure.

One could argue that for the EU to hold on to the unanimity principle constitutes a 'federalist deficit'. To become truly federal, all polities composed of more than two sub-units, 'coming together' into a federation, have at some point abandoned the unanimity principle for amending their fundamental order. They all have overcome – or at least reduced – the 'federalist deficit' on their way towards stronger integration. In all federal states the units composing them have a say when it comes to the amendment of the federal constitutional order. Typically, they have an equal say, independently of their size even though in some federal polities there is a certain weighting according to size or other criteria. Generally, however, federal states give disproportionately stronger power to their smaller sub-units and disproportionately weaker power to their larger sub-units, which, of course, underpins the original idea of federalism (Follesdal 2005). In the American case, for example, an amendment to the Constitution needs to be ratified by at least three-quarters of all states, with every state having the same weight. A simple majority of cantons is needed in Switzerland with, however, six out of the twenty-six cantons having only half a vote. While any move from unanimity towards qualified majorities constitutes a reduction of the federalist deficit, the Swiss case illustrates a system in which the federalist deficit has been completely overcome. It combines the federal principle of equal power of the sub-units (with the six exceptions just mentioned) and the democratic principle of simple majority voting.

It is true that integration – and the EU is a prime example of this – is possible without reducing or overcoming such a federalist deficit. For half a century, the EU has precisely done this. However, does this presage that the federalist deficit – the unanimity requirement for amending its fundamental order – will remain unproblematic in the future? If examined as an isolated feature, some may conclude that the federalist deficit will not hinder EU integration, just as it did not constitute an insurmountable obstacle for integration in the past. Therefore, why bother? This is a legitimate question and it may well be the case that there is no need to bother. Institutional features, however, rarely develop their effects in isolation and, unless one ignores the more complex institutional set-up of the EU integration process, the question 'why bother?' cannot remain rhetorical. Put simply, it can be argued that this is not just a rhetorical question but rather a fundamental one that needs to be considered.

Today, the EU is facing (at least) three fundamental structural and institutional developments that could lead to a particular constellation in which the overcoming of the federalist deficit may well become essential for future steps in European integration: (a) the expanded number of veto players through the recent (and future) enlargement of the EU; (b) the proposed Treaty on the European Constitution drafted as a detailed text with a clear division of competences; and (c) the increasing use of national referendums on EU integration.

## (a) The number of veto players

With the accession of the ten new EU member states on 1 May 2004 the (theoretical) veto probability for future integration steps has significantly increased. It goes without saying that increasing the number of veto players decreases the probability of unanimity. In practice, this theoretical rule can only be overturned if the additional veto players are perfect clones of the initial set of veto players. This, however, is clearly not the case (see also Tsebelis 2002 on the number and type of veto players; Obinger *et al.* 2005). Social, economic, political, geographic, linguistic and religious heterogeneity has significantly increased with the most recent round of enlargement. And should the accession negotiations with Bulgaria, Romania, Croatia and Turkey result in a twenty-nine member state EU, this heterogeneity would be amplified even further.

## (b) A detailed constitutional framework

As already mentioned, the European Convention has drafted – instead of opting for a lean constitution, containing but a small number of general principles *à l'américaine* – an *extensive* constitutional text that contains a large number of detailed provisions *à l'allemande* or *à la suisse*. It is sound to hypothesize that the more detailed a constitution defining the fundamental order of a polity, the more likely such a constitution's need to be amended. The American Constitution is one of the most stable in the world and has been amended on only six occasions since World War II. Of course, the stability of the US Constitution does not mean that constitutional law in the US does not evolve. It very much does so, above all through the role of the judiciary. By contrast, the German *Grundgesetz* has undergone over fifty amendments since 1949 and the Swiss Constitution has been altered more than a hundred times over the same period. There is no indication that would allow us to believe that the European Constitution would remain static; in fact, some future amendments are already being discussed with the Constitution not even ratified yet (i.e. future enlargements of the EU would alter the content of the European Constitution). As Swenden (2004: 388) accurately states: 'Comparative federalism makes it clear that detailed *and* rigid competence catalogues do not generally exist.' And even though the proposal of the German *Länder* to include such a detailed competence catalogue in the European Constitution was dismissed by the Convention at a rather early stage (Börzel 2003: 4), the Treaty establishing a European Constitution is very detailed indeed. A simple word count shows that the European Constitution is roughly fifteen times more voluminous than its American counterpart adopted by the Convention in Philadelphia (but only about three times as voluminous as the Swiss Federal Constitution).

## (c) National referendums

As Hug (2002: 115) remarks, no other subject has – cross-nationally – 'led to as many referendums as the process of European integration'. After the ratification process of the European Constitution, only three member states will remain that never held a referendum on an EU-related issue, namely Cyprus, Germany and Greece. In some of the member states, the holding of a binding referendum on amendments to EU Treaties is mandatory (Denmark, Ireland). Most of the new member states have a rather large array of direct democratic institutions embedded in their constitutions (Auer and Bützer 2001) and referendums on European integration are therefore, as Hug (2002: 115) rightly argues, 'likely to occur'.

But why would these three factors all of a sudden transform the federalist deficit into an integration-blocking feature? After all, it can be argued that – in itself – a larger number of veto players only *theoretically* increases the probability of failures in the integration process, as mechanisms have long been found – mainly in negotiations at the top – that allow for unanimous outcomes. The recent signing of the Treaty on the European Constitution as well as the opening of negotiations for Turkey's accession could well substantiate such an argument. The crux is that the risks of deadlock do not so much occur within the EU's 'summit diplomacy' (Lijphart 1968), but are heightened through a 'joint *popular* decision trap' (Scharpf 1985, 1988), created by the holding of national referendums, either because the latter are legally required or, more frequently, because governments of member states take an ad-hoc decision to hold a referendum. 'Summit diplomacy' enables consensual or unanimous decisions simply because the decision-makers are able to deliberate, bargain, co-operate and co-ordinate their actions. And here lies the fundamental difference with the simultaneous or consecutive holding of national referendums on the same issue: in referendums, the decision-makers – the electorates – have no means for closing deals with each other, no mechanisms for previously negotiated mutual agreements. They are isolated (if held simultaneously) or at best only marginally cross-influenced (if held consecutively) majoritarian decisions by millions of voters. In the EU context and under the rules of unanimity, a very small majority of voters within a very small country can block twenty-four member states.

Without any doubt the increased, and still rising, number of member states has augmented the probability of more frequent referendums on EU integration. And because of its constant need for adaptation the question arises as to whether the amendment procedure for the future EU constitutional order will not periodically run the danger of deadlock. The painful ratification procedures of both the Maastricht and the Nice Treaties showed that the federalist deficit loosens rather than strengthens the cords of the twenty-five swords of Damocles. So far, the EU could – in a sense – 'muddle through' its Treaty revisions, despite the referendum threat. However, could there be an increasing risk of future fundamental reforms going nowhere because of the EU's federalist deficit? It could be argued that with the recent enlargement (as well as those that are likely to be forthcoming) and the more frequent call for referendums, the uncertainty introduced into the procedure has grown and continues to do so. Popular veto points have been added and the 'joint popular decision trap' is looming larger and larger.

Additionally, with regard to the European Constitution, and unlike Schengen or European monetary union (EMU), where a Europe '*à deux vitesses*' is possible, one can hardly imagine a EU whose member states are divided into those belonging to a 'constitution zone' and those belonging to a 'non-constitution zone'. Worse still, it only needs one single referendum to go wrong and twenty-four states are prevented from adopting a Constitution unless they opt, as suggested by scholars, for a violation of the Vienna Convention on the law of Treaties. In this context one may add that Schmitter (2000: 118ff.) suggested the elaboration of two different constitutions, therefore creating a 'constitution-one zone' and a 'constitution-two zone'. However, as Schmitter himself recognizes, both systems would have to be inserted 'with the same overriding judicial procedure for resolving eventual conflicts'. In other words, there would still be some need for a super-constitutional order on which all member states agree and our initial problem would remain unresolved.

The adoption of the Constitution and – arguably, even more importantly – its future amendment process might suffer from this 'unfinished business of federalization'. In a twenty-five member state organization whose political, social, economic, religious and cultural heterogeneity is greater than in any previous alliance that gave rise to a federal arrangement, this may lead to a 'creeping sclerosis' or even an atrophy of the integration process (for a similar line of reasoning, see Follesdal 2002). Reducing or even fully overcoming the federalist deficit might therefore become of the utmost importance to the future process of European integration.

## 4. HOW THE UNITED STATES AND SWITZERLAND DEALT WITH THE FEDERALIST DEFICIT

Other confederal or quasi-federal alliances have had to face a very similar dilemma at some point in their history. Evidently, the transition from the Articles of Confederation to the US Constitution comes to mind. By opting for a qualified majority of nine out of the thirteen states for the adoption of the Constitution (Article VII), the Philadelphia Convention of 1787 violated the Articles of Confederation that could only be amended through unanimity (Article XIII of the Articles of Confederation). In addition, the framers built into the US Constitution a provision for a three-fourths majority for future amendments (Article V). Two years later, representatives of the eleven states that had ratified the Constitution gathered in the First Congress in New York and officially adopted the US Constitution. Ratification in North Carolina followed the same year and the only state that had refused ratification, Rhode Island, finally ratified it a year later. *Nota bene*, Rhode Island was not only unique in that it initially refused ratification, it was also the only state that used referendary mechanisms for ratification. In a certain way, this move towards a qualified majority constituted a revolutionary act, as a new regime was established through a process that did not follow the rules of the former regime.

On the other hand, as Rakove (1996: 129) observes, the framers and many federalists, by proposing novel concepts of ratification, did not seize power for themselves in Philadelphia: 'Their stroke was not a coup d'état but a démarche – a sudden bold movement that shifted the country from a condition of political torpor and entropy into a feverish burst of activity.' It is noteworthy that the easing of the federalist deficit (the question of the number of states needed for ratification) was by far not as heatedly debated as the procedure by which the new Constitution should be ratified, i.e. should the procedure be guided by a new form of (popular) legitimacy – through conventions – and would amendments to the proposed Constitution be legitimate during the ratification procedure (Rakove 1996: 94ff.)? In a sense the (illegal) reduction of the federalist deficit led to a truly new mechanism in the ratification process, aimed at giving the Constitution a higher form of democratic legitimacy than previous legal acts. Also, and we will come back to this point, further democratization of the American constitutional order was made possible by this reduction of the federalist deficit. For example, the first ten amendments – in the form of the Bill of Rights – were initially ratified between 1789 and 1790 by only eleven states but could nonetheless come into force at the end of the eighteenth century. As Dahl (2003: 27) notes: 'Incidentally, the two laggards, Georgia and Connecticut, finally did come around – but not until 1939!'

Interestingly enough, between the moment of adoption of the Constitution and its ratification by the two remaining states, North Carolina and Rhode Island, the latter were in some awkward position of 'non-alliance' as the Articles of Confederation ceased to exist with the adoption of the Constitution. The eleven ratifying states simply founded a new United States which only included the states that had ratified the Constitution with North Carolina and Rhode Island being (momentarily) ejected into some non-constitutional orbit. Would such a procedure serve as an example to be followed by the EU? Before proffering some thoughts in this respect, it is worth having a closer look at an alternative case, namely Switzerland and the way in which the Swiss, in 1848, overcame the federalist deficit contained in the 'Federal Contract' (*Bundesvertrag*) of 1815.

At the beginning of the nineteenth century, the government of the Swiss Confederation could be viewed as a sort of congress, the so-called '*Diet*'. The Draft Constitution of Switzerland was accepted by the *Diet* in the summer of 1848 and referred to the cantons for ratification. It is noteworthy that this decision of the *Diet* already contained the trick that made the overcoming of the federalist deficit possible (see Kölz 1992 for an excellent and detailed account; see also Auer 2004 on the same issue). The *Diet* in fact took two decisions. With the first, it agreed on the rules leading to the adoption of the Constitution. And these rules contained the majority principle and in this sense constituted a sovereign act. With the second decision, the *Diet* submitted the Draft Constitution to this procedure. The ratification process was difficult. While in some cases (Fribourg and Grisons) the cantonal Parliaments decided, most cantons had to refer to a popular vote. Nine out of the twenty-five cantons refused the Constitution, with rejecting majorities reaching up to 96 (!) per cent.

During the fall of 1848, the *Diet* gathered again and adopted the Federal Constitution, with the cantons having refused the ratification not taking part in the vote on the adoption but nevertheless accepting that the Constitution was imposed on them. Here lies the fundamental difference with the process leading to the adoption of the US Constitution. Not only did the non-ratifying cantons accept their fate and become part of the newly created federal state, but also the cantons that had ratified the Constitution accepted the non-ratifying cantons among them. Finally, contrary to the adoption of the American Constitution, the *Diet* grounded its decision to adopt the Federal Constitution on the explicit idea that a double majority was attained in the ratification process, a majority of the voting population and a majority of the cantons.

## 5. SHOULD THE EU OVERCOME ITS FEDERALIST DEFICIT AND, IF YES, HOW?

What can we learn from the Swiss experience with regard to the adventure of the European Constitution? The Swiss were facing a very similar dilemma to that which befalls the EU now. They had similar problems to solve not only for the adoption of the Constitution, but for its future revisions. In the Swiss case it was clear, from the beginning, that unanimity among the twenty-five cantons could not be an option. In this respect, the framers of the American Constitution came to a similar conclusion during the summer of 1887 (Rakove 1996). Also, in the Swiss case, it was clear that some, if not most, of the cantons would have to give the final word for ratification to their electorates.

Furthermore, the Swiss may have suspected that the ratification of their new constitution was only an initial act, to be followed by inevitably necessary constitutional changes for which a unanimity rule would represent a very high hurdle. Indeed, following its adoption in 1848, the Federal Constitution has thus far been amended 156 times. For such amendments to occur, a referendum has to be held in which both the people's and the cantons' *simple* majorities need to be attained. In this context, it has been erroneously stated (Swenden 2004: 379) that this high number of successful constitutional revisions stems from amendments that emerged from the grass roots in a bottom-up process. In fact, only fourteen popular initiatives were successful at the polls and only nineteen proposals (so-called counterproposals) directly linked to popular initiatives resulted in constitutional change. The bulk of all constitutional amendments (123) resulted from a top-down process.

Let us counterfactually imagine that unanimity among the cantonal electorates would have been required for these amendments. The success rate would have dropped to one-third (54) of the 156 constitutional changes. In other words two-thirds of the successful amendments would have been blocked by one or more cantons. Figure 1 depicts the cantonal majorities in the successful amendment votes since 1848.

If the system had allowed for a *quasi-unanimity* – with only one canton dissenting from the others – to suffice for the ratification of the proposed amendment, the success rate would have already reached 50 per cent. If a qualified majority of four-fifths of the cantons had been needed, three out of four amendments would have gone through. With a qualified majority of two-thirds, the success rate would have gone up to almost 90 per cent. In other words, reducing the federalist deficit in Switzerland, even by the introduction of highly qualified majorities, would have drastically reduced the veto power of a single or a very small group of cantons.

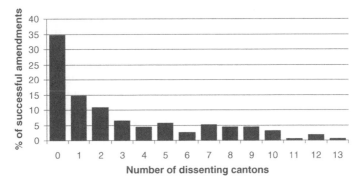

*Figure 1* Number of cantons opposing successful constitutional amendments in Switzerland (1848–2004)
*Sources*: c2d.unige.ch, www.admin.ch, own calculations

To be sure, such counterfactual reasoning and its extrapolation to the European context should be treated with a great deal of precaution. However, the Swiss experience shows the devastating effect of unanimity requirements if the agreement of a member state, in this case a canton, cannot be negotiated but must flow from a referendum. The question of reducing or even overcoming the federalist deficit within a polity in which *the consent of member states is dependent on a referendum vote* is not only legitimate but potentially crucial for the polity's capacity to adapt its fundamental order over time. And should national referendums become more generalized among EU member states, then the EU has to ask itself if the time has come to address the federalist deficit. But how? At least three options deserve consideration.

First, the EU could attempt to follow the American example and solve the problem by a similar revolutionary-type trick at this very moment, during the ratification procedure of its Constitution. Admittedly, when compared to the revolutions in the American and Swiss cases, it might be viewed more as a case of evolution given that in the EU qualified majority voting exists for infra-constitutional acts. Such an option is, however, problematic. For example, let us imagine a Rhode Island-type of scenario in which a member state rejects the Constitution in a nationwide referendum vote, but the Constitution is nevertheless adopted without this member state. The problem would be that as the adoption of the Constitution would put the EU Treaties out of operation, the non-ratifying member state would find itself in some 'non-constitutional-non-treaty-orbit'. This would correspond to a *re-foundation* of the EU, with the dissenting member state simply being 'kicked out' of the previous compact (for a discussion on this possibility, see De Witte 2004: 17f.).

The second option could be for the EU to follow the Swiss federalization process. While it can be doubted that the members of the European Convention consciously drew a parallel with the Swiss case, the similarities to the solution of the *Diet* are quite astounding. In the Spring of 2003, right at the end of the European Convention process, a declaration was added to the Constitution, stating that: 'if, two years after the signature of the Treaty establishing the Constitution, four fifths of the Member States have ratified it and one or more Member States have encountered difficulties in proceeding with ratification, the matter will be referred to the European Council.' It is of utmost importance to note that this formulation is the exact copy of the amendment procedure contained in the EU Constitution (Art. IV-443 EU Constitution). This – in De Witte's (2004: 17) words – 'intriguing declaration' can be looked upon as some precursor to the announced 'Plan B', a Franco-German proposal to make the adoption of the Constitution possible if at least twenty member states (four-fifths) ratify it.

Could 'Plan B' reduce the federalist deficit? While I believe this to be the case, it could also be argued that the core aspect of the federalist deficit would remain, as even if four-fifths – but not all member states – accepted the Constitution, the final decision over the adoption would be referred to the European Council. And European Council decisions must be taken, in principle, consensually or unanimously. However, the reduction of the federalist deficit would reside in the political possibility for the Council to take a unanimous decision despite some rejecting national referendums. Of course, this would constitute a breaching of the law and, in particular, Article 48 EU Treaty (De Witte 2004: 17) but, it seems, revolutions do not occur without such legally non-justifiable breaches of the law. It would be a purely political, though illegal, act. In this sense the 'revolutionary-type' declaration added to the EU Constitution (including its identical amendment procedure) comes – functionally – very close to the Swiss procedure of 1848.

Of course, the government of a country that accepts the Constitution within the European Council despite its electorate having rejected it in a referendum would certainly face a domestic legitimacy crisis, to say nothing of possible legal complications owing to the binding character of some of the national referendum provisions. It is at this point that the voluntary unilateral secession option could become important.

Finally, there could have been a third and novel option. The declaration – and consequently 'Plan B' – could have been dropped, with the EU Constitution therefore having to go through the 'referendum roulette' in which a single 'no' would be deadly to the Constitution. The Constitution itself could have introduced an amendment procedure based on a qualified majority. If the Constitution would survive the unanimous ratification procedure it would avoid any legitimacy-threatening revolutionary type of act. And by virtue of the majority principle for amendments, the federalist deficit would have been overcome. However, for now this option is consigned to the dustbin of history, unless the whole constitutionalizing exercise is reopened following a negative outcome of the current ratification process. The European Council adopted the EU Constitution without removing the famous declaration on ratification, therefore adopting the second 'Swiss-type' option.

## 6. CONCLUSION

This contribution has sought to draw attention to the question of the federalist deficit and its pertinence to the future integration process. But an important caveat should be added. It might well be that the EU does not want and does not even need to reduce or completely overcome this federalist deficit. In the absence of a clearly stated *finalité politique*, 'integration as usual' could be pursued in the future. However, if such is the case, the EU might actually do better without a Constitution. Or, at best, with a Constitution that states the big principles and that, in the name of efficiency, would not need to be as regularly adapted as the detailed provisions contained in the EU Constitution.

But has it not become a bit late for arguing against the drafting of a detailed EU Constitution? Has the Constitution not gone too far already, such that it cannot be shipwrecked without very negative effects on the whole integration process? We know that many confederal arrangements, including the Swiss and the US, have become federal because of internal and external threats. Endogenous threats are now also appearing in relation to the future integration process of the EU. And with twenty-five governmental and parliamentary veto players, of which about one-third delegates this veto power to the people by means of referendums, effectively expanding an already existing 'joint popular decision trap', the future importance of the federalist deficit should not be underestimated.

One last point: could it be that the reduction or complete overcoming of the federalist deficit may be useful and desirable – if not bluntly necessary – to reduce the democratic deficit of the EU? So far, the EU has managed to democratize various aspects of its institutions and functioning despite the federalist deficit. Yet, as this contribution has contended, the federalist deficit has the potential to block further integration – and likewise democratization of the EU polity. The Swiss, and to some extent the American, examples show that this has happened before. To give but a few examples: the introduction of the Bill of Rights; several extensions of the right to vote, the direct elections of senators; the introduction of new, and the extension of existing, instruments of direct democracy would not have gone through (or at least not without further attempts) under the rule of unanimity. Hence, could it be credible to affirm, without seeking to ring any alarmist bell, that, for the EU, future democratization – paradoxically enough – may be dependent on the prior easing of the federalist deficit?

**Addresses for correspondence:** Alexander H. Trechsel, Department of Political and Social Sciences, European University Institute, Via dei Roccettini 9, I-50016 San Domenico di Fiesole (Fl), Italy. Tel: (+39) 055 4685 442. Fax: (+39) 055 4685 201. email: Alexander.Trechsel@iue.it and Research and Documentation Centre on Direct Democracy (c2d), Faculté de droit, Université de Genève, 40, bd. du Pont-d'Arve, CH-1211 Geneva 4, Switzerland. Tel: (+41) 22 379 8533. Fax: (+41) 22 379 8536. email: Alexandre.Trechsel@droit.unige.ch

# REFERENCES

Abromeit, H. (2002) 'Contours of a European federation', *Regional and Federal Studies* 12(1): 1–20.

Auer, A. (2004) 'Referenden und europäische Öffentlichkeit', *Zeitschrift für Staats-und Europawissenschaften* 2(4): 580–96.

Auer, A. (2005) 'The constitutional scheme of federalism', *Journal of European Public Policy* 12(3): 419–431.

Auer, A. and Bützer, M. (eds) (2001) *Direct Democracy: The Eastern and Central European Experience*, Aldershot: Ashgate.

Bednar, J., Ferejohn, J. and Garrett, G. (1996) 'The politics of European federalism', *International Review of Law and Economics* 16(3): 279–94.

Benz, A. (2003) 'Demokratiereform durch Föderalisierung?', in C. Offe (ed.), *Demokratisierung der Demokratie. Diagnosen und Reformvorschläge*, Frankfurt/ New York: Campus, pp. 169–92.

Börzel, T.A. (2003) 'What can federalism teach us about the EU? The German experience', *The Federal Trust for education and research online paper 17/02*, available at http://www.fedtrust.co.uk/uploads/constitution/17_03.pdf

Börzel, T.A. and Hösli, M.O. (2003) 'Brussels between Berlin and Bern: comparative federalism meets the European Union', *Governance* 16(2): 179–202.

Burgess, M. (2000) *Federalism and European Union*, London: Routledge.

Butler, D. and Ranney, A. (1994) *Referendums around the World. The Growing Use of Direct Democracy*, Washington DC: The AEI Press.

Dahl, R.A. (2003) *How Democratic is the American Constitution?*, 2nd edn, New Haven: Yale University Press.

Delley, J.-D. and Mader, L. (1986) *L'Etat face au défi énergétique*, Lausanne: Payot.

Deutsch, K.W. (1976) *Die Schweiz als ein paradigmatischer Fall politischer Integration*, Bern: Haupt.

De Witte, B. (2004) *The National Constitutional Dimension of European Treaty Revision. Evolution and Recent Debates*, Second Walter van Gerven Lecture, Leuven Centre for a Common Law of Europe, Groningen: Europa Law Publishing.

Dobson, L. and Follesdal, A. (eds) (2004) *Political Theory and the European Constitution*, London: Routledge.

Donahue, J.D. and Pollack, M.A. (2001) 'Centralization and its discontents: the rhythms of federalism in the United States and the European Union', in K. Nicolaidis and R. Howse (eds), *The Federal Vision. Legitimacy and Levels of Governance in the United States and the European Union*, Oxford: Oxford University Press, pp. 73–117.

Filippov, M., Ordeshook, P.C. and Shvetsova, O. (2004) *Designing Federalism. A Theory of Self-Sustainable Federal Institutions*, Cambridge: Cambridge University Press.

Follesdal, A. (1997) 'Democracy and federalism in the EU: a liberal contractualist perspective', in A. Follesdal and P. Koslowski (eds), *Democracy and the European Union*, Berlin: Springer, pp. 231–53.

Follesdal, A. (2002) 'Drafting a European Constitution – challenges and opportunities', *Constitutionalism Web-Papers* ConWEB No. 4/2002, available at http://les1.man.ac.uk/conweb/

Follesdal, A. (2005) 'Towards a stable *finalité* with federal features? The balancing acts of the Constitutional Treaty for Europe', *Journal of European Public Policy* 12(3): 572–589.

Friedrich, C.J. (1968) *Trends of Federalism in Theory and Practice*, New York: Praeger.

Hesse, J.J. and Wright, V. (eds) (1996) *Federalizing Europe? The Costs, Benefits, and Preconditions of Federal Political Systems*, Oxford: Oxford University Press.

Hug, S. (2002) *Voices of Europe. Citizens, Referendums, and European Integration*, Lanham: Rowman & Littlefield.

Kelemen, D. (2000) 'Regulatory federalism: EU environmental regulation in comparative perspective', *Journal of Public Policy* 20(3): 133–67.

Kelemen, D. (2003) 'The structure and dynamics of EU federalism', *Comparative Political Studies* 36(1–2): 184–208.

Kölz, A. (1992) *Neuere Schweizerische Verfassungsgeschichte. Ihre Grundlagen vom Ende der Alten Eidgenossenschaft bis 1848*, Bern: Stämpfli.

Kriesi, H. (1998) *Le système politique Suisse*, Paris: Economica.

Kriesi, H. and Trechsel, A.H. (2005) (forthcoming) *The Politics of Switzerland. Continuity and Change in a Consensus-Democracy*, Cambridge: Cambridge University Press.

Kymlicka, W. (1995) *Multicultural Citizenship. A Liberal Theory of Minority Rights*, Oxford: Clarendon Press.

Lijphart, A. (1968) *The Politics of Accommodation: Pluralism and Democracy in the Netherlands*, Berkeley: University of California Press.

Lijphart, A. (1984) *Democracies. Patterns of Majoritarian and Consensus Government in Twenty-One Countries*, New Haven: Yale University Press.

Linz, J. and Stepan, A. (1996) *Problems of Democratic Transition and Consolidation: Southern Europe, South America, and Post-Communist Europe*, Baltimore: The Johns Hopkins University Press.

Mair, P. (1998) 'Comparative politics: an overview', in R.E. Goodin and H.D. Klingemann (eds), *A New Handbook of Political Science*, Oxford: Oxford University Press, pp. 309–35.

Marquand, D. (1979) *Parliament for Europe*, London: Jonathan Cape.

McKay, D. (1999) *Federalism and the European Union. A Political Economy Perspective*, Oxford: Oxford University Press.

McKay, D. (2001) *Designing Europe: Comparative Lessons from the Federal Experience*, Oxford: Oxford University Press.

McKay, D. (2004) 'The EU as a self-sustaining federation: specifying the constitutional conditions', in L. Dobson and A. Follesdal (eds), *Political Theory and the European Constitution*, London: Routledge, pp. 23–39.

McKay, D. (2005) 'Economic logic or political logic? Economic theory, federal theory and EMU', *Journal of European Public Policy* 12(3): 528–544.

Mendez, F. (2005) 'The European Union and cybercrime: insights from comparative federalism', *Journal of European Public Policy* 12(3): 509–527.

Mény, Y. (2003) 'De la démocratie en Europe: old concepts and new challenges', *Journal of Common Market Studies* 41(1): 1–13.

Moravcsik, A. (2002) 'In defence of the "democratic deficit": reassessing legitimacy in the European Union', *Journal of Common Market Studies* 40(4): 603–24.

Nicolaidis, K. (2004) 'We the peoples of Europe . . .', *Foreign Affairs* 83(6): 97–110.

Nicolaidis, K. and Howse, R. (eds) (2001) *The Federal Vision. Legitimacy and Levels of Government in the United States and the European Union*, Oxford: Oxford University Press.

Obinger, H., Leibfried, S. and Castles, F.G. (2005) 'Bypasses to a social Europe? Lessons from federal experience', *Journal of European Public Policy* 12(3): 545–571.

Papadopoulos, Y. (2005) 'Implementing (and radicalizing) art. I-47.4 of the Constitution: is the addition of some (semi-)direct democracy to the nascent consociational European federation just Swiss folklore?', *Journal of European Public Policy* 12(3): 448–467.

Rakove, J.N. (1996) *Original Meanings. Politics and Ideas in the Making of the Constitution*, New York: Vintage Books.

Riker, W.H. (1975) 'Federalism', in F.I. Greenstein and N.W. Polsby (eds), *Handbook of Political Science. Volume 5: Governmental Institutions and Processes*, Reading: Addison-Wesley, pp. 93–172.

Scharpf, F.W. (1985) 'Die Politikverflechtungs-Falle: Europäische Integration und deutscher Föderalismus im Vergleich', *Politische Vierteljahresschrift* 26(4): 323–56.

Scharpf, F.W. (1988) 'The joint-decision trap: lessons from German federalism and European integration', *Public Administration* 66(3): 239–78.

Schmidt, V.A. (2002) 'Europeanization and the mechanics of economic policy adjustment', *Journal of European Public Policy* 9(6): 894–912.

Schmitter, P.C. (2000) *How to Democratize the European Union . . . And Why Bother*, Lanham: Rowman & Littlefield.

Schmitter, P.C. (2004) 'Is federalism for Europe a solution or a problem: Tocqueville inverted, perverted or subverted?', in L. Dobson and A. Follesdal (eds), *Political Theory and the European Constitution*, London: Routledge, pp. 10–22.

Stepan, A. (1999) 'Federalism and democracy: beyond the US model', *Journal of Democracy* 10(4): 19–34.

Swenden, W. (2004) 'Is the European Union in need of a competence catalogue? Insights from comparative federalism', *Journal of Common Market Studies* 42(2): 371–92.

Tsebelis, G. (2002) *Veto Players: How Political Institutions Work*, Princeton: Princeton University Press.

Watts, R.L. (1994) 'Contemporary views on federalism', in B. de Villiers (ed.), *Evaluating Federal Systems*, Dordrecht: Martinus Nijhoff, pp. 1–29.

Weiler, J.H.H. (2001) 'Federalism without constitutionalism: Europe's sonderweg', in K. Nicolaidis and R. Howse (eds), *The Federal Vision. Legitimacy and Levels of Governance in the United States and the European Union*, Oxford: Oxford University Press, pp. 54–70.

Zweifel, T.D. (2002) '. . . Who is without sin cast the first stone: the EU's democratic deficit in comparison', *Journal of European Public Policy* 9(5): 812–40.

# The constitutional scheme of federalism

Andreas Auer

## INTRODUCTION

Federalism has definitely something to do with the constitution. But what exactly? The answer to this question is difficult, not only because both, federalism and the constitution, have many different meanings, but also because they are not, so to say, singing the same melody. Federalism is basically a state structure, whereas the constitution is the fundamental law of the state. One is a specific configuration of political entities, the other is a legal norm. Both notions thus refer to the state, showing how the latter is construed and indicating its legal foundation. Neither federalism nor the constitution exists elsewhere than in our minds, yet both have a significant political, economic and social impact. Federalism and the constitution are basic, and even very basic legal concepts. At the same time, they are ideologies, very basic ideologies. This paper will try to bring them together, both as legal concepts and as ideologies.

In the first place, history shows that federalism has contributed much to modern constitutionalism (I). Second, federalism can be defined on the basis of three main principles, which necessarily have a constitutional impact (II). Third, federal constitutions are different from non-federal constitutions, as they perform some specific functions (III). As a result, federalism can be seen as a main factor for fostering the legal, as opposed to the political, nature of the constitution (IV). Finally, I will turn to the question of whether the European Union (EU) can or must be seen as a federal-type construction, although denials of this existence strongly outnumber the affirmations of it, and even though the answer has undoubtedly an academic flavour (V).

## I. FEDERALISM AND CONSTITUTIONALISM

History of modern constitutionalism shows that federalism has played an important role in its appearance and further development. The importance of this role has hardly declined in recent times. From the Philadelphia Convention of 1787 to the European Convention of 2003, federalism has probably been the one structural feature which has most strongly fostered and promoted the idea as well as the necessity of constitution framing.

The most famous political documents arguing in favour of the enactment of a constitution were, of course, the 'Federalist Papers', a collection of pamphlets written by Alexander Hamilton, James Madison and John Jay in 1787/1788. The Founding Fathers of the American Constitution, which is still in force today, were convinced that the dilemma between the economic need for a stronger union and the political necessity of maintaining the sovereignty of the states could only be solved by inventing an entirely new state structure: two levels of government – the state and the Union – acting simultaneously on the individual citizen.[1] The idea of possible coexistence, within the same territory and the same legal order, of two governments, each one with its own constitution, its own institutions, its own laws and its own taxes, acting simultaneously on the same population, was a new[2] and indeed a revolutionary idea at the end of the eighteenth century. Federalism can thus be said to stand – more than the constitution itself, more than separation of powers and much more than democracy – as the one most outstanding invention of the American Founding Fathers. Nothing of what has happened in constitutional history since these early days – and many things have happened as we all know – can alter the fact that the very first national constitution was indeed a federal constitution.

The Swiss experience in constitution framing owes much to the American model. The failure of the first Helvetic Constitution of 1798, imposed by a French conqueror named Napoleon Bonaparte, was mainly due to its stubborn ignorance of the living strength of the cantons, refractory to any uniformity, be it in the name of the revolution. Yet economic pressures made it necessary to overcome the traditional confederate state structure, going back to the Middle Ages, which had proved to be unable to promote and to protect efficiently the free movement of persons and goods among the different constituencies of the country. The Constitution of 1848 owes its undeniable success mainly to its federal nature, which has resisted two major constitutional revisions (1874 and 1999) and up to as many as 216 constitutional amendments submitted to the people.[3] The Swiss Constitution, and indeed Switzerland, cannot be but federal.

The dilemma faced by those who were called in 2003 to invent a new institutional framework for Europe is in some ways similar to the challenges with which the makers of the American and the Swiss Constitutions were confronted. Again, there was considerable need, both economic and social, for a stronger union among the peoples of Europe. Again, there was an equally strong political pressure for maintaining the sovereignty of the member states, 'masters of the treaties'. And again, the solution of this powerful contradiction was seen to result from the adoption of a constitution. Even if, mainly for political reasons, the concept of federalism was banished from the Convention, the process of framing the Constitution for Europe owed much to the typically federalist-type problems which modern Europe has to face, especially in the present context of enlargement. The very first Article of the Treaty establishing a Constitution for Europe (Cst.E) is full of concepts and terms which are familiar to every federalist state: 'conferred competences', 'common objectives', 'co-ordinated policies', 'the community way' of exercising competences, etc.

Of course, constitutionalism cannot be reduced to the federal phenomenon. There are many more non-federal constitutions in the world than there are federal ones. And it is well known that every single federal constitution is different from the others, to the point that comparisons become increasingly difficult. Yet many non-federal constitutions have to deal with, without saying so, typically federalist problems. The on-going process of decentralization and devolution in most modern so-called unitary states is nothing but a specific way of combining some degree of diversity with some degree of unity. Needless to say, the constitution is often called to give strength to, and to structure, this delicate balance. This is precisely what federalism is all about.

## II. THE BASIC CONSTITUTIONAL PRINCIPLES OF FEDERALISM

How can one explain the difficulties in defining federalism? Mainly because there are as many federalisms as there are federal states, each one considering its own specificities as being absolutely essential to the very concept of federalism. Political scientists and lawyers, politicians and journalists have long been trying to break that diversity down to some common rules.[4] Three basic principles or guidelines can be distinguished and must be combined in order to reveal the existence of a federal state experience: autonomy, superposition and participation.[5]

**Autonomy** means that the constituent units of a federal state structure enjoy more than just some delegated competences. They are autonomous in many ways: they have their own institutions and organs; they have their own laws and regulations; they have a constitution; they have legislators, governments and judges; they have at least some financial autonomy, meaning that they may raise taxes and decide freely upon their affectation. Constituent units thus have their own legal order. Being autonomous, they are just like sovereign states, without being sovereign states. This is so because their sovereignty is limited by the second principle, the principle of superposition.

**Superposition** means that the powers of constituent units and the way they make use of these powers are subordinate to the requirements of a superior legal order, i.e. the one formed by the federal unit. Laws and decisions of the federal unit are, and must be, binding for the constituent units. Federalism is not a supermarket where one may buy whatever one wants to. American and Swiss constitutional history shows that theories of 'nullification' or 'interposition', allowing constituent units to oppose their sovereignty to the application of a federal measure they dislike, amount to the very negation of federalism. Nothing prevails, in law, over the simple rule that federal regulations must be, in case of conflict, superior to state regulations. Another question is, of course, who is entitled to have the final word about questions where competences are contested between constituent and central units (see below, III C).

**Participation** basically means that the legal orders of the central unit and the legal orders of the constituent units are not strangers to each other. They are, on the contrary, so closely intertwined and connected as to appear to form but one legal order. Participation between two superposed legal levels is probably the most decisive feature of federal government (interlocking federalism[6]). But it is essential to recognize that participation must go both ways, bottom-up and top-down.

On the one hand, the constituent units have the possibility and, indeed, the obligation to participate in the process of defining, of enacting and of implementing federal rules and policies: the existence of a second chamber representing directly the constituent units, the power to initiate legislation, the right to be consulted before the enactment of a federal regulation or the conclusion of an international treaty, the possibility to apply to the constitutional court, and, most important, the obligation to implement and to enforce federal rules. By these means, and many more, the constituent units become directly involved in the process of defining and implementing the will and the policy of the federal unit.

On the other hand, the federal unit has also to contribute in some way to the adoption or the implementation of the laws and regulations of the constituent units. It cannot remain completely indifferent to the exercice of state autonomy. The central unit must not only recognize the existence and the autonomy of the constituent units. It also has to guarantee, on the international as well as on the national level of government, full respect and enforcement of the regular exercise, by the constituent units, of their powers and regulations. In other words, the federal unit has to somehow become involved in the process of formulating and implementing the will of the constituent units.

Federalism thus consists of a specific combination of self-rule (autonomy), of limited rule (superposition) and of shared rule (participation). The two levels of government are strongly and closely dependent on each other. Without the constituent units, the federal unit cannot exist. Without the latter, the former cannot be autonomous. Both have to work together, through a set of specific procedures, in order to accomplish their respective goals.

The three basic principles of federalism necessarily have constitutional significance and impact. Constitutions of federal states cannot but recognize the binding force of these principles, by defining their meaning, by protecting their coexistence and mutual reinforcement, and by guaranteeing their application. The words employed by constitutions may not matter so much. It is not essential that federal state systems be called by their real name. They may refer to other terms, like Switzerland wrongly calling itself a 'Confederation' since 1848. They may refer to the formula of 'an ever closer union', like the EU used to, or to 'the Community way' to exercise competences (Article 1 Cst.E). What is essential is not what constitutions say, but what they do, even without saying. If law as a norm is mainly fiction, it can also employ fictitious names. In other words, federalism may well exist, and does sometimes exist, without ever refering to the F-word. The opposite, of course, is also true: the mere reference to federalism does not necessarily create a federal state system.

## III. SPECIFIC FUNCTIONS OF FEDERAL CONSTITUTIONS

Federal constitutions are not like ordinary constitutions. Whatever the differences among them may be – in style, structure, function and wording – there are some points which only federal constitutions have to deal with. Three main points can be singled out: defining the units, allocating powers, and setting up a conflict resolution scheme.

### A. Defining the constituent units

Firstly, federal constitutions most often enumerate the constituent units which, together, form the federal or central unit. This enumeration means, in legal terms, that the existence of the constituent units is constitutionally guaranteed. In consequence, any change in the composition of the central unit – enlargement, secession, merger, division – implies a constitutional amendment, according to the specific procedure set forth by the constitution itself. There are exceptions, as we all know. But exceptions do not abolish, they confirm the rule and the rule requires some kind of constitutional anchorage of the constituent units. There is no higher legal recognition of the component units than their enshrinement in the federal constitution. In a federal system, constituent units are thus federally embedded units.

A constitution which does not mention any constituent unit can hardly be a federal constitution. And if there are non-federal constitutions that do mention the existence of some or of all decentralized units, there might be a case for asking if, in spite of the wording, they are not building up a federalist type of government.

In setting up the federal government and in recognizing and guaranteeing the existence of the constituent units, federal constitutions reveal their double face, so typical of the federalist experience. Federal constitutions are not merely constitutions of the central unit, enriched by some reference to constituent units. Federal constitutions belong to and 'constitute' both units, federal as well as constituent. They are superior to each one. Of course, they regularly have more sections and articles relating to the federal government than provisions concerning the constituent units. But that does not matter. What matters is that the conjunction, within the same constitution, of two types of provisions, one relating to the centre and the other to the periphery, is a strong factor for indicating that we are dealing with a federal constitution.

## B. Distribution of powers

Second, federal constitutions typically distribute state powers by attributing specific competences to the federal unit and/or to the component units. It is inconceivable that each component unit deals with whatever matter it wants to. It is equally unacceptable that the federal unit arbitrarily chooses to regulate any matter it feels fit to. Powers, competences and responsibilities are necessarily split or shared between the two levels of government and it is up to the constitution to operate this distribution.

The distribution of competences by the constitution typically implies three distinct though closely related operations, i.e. defining the distribution formula, operating the initial distribution, and providing for a procedure for changing this initial distribution.

**Defining the distribution formula** means that the constitution has to set up the general principle according to which powers are being shared. It may attribute the general clause of competences to the component units. In that case, the constitution enumerates all powers, and only the powers, of the central unit, the remainder being left to the component units. It may, alternatively, list all the competences of the component units, leaving the remainder to the central unit. Finally, it may enumerate both the powers of the central unit and the powers of the constituent units. Most federal constitutions rely on the first model.

**Operating the initial distribution** means that the constitution, at the time of its adoption, enumerates the legislative, executive and financial competences of the centre, or of the periphery, according to the chosen distribution formula. Federal constitutions hence regularly contain a list of distinct competences conferred to the federal unit, such as national defence, criminal and civil law, social security, protection of the environment, economic policy, nuclear energy, foreign relations, and so forth. In doing so, the constitution shapes the specific meaning of its federalist nature. It may centralize large parts of state powers, leaving only crumbs to the component units. Or it may put heavy weight on the powers of the component units, delegating to the central unit only the powers which are felt to be absolutely essential. Between those extremes, there is an infinite variety of combinations, both quantitative and qualitative, with the result that every federal system has its own physionomy.

This is why federalism is such a flexible structure of government, to the point that it is sometimes accused of being so flexible that it gives 'everything to everybody'.

**Defining a procedure for changing the initial distribution** means that the constitution has to take into account the indisputable fact that things – the social, economic and political needs and priorities of state and society – necessarily change and that, with time, there is considerable pressure for centralizing or for decentralizing powers otherwise than the original or the actual constitution provides for. To operate modifications of the initial distribution of competences, several methods and techniques are available. Again, it is up to the constitution and its practice to set up those methods and techniques, ranging from direct and representative democracy to constitutional adjudication, and even customary law.

In Switzerland, for instance, as the constitution is amendable according to quite a flexible procedure, every single change in the distribution of competences between the federal and the constituent units implies a formal amendment to the constitution, subject to approval by a majority of the people and of the majority of the cantons. It is up to the citizens to decide upon the state of equilibrium between federal and cantonal powers. Two-thirds approximately of all constitutional amendments submitted to the people since 1874 dealt with some question of power-sharing between the Confederation and the cantons. Direct democracy therefore is the 'technique' chosen by the Swiss constitution in order to change the distribution of authority between the Confederation and the cantons.

In the United States, the constitution is extremely rigid and almost impossible to amend. According to the doctrine of implied powers set forth by the framers (Article I, Section 8, Clause 18) and developed by the Supreme Court as early as 1819, Congress is entitled to enact all laws that are 'necessary and proper for carrying into execution the foregoing (enumerated) powers'. Through a very extensive interpretation of this single constitutional clause, Court and Congress have been able to expand continually the powers of the Union without any formal change of the constitution. Statutory law, as well as judicial review, are thus the specific methods of adapting the distribution of powers retained by American constitutional practice to the tremendous changes that have occurred in the economic, social and political spheres of government.

## C. Conflict resolution scheme

As powers and competences are shared between the central unit and the component units, and as each unit is called to abide by this constitutional sharing, there will inevitably be conflicts, both negative and positive, relating to the exercise of these powers by either of the two spheres of government. Federalism is a complex feature for governing modern states. Complex systems must provide for some means to reduce complexity through litigation, arbitration, judicial decision or political authority. It comes as no surprise that every single federal state structure appoints some sort of umpire who is called to resolve federal-type conflicts. Being called to allocate powers and authority defined by the constitution, the conflict regulation scheme itself must be of constitutional value too. Yet again, there are all kinds of methods for conflict resolution.

There is one method, however, which is not only widespread, but also hardly avoidable: constitutional adjudication. Federalism has been the one most decisive factor for the establishment of constitutional adjudication. For Dicey, 'federalism, lastly, means legalism – the predominance of the judiciary in the Constitution'[7] and according to Kelsen, 'the institution of the constitutional tribunal achieves legally the political idea of federalism'.[8] In the United States, in Canada, in Germany, in Austria, Switzerland, Spain, Portugal and elsewhere, judicial review and constitutional adjudication were mainly established as a response to the challenge of federalist-type conflicts which regularly arose in the functioning of state power.

Various techniques have been developed to submit federalist-type conflicts to the constitutional judge. In centralized systems of constitutional adjudication, both the central unit and the component units are regularly entitled to appeal to the constitutional tribunal whenever an act adopted by one level violates the distribution of powers defined by the constitution. In decentralized systems of constitutional adjudication, too, acts and decisions adopted by one level can often be challenged before the constitutional judge for reasons relating directly to the division of authority.

Probably the most efficient device for solving conflicts arising between powers and regulations used and enacted by one or the other units composing the federal state is to enable individuals to bring these conflicts before the constitutional court. In other words, the pre-eminence of federal law over state law, as a by-product of the principle of superposition, is often recognized as a specific constitutional right. Rights, as Joe Weiler put it, are an important tool for integration. The legal remedies called *Verfassungsbeschwerde* in Germany, *amparo* in Spain or *recours de droit public* in Switzerland have the advantage of entrusting the procedural defence of the power distribution scheme provided for in the constitution to each individual and to his personal legal interests. Procedurally channelled egoism is thus an efficient and subtle instrument for preserving the division of powers between the federal and the component units.

The same applies to conflicts arising between different constituent units. Federal constitutions have to provide a way for resolving these conflicts and, again, the constitutional court is probably the most appropriate to do so.

## IV. THE LEGAL NATURE OF CONSTITUTIONAL LAW IN FEDERAL STATES

As a result of the constitutional significance of the three basic principles of federalism and as a consequence of the specific functions that federal constitutions regularly have to perform, constitutional law in federal states has long been recognized as being of a predominantly legal nature. In many non-federal states, such as France for instance, constitutional law has often been considered as consisting of nothing more than a simple set of political rules (Burdeau), which have little, if any, legal value. 'True' (i.e. civil) lawyers thus had problems in recognizing constitutional law as being part of law, and did not even think of comparing it, in legal terms, to contracts, trusts or criminal law. This was so because of the openly political nature of constitutions and the fragility which apparently results from this nature.

As federalism fosters and promotes constitutional adjudication procedures, courts are entrusted, entitled and indeed obliged to decide upon constitutional questions. Federalism was first in bringing the constitution to the courts, long before civil rights and liberties did the same. Courts cannot decide questions, constitutional or otherwise, without referring to legal arguments and without establishing precedents. If constitutional adjudication is a method of trying to domesticate politics (Favoreu), it is also a way to 'juridize' the constitution. As courts were slowly but steadily building up a body of judicial constitutional law within the field of federalism, the power of the political authorities to play in this field has been reduced, just as the rights of the citizens have been reinforced and protected. Federalism has contributed much to the evolution of the constitution from a political recipe to a legal norm.

This evolution also has an impact on legal education. If constitutional law nowadays is regularly taught and studied in law schools as an important branch of the legal order, and not only as an aspect of political science, it owes this mainly to federalism. In the end, it might well be that the constitution owes more to federalism than federalism owes to the constitution.

## V. THE EU AS A FEDERAL-TYPE CONSTRUCTION

It is a widely shared opinion, both in law and in political science, that the EU is something other than a federal-type construction.[9] Deprived as it is supposed to be of a common *demos*, the EU is not even considered as a state. Traditional concepts like 'federal state' or 'confederation' are thus abandoned in favour of vague formulas like 'a union of peoples and states', *Staatenverbund* or the like. According to this view, federalism is, at best or at worst, the future, but certainly not the present, of Europe. In order to realize that future and to become federal, the EU would have to accomplish determined steps and meet special, actually unfulfilled conditions on both the institutional and the political level.

On political battlefields and in the media, it might be a good point to draw the picture of a federally united Europe, and it might be worth questioning this perspective, which is so promising for some, and so frightening for others. Precisely because federalism as an ideology acts at the same time, but at different places and in different minds, as an ideology of centralization and as an ideology of decentralization, it can be used both ways. It is well known that in the US and on the EU level, the 'federalists' are supposed to favour a more closer union, whereas in Switzerland and Germany, the very same denomination advocates stronger cantons and *Länder*. It is somewhat surprising to realize how deeply and how directly the values of federalism are determined not by rational arguments and real experience, but by prejudice and presumptions based on these contradictory assumptions. Just as you will hardly find a French or a British scholar arguing scientifically in favour of federalism, you will have trouble finding a Swiss or a German scholar criticizing federalism as being inherently inappropriate. On the EU level, those who oppose both a stronger Europe and correspondingly a weakening of the nation states argue that the EU cannot and must not become federal. Federalism in this view is inherently bad, because the concept is identified with centralism. Those who are in favour of a stronger EU and accept that member states might become a bit weaker do not dare to advocate federalism either, because they are afraid that the F-word will do more harm than good in promoting their political goal. It comes therefore as no surprise that, for politicians, journalists and social scientists, the question of the federal or non-federal nature of the EU might well be asked and can be debated, but is very unlikely ever to receive a clear-cut answer.

In legal terms, in view of the well-established constitutional characteristics of federalism and in comparison with the wide variety of federal-type experiences on the level of national government, the answer leaves little if any doubt. The EU already is, and plainly is, nothing other than a multinational federal state construction. It can even be said to be more federal than many national federal states, like Canada or Belgium.

The member states of the EU are autonomous. They have their own legal orders, their own constitutions, their own institutions, their own resources and their own problems. They are sovereign, if sovereignty means that the member states are indeed the original, the first and the basic public entities in the Union and that they will keep on playing this decisive role. According to Article I-5 Cst.E, the EU 'shall respect (the) essential state functions (of the member states)'. However, they are no longer merely individual nation states. They have become member states, and as such they are part of a whole, the EU. Their sovereignty is clearly limited by EU law and policy.

The EU is superposed to the member states. Article I-10 Cst.E clearly states that 'the Constitution, and law adopted by the Union's institutions in exercising competences conferred on it, shall have primacy over the law of the member states'. Long before the adoption of the Constitution, the Community had developed its own legal order which the Court of Justice held to be, within its boundaries and powers, superior to the legal orders of the member states. The principles of primacy,[10] of direct effect[11] and of direct applicability[12] of community law, framed by the Court during the 1960s and the 1970s of the last century, the functional co-operation between the European and the national courts, the constant shift of significant state powers from the member states to the EU had the effect of evicting national law which was in conflict with community law. Today, it is fully admitted, although sometimes regretted, that EU legislation has a direct effect on EU citizens.

The EU and the member states both participate in the formulation of their respective policies and regulations. The European Council; Council of Ministers; European Parliament; European Commission; ratification, amendment and membership enlargement procedures – the member states are omnipresent in the institutional framework of the EU (Articles I-18–I-28 Cst.E). They apply the legal acts of the Union, both legislative (laws and framework laws) and non-legislative (regulations and decisions), thus acting within their legal orders on behalf of the EU. Their courts are bound by the legal acts of the Union, which prevail over conflicting national law. Those acts, as the Court noted early on, confer not only obligations but also rights to the individuals, rights which have become part of their legal heritage. On the other hand, the EU takes very much into account the existence and the legal orders as well as the policies of the member states (Article I-5 Cst.E). Being ratified and signed by all member states, the Constitution clearly designates them as the constituent units of the EU.

There is a clear division of powers and competences between the EU and the member states, defined and developed by the Constitution according to the principles of conferral (Article I-9.2 Cst.E), of subsidiarity (Article I-9.3 Cst.E) and of proportionality (Article I-9.4 Cst.E). The Constitution defines the distribution formula by stating that 'competences not conferred upon the Union in the Constitution remain with the member states' (Art. I-9.2). There is an initial attribution of powers, by defining areas of exclusive competences (Art. I-12 Cst.E), of shared competences (Article I-13 Cst.E) and of supporting, co-ordinating or complementary action (Article I-16 Cst.E). There are procedures for expanding or reducing the actual distribution of powers, either through the flexibility clause (Article I-17 Cst.E), or through revision of the Constitution (Article IV-7 Cst.E).

And finally, conflicts between EU law and national law are solved by a sophisticated and quite efficient set of judicial and political institutions and remedies. The Court of Justice is the central, although not the only, actor of conflict resolution within the EU (Articles III-266; III-267 Cst.E).[13]

So much being said, little is resolved. To be or not to be a federal-type construction does not, for the EU or any national state, answer the decisive questions relating to the relationships between the centre and the periphery, to the optimal degree of centralization or devolution, to the scope of primacy rule, to the meaning of subsidiarity, to the limits of direct effect, to the extent of judicial review. Yet it does, although this might well be a mainly academic consideration, remind those who have to give answers to these questions that the experience of European integration is unique, but only within a well-established set of federal traditions going back to the very early days of modern constitutionalism.

## CONCLUSION

The inherent diversity, great flexibility and surprising dynamics of federalism make it difficult to define this particular state structure in precise terms.

Federalism is a process much more than a given state of institutions and regulations. Yet it is strongly dependent on the latter. Since Maastricht at least, and even more so under the new Constitution for Europe, the dynamics of European integration have reached an intensity, both in qualitative and in quantitative terms, that meets all the legal requirements and characteristics which are attached in some way to federalism. Federal Europe has thus become a legal reality, even if the political debate about its nature and future will and shall continue.

**Address for correspondence:** Andreas Auer, Department of Constitutional Law and Research and Documentation Centre on Direct Democracy (c2d), Faculté de droit, Université de Genève, 40, bd. du Pont-d'Arve, CH-1211 Geneva 4, Switzerland. Tel: (+41) 22 379 8531. Fax: (+41) 22 379 8536. email: Andreas.Auer@droit.unige.ch

## NOTES

1 'The government of the Union, like that of each state, must be able to address itself immediately to the hopes and fears of individuals; and to attract to its support the strongest influence upon the human heart', The Federalist Papers, No. 16 (Hamilton); 'We must abandon the vain project of legislating upon the States in their collective capacities; we must extend the laws of the federal government to the individual citizens of America', ibid. No. 23 (Hamilton).
2 But see already Althusius, *Politica Methodica Digesta* (1603).
3 http://c2d.unige.ch
4 Among the fathers of the theory of federalism are Althusius, Hume, Proudhon, Laband, Jellinek, Scelle, Mouskhély, Wheare, Hughes, Friedrich, and many others.
5 Georges Scelle retained four elements, four laws: participation, superposition, division of competences and the 'governmental character of the local representatives', *Précis de droit des gens*, Vol. I, Paris 1932, 190 ss.
6 A. Follesdal, *Federalism*, Stanford, 2003.
7 A.V. Dicey, *An Introduction to the Study of the Law of the Constitution* (1855), London, 1959, 175.
8 H. Kelsen, Wesen und Entwicklung der Staatsgerichtsbarkeit, Veröffentlichungen der Vereinigung Deutscher Staatsrechtslehrer, 1929, 81.
9 For an informed yet rather sceptical discussion on the EU's federal features, see Scharpf (2001); Moravcsik (2001); Schmitter (2000); Riker (1996); Elazar (2001).
10 *Costa* v. *ENEL*, Case 6/64, 15 July 1964.
11 *Van Gend en Loos* v. *Netherlands Fiscal Administration*, Case 26/62, 5 February 1963.
12 *Italian Minister for Finance* v. *Simmenthal S.p.A*, Case 106/77, 9 March 1978.
13 C. Timmermans (2004) 'The European Union's judicial system', *CMLR* 41: 393–405.

## BASIC REFERENCES

Auer, A., Malinverni, G. and Hottelier, M. (2000) *Droit constitutionnel suisse*, Vol. I, *L'Etat*, Berne, Nr 865–96.

Blindenbacher, R. and Watts, R.L. (2002) 'Federalism in a changing world – a conceptual framework', in R. Blindenbacher and A. Koller (eds), *Federalism in a Changing World – Learning from Each Other*, Montreal pp. 7–25.

Croisat, M. (1995) *Le fédéralisme dans les démocraties contemporaines*, 2nd edn, Paris.

Dashwood, A. (2004) 'The relationships between the member states and the European Union/European Community', *CMLR* 41: 355–81.

Elazar, D.J. (1987) *Exploring Federalism*, London.

Elazar, D.J. (2001) 'The United States and the European Union: models for their epochs', in K. Nicolaidis and R. Howse, (eds), *The Federal Vision: Legitimacy and Levels of Governance in the United States and the European Union*, Oxford: Oxford University Press.

Fleiner, T. (2001) 'Föderalismus als Ordnungsprinzip der Verfassung', in Thürer, Aubert and Müller (eds), *Verfassungsrecht der Schweiz*, Zurich, pp. 429–42.

Follesdal, A. (2003) *Federalism*, Stanford.

Moravcsik, A. (2001) 'Federalism in the European Union: rhetoric and reality', in K. Nicolaidis and R. Howse (eds), *The Federal Vision: Legitimacy and Levels of Governance in the United States and the European Union*, Oxford: Oxford University Press.

Norman, P. (2003) *The Accidental Constitution*, Brussels.

Poncins, E. de (2003) *Vers une constitution européenne*, Paris.

Riker, W.H. (1996) 'European federalism: the lessons of past experience', in J. Hesse and V. Wright (eds), *Federalizing Europe? The Costs, Benefits and Preconditions of Federal Political Systems*, Oxford: Oxford University Press.

Scharpf, F. (2001) 'Notes toward a theory of multilevel governing in Europe', *Scandinavian Political Studies* 24(1): 1–26.

Schindler, D. (1992) Schweizerischer und europäischer Föderalismus, Zentralblatt für Staats- und Gemeindeverwaltung, 193 ff.

Schmitter, P. (2000) 'Federalism and the euro-polity', *Journal of Democracy* 11(1): 40–7.

Witte, B. de (ed.) (2003) *Ten Reflections on the Constitutional Treaty for Europe*, Florence.

# Asymmetric federalism between globalization and regionalization

Klaus von Beyme

## 1. INTRODUCTION

The question 'who speaks for the Europeans?' involves a basic contradiction in European constitutional engineering: federalist autonomy developed against democratic representation on the basis of popular sovereignty of equal citizens. Working on a European Constitution includes the search for a fair balance between the modes of representation. This paper shows, however, that the balance remains precarious. Asymmetries in de iure institutional settings and in de facto social and economic developments permanently reshuffle the balance. The classical 'coming-together federations', such as the USA, Switzerland or Australia, admit greater asymmetries than later federations, such as Germany or Austria. Recent 'holding-together federations', such as Belgium, Spain or India, which developed out of former central states, create a new type of symmetry. Stepan (1999: 32f.) showed that these new federations, in contrast to the American model, are already constitutionally asymmetrical and more demos-enabling than demos-constraining. The European Union (EU) – more heterogeneous than any of the existing federations or decentralized states in Europe – will suffer from the contradiction that a high degree of de facto inequality has to be reconciled with as much of a constitutional symmetry as possible.

When Spain after Franco worked on a new constitution, many German political scientists were invited to discuss federalism, because Germany seemed to be the only system (Belgium at that time was still fairly centralized) within the European Community which practised authentic federalism. The scholars recommended federalism and were disappointed that no coherent federal system was created. Instead of a clear constitutional device, one 'pre-autonomia' – e.g. autonomous rights to certain regions before the whole system was settled – after the other was granted. Regions which claimed their autonomy most vehemently got most. The result was a patchwork of regulations, but no coherent logic of action within the system. Looking back, we became more tolerant towards this kind of procedure. Institutionalist palaeo-federalism – old federalism contrasted to neo-federalist devices – was oriented towards the arch-federations with equal rights, such as the USA and Switzerland, the classical 'coming-together' federations in history. In this light, post-war federations, such as the Federal Republic of Germany – with its different votes according to the size of the *Länder* – were initially dubbed only 'quasi-federal' (Wheare 1963: 26). Germany in its constitutional history had to fight the prejudice that federalism and a parliamentary system were incompatible. The 'authentic' federations, USA and Switzerland, were not parliamentary systems by chance. Parliamentary sovereignty seemed to be incompatible with a doctrine of 'states' rights'. Among continental lawyers there was little knowledge that countries working in a British tradition of parliamentary sovereignty, such as Canada and Australia, had long falsified the assumption of such an incompatibility (cf. Bowie and Friedrich 1954: 71). Continental constitutional lawyers in particular had a haughty attitude towards the experiences of 'the colonies' – as they dubbed them – and did not accept the Commonwealth countries as a model. But even Friedrich (in Bowie and Friedrich 1954: 823) preferred, in his recommendations for a European Community, an executive – elected by two chambers – with a fixed term, according to the Swiss model.

Older archaic theories of federalism started from a rational model of symmetric states' rights. All the units – little Connecticut as well as big New York – had the same competences. This model was typical for classical modernism. Postmodernist thinking with its patchwork scenarios from personal lifestyles to art has developed much more tolerance towards asymmetries. A neo-liberal theory, promoting individualization, has strengthened the thinking in asymmetries. Older institutionalists still thought they could answer global theories such as 'how federal government should be organized' (Wheare 1963: 53).

This approach has by now been substituted by an 'enlightened neo-institutionalism'. It was frequently combined with the rational choice approach. Interests of actors were analysed in a dynamic way. The motives of the process of new asymmetries in existing federations – originally conceived of as symmetric – have been analysed and are no longer labelled as 'deviant behaviour' undermining federalism. Two dynamics have strengthened the process of asymmetries:

- The revolt of regions and ethnic groups which found themselves underprivileged in the process of nation-building.
- The economic imbalances which are permanently increased by Europeanization, globalization, migration and environmental destruction.

In the classic federations real symmetry has long been undermined, even if equal representation in a second chamber seems to indicate a balance of states' rights. The rationalistic question as to how to organize federalism – sometimes brought to the agenda by 'constitutional engineers' – is frequently substituted by the question as to how federations can survive under the attacks of new social dynamics.

The third wave of transition to democracy in South and East Europe, with a number of constitution-making processes which had no historical precedents, has sharpened our understanding on inevitable asymmetries. The three federations in the Communist camp (Soviet Union, Yugoslavia, Czechoslovakia) perished. Only Russia has tried a new federal start. But after the loss of all the Union Republics of the former Soviet Union the counterweights to huge Russia, extending from Kaliningrad to Vladivostok – such as Ukraine or Kasachstan – were missing. The new federation was doomed to be a wedding of mice with an elephant, i.e. asymmetry was extreme from the outset.

The neo-liberal paradigm leads away from 'participatory federalism' in the direction of a 'federalism of competition'. The idea of competition necessarily undermines the advocates of equality. Competition causes asymmetry. Otherwise incentives for regional innovations could not be developed (Sturm 2000: 32). 'Class struggle from below' – the demands of the poorer federal units – has been complemented by 'class struggle from above'. Rich German *Länder* such as Bavaria and Baden-Württemberg criticize egalitarian devices of distribution as a kind of '*malus*' – e.g. a kind of punishment for a sound regional economy which does not rely on horizontal or vertical redistribution of funds. Germany has been counted among the 'unitary federations' not just because of its integrative and egalitarian ideology. German history produced the ideology as well as the actor who promoted unification. In a process of late modernization the equalization of life conditions seemed essential. This was not just the remainder of bureaucratic Prussian '*Machbarkeitswahn*' (obsession that everything can be manipulated). In a country with 12 million refugees after 1945, the integrative message of Art. 72 Basic Law in the chapter of concurrent legislation seemed to be a necessary concession to the poorer regions that life conditions will be unified. In Prussia this ideology was also the product of active social Christianity in the pietistic movement and the rational bureaucratic enlightenment which became the creed of the Prussian bureaucracy, as it was taught at the main Prussian university: Halle. '*Polizey-Wissenschaft*' – policy science – was the cameralistic forerunner of modernization ideology which also affected the federal subunits after the formation of the German Reich. It was an ideological compensation of the fact that the life conditions in Prussia extending from the Belgian to the Russian border were more unequal than in any other German territory. 'Unification of the conditions of life' in the constitution has been smoothed down after reunification to '*Gleichwertigkeit*' – equivalent conditions, close to the old '*suum cuique*' and no longer inviting too many raised hopes. The new federal president Köhler caused much dissatisfaction in 2004 when he confessed that Germans will have to live with great differences in wealth for the coming decades. But even the version of 'equivalent conditions' is fairly remote from Anglo-Saxon conceptions, at least in the USA and to a lesser degree in Canada. Rarely do equalizers blame the system which allows six times more social transfers in California than in Alabama (Majone 1996). In federations with huge distances, the life conditions of the capital are of minor importance for populations at the periphery who frequently get to the capital only via TV. This is true even in Russia, though the Far East and Siberia have lived for more than seventy years under the equalizing doctrine of Communism. Federations with different ethnic groups are also inclined to accept more easily deviances from the demand of equality of life conditions because their cultural identity is their main concern. Galicia or Sicily will, of course, always ask central government for more help. But the slowness of the equalization process seems to be tolerable as long as regional autonomy in questions close to the hearts of the people in the subunits can be practised.

Enlightened neo-institutionalism is less interested in legal considerations of how federations should be organized than in aiming at a policy-oriented approach. Institutions can be variable, according to different policy areas. In transformation processes, however, two legal minimal conditions had to be met:

- legal autonomy for the subunits;
- the creation of fair chances for minorities in the electoral system.

This was one of the reasons why the winner-takes-all systems – which were practised under Communism and preferred by most post-Communists – have not prevailed in most countries of transition. The institutional mix as a product of constitutional engineering in East Europe was mostly some autonomy for the subunits in combination with proportional electoral law. Only in federations with a British tradition, such as Canada, was the Westminster tradition so strong that proportionalism did not prevail. In a non-federal state, such as New Zealand, this tradition was interrupted in 1993 for reasons of sub-autonomy for the native population, the Maori. In Russia the choice of a 'parallel system' led to results which were closer to the practices of majority systems (Nohlen and Kasapovic 1996: 34ff.). But the local élites were strengthened and became more independent of central decision-making. The Russian mix of institutions therefore furthered centrifugal tendencies. Equality of competences – with some exceptions as found in Germany or Austria – was only a myth. Russia is a hybrid in a matrix of the typical transitional mix of institutions (equal–unequal competences, and majority or proportional electoral systems).

|  | federalism | |
|---|---|---|
|  | *equal rights* | *unequal rights* |
| proportional electoral law | moderate egalitarian: Germany, Austria; egalitarian: Belgium, Switzerland | modified autonomy: Spain, Italy |
| majoritarian | equal rights: USA | Russia, India devolution: Britain |

*Matrix*    Institutional mix for mitigating territorial conflicts

This graphic typology should not obscure the fact that the 'snapshot' represents only a moment in a permanent dynamic. British devolution after the creation of Parliaments for Scotland and Wales in 1999 can quickly develop in a Spanish direction which only deviates from the Spanish model because of a different electoral law. But even the electoral law in Britain is no longer a 'holy cow' as Britain shows in the European elections. Russia is particularly indeterminate in this picture. The country has combined American, German and Spanish solutions in a contradictory system. It is comparable in many respects only to India (Traut 1995: 118). The constituent powers of the sub-units in these federations are partly dependent on the central decision-making system. Where this central prerogative has been contested the central administration has reacted mostly in an asymmetric way. The separation of Chechnya and Ingushetiya (1991) was accepted. Further claims of Chechnya in the direction of sovereignty were blocked in a bloody way. The attempt to create a Ural Republic with Yekaterinburg (Sverdlovsk) as the capital has also been vetoed (1993). From Spain to Russia the new federations have reacted in a pragmatic way and increased asymmetries. The ideal of a federation with symmetric rights and proportional electoral law is partly realized only in Belgium and Switzerland. Bipolar classifications are a first step towards orientation. But they are too schematic for a detailed analysis which has to include:

– de iure asymmetries in constitutions and laws;
– de facto asymmetries in the sphere of economic, social and political dynamics.

## 2. DE IURE ASYMMETRIES

The first contribution to a theory of asymmetric federalism (Tarlton 1965) has mainly worked on the de iure asymmetries. They are important even today.

(1) De iure asymmetries paradoxically arise in old federations such as the USA or Switzerland because the federal constitutions contain little hints about the internal structure of states or cantons. The other extreme is represented by India with a federal regulation of the state constitutions. The Russian Federation did not follow a consistent policy in so far as it postulated (Art. 5.4) equal rights for the federal 'subjects' (this authoritarian term is hardly promising!) and on the other hand recognizes statehood for federal subjects only for a minority of ethnic entities. Russian districts (*oblasty*) do not have a constitution and their statutes grant very limited legislative rights (Art. 5.2). The group of republics with a non-Russian ethnic majority was sometimes changed – similar to Spain – according to political pressure. Their number was increased from sixteen (1989) to twenty-one (1993). In some cases this increase was due to separation (Chechnya and Ingushetiya); in most cases certain units were upgraded (Altai, for instance). Only this group has the right to impose bilingualism on its institutions. In Italy the statute for Sicily, which was created before the Italian constitution was passed, was never co-ordinated with the constitution. Threats of secession led to a kind of 'pre-autonomia' (preliminary granted autonomous rights). The five ethnic 'special regions' and fifteen normal regions have different legal qualities in the statutes and different political competences (Pizzorusso in Kramer 1993: 48ff.).

(2) A second asymmetry arises in federal systems where the federation has the right to consider territorial reorganization. Nobody would dare to think about the abolition of Appenzell or Vermont in their respective countries. Gerhard Lehmbruch (2000: 89) has rightly emphasized a contradiction in Germany: competitive federalism is applauded, but the unitary way of thinking prevails when a reshuffling of the *Länder* is discussed by committees in the central decision-making system. Two criteria were mentioned in the creation of *Länder*: regional traditions, '*landmannschaftliche Verbundenheit*' sounds almost tribalistic. But regional traditions were countervailed by centralizing ideas about 'economic efficacy' in size and distribution of the sub-units (Art. 29 Basic Law). Federations in the Third World such as India, Nigeria and even South Africa have not only discussed federal reform but have implemented it. The case of Belgium, which is occasionally mentioned in this context (Agranoff 1999: 36), does not fit, however, because the whole state – not from above, but because of pressure from the Flemish parts of the country – had to be reorganized in order to avoid secession. In Belgium territorial reorganization, which divided one province like Brabant according to linguistic groups, was the outcome of a 'federalism of dissociation' (Delwit *et al.* 1999: 53) – a new form of creating legal asymmetries in federal systems. Canada is a good example because there were many proposals for

a merger of the poor provinces. A 'maritime union' was envisaged. Even the division of large provinces was discussed. But all this was impossible to implement against the will of Quebec which preferred either a bipolar federation according to the Belgian model or a federation of Quebec with the rest of the provinces of Canada (Watts 1999: 135).

All the devices of territorial reapportionment have a drawback in that they try to expel the 'devil of economic asymmetry' with the 'Beelzebub of centralist rationalism'. In Germany such a reorganization seemed to be necessary after reunification. The German Democratic Republic (GDR) had already abolished her *Länder* in 1952. But in the short period of sovereignty for a free GDR in 1989/1990 the five *Länder* were important strongholds of grassroots democratization so nobody dared to implement de Maizière's plans for a reduction to two or three eastern *Länder*. After legal reunification on 3 October 1990 it was impossible to uproot the budding plant of regional autonomy, the more so as – with the exception of Saxony-Anhalt, an agglomeration of former Prussian territories with enclaves of the ministate of Anhalt – all the territorial units deployed more regional and historical identity (*landsmannschaftliche Verbundenheit*) than some West German *Länder* such as North Rhine-Westphalia or Rhineland-Palatinate, artificial creations by the occupation forces after 1945. The economic weakness of East Germany was thus able to reinforce the asymmetries of West German federalism. Germany, the oldest federation in the world if we include the first Empire up to 1806, was characterized by consensual political culture and a tradition of '*amicabilis compositio*' – a tradition dating from the end of the religious wars through friendly 'coming-together' regulations – on the one hand, and the unitary tendencies which developed under Prussian dominance in the process of the constitution of the second German Reich (1871–1918), on the other.

(3)  In many federations from Canada to Russia asymmetry exists via the different rights of federal units. In Russia, this is excessively developed in a hierarchy of competences. Legislative rights de jure are small in the case of the districts Moscow and St Petersburg. But de facto asymmetry compensates for this minor de iure competence because they are the centre for important banks and businesses. Economic weight overrides de iure weaknesses. Russia and Canada developed such asymmetries under the pressure of dissociative movements. In a 'Canada round' of reform of federalism the Charlottetown proposals hinted at further asymmetries (Watts 1999: 130f.). 'Equity of provinces' (section 1.2 (1) d) as a basic principle has to be harmonized with the recognition of Quebec as a 'distinct society' (section 1.2 (1) c and d). For New Brunswick the equality of two languages, English and French, has been inserted. Three of nine Supreme Court judges have to be recruited from the 'civil law bar of Quebec' (section 18). To fight disruptive tendencies, even future amendments to the Constitution have been envisaged: the federal constitution can never be changed without the consent of Quebec. Special solutions for the aborigines have developed

asymmetries in the federations of Australia and Canada. The Canadian process of reform of federalism displays, however, a basic dilemma: high barriers against constitutional amendments are meant to protect existing asymmetries. New balances of federalism are hard to find because the procedure of amending the constitution is complicated – as in the United States. Thus most proposals for federal reform have never been ratified.

In systems of 'devolutionary federalism', such as Spain, where competences to the subunits have been given according to political opportunity and pressure, asymmetrization of federalism is almost a programme (Moreno 1999: 167). Federalism has long been considered as a basic goal in heterogeneous societies. On the road to more asymmetric autonomies for the most militant ethnic groups, however, federalism declines to a programme which is permanently amended (*Eventualprogramm*) and reduced to tentative goals for policies.

(4) Only federations which were developed out of a confederation of states normally have a second chamber in which all units are symmetrically represented with the same number of votes. These federations had to deviate from the democratic principle because the smaller units were overrepresented. In old federations the second chamber, like the Senate in Australia and the USA, is not an organ of representation of states. The states' representatives do not consider themselves as agents of their home states. Therefore, conflicts between American governors and senators were not infrequent. In Spain there is a senate as a territorial chamber, but the autonomous communities do not participate via the senate. In 1994 a 'General Commission for the Autonomies' was created in order to increase the influence of the regional entities (Grau i Creus 2000: 59). Belgium, after the federalization of the state in 1993, transformed the senate into a chamber of the linguistic communities – not of the regions. There are four groups of senators, regulated through ethnic quota – the King's children as senators being the exception. The attempt to create symmetry makes the composition of this institution unusually complicated (Deschouver 2000: 109).

Germany was a unique case. The Federal Council, as the representatives of *Länder* government who have to cast their votes en bloc and not according to party affiliation, is the result of a confederative tradition since the first Empire (until 1806) and the German Confederation (1815–1866). The historical remainder of this executive structure of the regional chamber was mistrusted by the Allies in 1949. But the institution survived democratic legalization even after reunification and thus illustrates that institutional developments are dependent on historical development. A path once chosen in history cannot easily be left. The German language with its preference for nouns dubbed it: '*Pfadabhängigkeit* of constitutional reform' (Lehmbruch 2000: 78f.). After reunification a committee for constitutional amendments changed the number of seats in the Federal Council in order to avoid the large states being overriden by a majority of small *Länder*. All the East German *Länder* had to be counted among this group.

(5) Among the legal asymmetries is the question as to whether the Federation has an administration of its own. Most federations, with the exception of Germany, have tried to hand over legislation and its implementation to one level. Germany is an irregular case because the implementation of laws and its costs are a burden for the *Länder* in most policy areas. This leads to increasing centralization. In Switzerland a mixed form of decentralized models, as in the USA, and a system of functional division of tasks have been developed (Rentzsch 2000: 54). Where *Länder* or cantons bear the main burden of implementation, asymmetries are reinforced because the larger units have more discretion in the process of administration. In Germany stronger units, such as Hessen – then the 'reddest' among the Social Democratic states – could afford not to implement all the provisions of Adenauer's housing policy, and Bavaria – the 'blackest' of the Christian Democracy governed territories – took its revenge against the social policies of the social-liberal coalition (cf. von Beyme 1997: 313ff.). The smaller and poorer units in many federations have higher rights to acquire subventions in fiscal policies. But even in old federations these smaller units proved to have so little planning capacities that they were unable to mobilize a proper share of the federal subsidies (Armingeon 2000: 115). Asymmetries are reinforced when de iure and de facto asymmetries cumulate their impact in an unhealthy way. On the other hand, the Federation frequently has little steering capacity with its politics of the 'golden bridle' (*goldener Zügel*) when the Constitution regulates the competences between Federation and the subunits in a very detailed way – as it normally does in the younger federations. A fiscally oriented 'theory of legislation' – in the tradition of rational choice – starts from the assumption that the subunits via the construction of fiscal federalism are frequently seduced to take the wrong decisions (Peterson 1995: 39).

## 3. DE FACTO ASYMMETRIES

(1) The most normal asymmetry in federalism is the product of different sizes and economic strengths of member states. In Canada the smallest province, Prince Edward Island, comprises only 1.4 per cent of the population; in Australia, Tasmania only 2.8 per cent. In the USA in three states (Wyoming, Alaska and Vermont) only 0.2 per cent of the population reside. Switzerland contains Appenzell-Innerrhoden with 0.2 per cent, Spain, Rioja with 0.7 per cent, India, Sikkim with 0.05 per cent, and Germany, Bremen with 0.8 per cent. The mini-states are overwhelmed by the sheer weight of big neighbours. They compensate for this weakness by the 'power to blackmail' the bigger states, which was criticized by William Riker as early as 1964 (1964: 155). This capacity to blackmail is evident in the most decentralized systems such as Switzerland. Fortunately, the worst-case scenario rarely happens: before the introduction of the new

Constitution in 1999 51 per cent of the smallest cantons – at that time nine and a half units – which voted against an innovation, were theoretically able to let 9 per cent of the Swiss population prevail over a majority of 91 per cent of the citizens (Germann 1991).

(2) Institutions of 'intergovernmental decision-making' (*Politikverflechtung*) are mostly not regulated formally among the de iure asymmetries. The same holds true of many forms of horizontal and vertical co-operation in a 'participatory federalist system'. 'Executive federalism' was strengthened in most systems (Painter 2000: 142). Executive interstate negotiations prevail over the legal decisions of national institutions in Canada. Fritz Scharpf (1988) has discovered the 'joint-decision trap' (*Politikverflechtungsfalle*) and made famous an untranslatable German noun. It is characterized by a coincidence of individual rationality and collective irrationality and, of course, by increasing asymmetries. Collective irrationality does not spread in all the federations in the same way. In Switzerland, in spite of asymmetries and economic differences among the cantons, the same logic of 'bargaining and compromise' prevails (Armingeon 2000: 121). The interlacing of decisions remains mostly horizontal, as in the conference of the directors of education departments. Political élites who permanently pursue a strategy of conflict are not rewarded in such a system. Conflicts are mitigated because the cantons – similar to American states – do not chase after the German phantom of 'equal life conditions' throughout the country. Germany falsifies the rule that federations develop brakes against increasing welfare policies because the number of veto-players and codecision-makers is too large (Wachendorfer-Schmidt 2000: 244). 'Dual federalism' in the USA and in Switzerland certainly has some advantages over the models of 'centralized federalism' as it developed in Austria and Germany. Combined federalism has the tendency to grow into a 'supportive federalism'. '*Föderalismus*' in a German play on words develops into a '*Förderalismus*', e.g. a cartel of mutual support for the respective interests of the subunits (Schneider 1998). Unfortunately, the inner German discussion on this drawback is not yet grounded on empirical comparative studies of fiscal federalism in various countries. The counter-model, the American system of grants-in-aid, so highly recommended to the West German decision-makers in 1949 by the American High Command, produces other irrationalities and does not favour the poorer areas with a weak infrastructure.

In strongly asymmetric systems of an 'incomplete federalism', as it exists in Spain or Russia, initially bilateral negotiation shaped the systems. In Russia some subunits, e.g. Tartarstan, could blackmail the centre as long as it had not yet complete power over the vast territories in the country. Only Putin's reform of federalism has smoothed down some of the centrifugal tendencies of the system (cf. von Beyme 2000). Spain is an example of growing horizontal negotiations in sectoral conferences with consolidation of the system. The Spanish Constitutional Court has recommended some of these innovations and was in this respect more influential than its Russian counterpart. The conferences of the seventeen autonomous units in Spain are, however, not institutions of decision-making but rather a forum for discussion. In terms of game theory these conferences are not games of seventeen plus one actors, but rather a game of eighteen separate players (Grau i Creus 2000: 62, 73).

(3) Party systems have strengthened the 'asymmetrization of federations'. In older constitutions they were not provided for, and federalist ideology thought in terms of regions, not of party divisions. Where regional parties are strong, as in the Basque Country and in Catalonia, in South Tyrol, Bavaria or Scotland, the veto-power of regional parties creates new asymmetries. In federations with one party system throughout the country, as in Germany (with the exception of the CSU in Bavaria and the PDS in East Germany), centralizing tendencies are strong. In other federations, as in Canada, the old federal two-party system eroded and increased the potential for blackmail among the smaller provinces – in spite of the fact that Canada stuck to the Westminster model of an electoral law. Special developments in certain federations have falsified the old assumption of the Hermens school of electoral law that a winner-takes-all system serves as a stronghold against party fragmentation. Where regional parties are strong, the federal actors have developed a differentiated attitude towards the autonomous subunits. Strong élites, such as Felipe González in Spain, kept aloof from the conflicts of the regions. Less strong leaders, such as the conservative leader of Galicia, Fraga, on the other hand, used the autonomy to strengthen their party political position.

(4) Federal finance systems are normally a mixture of de iure and de facto asymmetries. Even in the dual federalism of the USA, with an unlimited right to tax and clearly separated fiscal administrations, the competences of some levels of domestic policy are not clearly defined so that conflicts are possible. Nevertheless, the USA never thought of the creation of common taxes between federation and states as a way out of uncertainty (Rentzsch 2000: 44).

With growing globalization and internationalization fiscal federalism was in many cases more important than constellations of party politics. Even in Germany negative alliances, combining the forces of the two political camps, have been formed among the prime ministers of the *Länder*. Castles (2000: 192) went so far as to declare that the relations between decentralization and economic efficiency are more dependent on budget policy than on the political structures of the respective systems. Germany developed the most centralized and highest density of regulations among the federations (Rentzsch 2000: 50), independent of the question as to which party coalitions prevailed. Financial needs create a pressure for asymmetries and the way out is in many cases a blending of the financial systems with elements of a divided and an integrated system. Even in not-yet-really federalist systems such as Spain this tendency can be evident (Wendland 1997: 237).

No federation can do without transfers to the member states. The financing of the federation is normally not done via 'matricular contributions' as in the Imperial German Reich until 1918 or in the EU. The more welfare-oriented a federation tends to be, the more the financial powers of the weakest subunits have been promoted as in Australia, Canada and Germany. This has been linked to a political system's variable: all the three federations live in a parliamentary system (Rentzsch 2000: 54), but probably ideological traditions are as important as the institutional arrangement between government and parliament.

## 4. CONCLUSION

Growing scepticism concerning the steering capacity of states in postmodern times of non-planning has increased tolerance towards the asymmetric and undemocratic remainders of federalism. In the nineteenth century in late nation states such as Italy and Germany, the centrifugal forces in federal systems were under attack in political theory (von Treitschke 1921: 83). In the polemics of modernizers versus states' rights ideologues, such as Calhoun in America and the Bavarian Max von Seydel, symmetry of federalism was not a goal. 'Concurrent majorities' were more important than a nation-wide popular majority. In postmodern times the problems of the retreating forces of federalism were no longer criticized as among former modernizers. Federalism was recognized as a 'progressive structure in the evolution' (Mayntz 1989: 9). Polycentric forms of organization were no longer an attack on state sovereignty. Territorial and functional fragmentation in decision-making systems corresponded to postmodern lifestyle and theory by 'thinking in fragments'. Federalism seemed to be an appropriate compromise. The nation state was too small for really big problems in the age of globalization, but at the same time it was too small for most of the minor regional problems (Bell 1988: 2).

Recent literature no longer advocates an evolutionary progressive structure but tries in an empirical way to compare the performance of federal systems. Very few authors are satisfied with the 'mystical origins of federalism' in a biblical way (Görner 1996: 5). The general superiority of federal states was no longer assumed (Keman 2000: 222). Recent studies ask to which degree federal structures are functional. Even champions of the rational choice approach are no longer 'blue-print rationalists'. Indian and Canadian data showed that the accommodation of ethnic groups requires frequently irrational ad hoc decisions in order to preserve the integrity of the federation (Mitra 2000: 55). With special arrangements for the entry of Cyprus into the EU, the first proof is evident that the same pragmatic policies will prevail in Europe and create asymmetric federalism.

Conflict management in the age of globalization and regionalization is done with a variety of instruments – from genocide to separation (Smith 1995: 300). Federalism as an instrument is typical for middle-of-the-road measures. But federalism does not guarantee *per se* permanent social peace.

Belgium, Canada, Spain, Nigeria and India had to live with this experience in a permanent crisis. Social dynamics cannot be regulated in the long run. Switzerland and Belgium went farthest in a detailed regulation of ethnic school districts and language requirements in the administration. The conflict is easier to handle when it has dyadic structures as in Belgium, Canada and, to some extent, Switzerland. In mixed ethnic areas, as in Brussels, Bosnia-Herzegovina and in many East European countries, the balance found via constitutional engineering always remained precarious and unstable.

More important than the search for 'eternal solutions' in fighting the asymmetric rights of the subunits of federalism is the degree to which civil society is internalized and the amount of protection for minorities in society (Knop *et al.* 1995: 7). Migrations in the age of globalization will undermine any artificially stabilized borders and legal arrangements. The rational dream of classical modernism for symmetry is permanently under attack from new postmodern de facto asymmetries. Rational instruments of accommodation are precarious because pre-modern remainders of feelings of identity are not easily out-manoeuvred by rational options for political actions (Evers 1994: 64).

The EU has tried to escape this dilemma by launching the notion of 'subsidiarity' instead of the term 'federalism'. This notion stems from the debate on functional interest groups in the social doctrines of the Catholic Church and entered Calvinist political thought in the theories of Althusius. Europe has territorialized this term, but the European Parliament made it clear in a majority decision that 'subsidiarity' in case of doubt meant 'federalism' – not preferred by larger centralized national states such as France and Britain. The discussion on the appropriate form of federalism in Europe is continuing. Every year new terms create new 'epitheta-federalisms': such as 'interlaced' or 'subsidiary federalism', 'differentiating' or 'participatory federalism', etc. The semantic struggles are the more intensive as they reach a normative level, e.g. the question as to which form of federalism is appropriate for the EU (Sidjanski 2001: 73).

'Conflict management' and 'conflict solution' have been differentiated in this debate (Burgess and Gagnon 1993: 18). Conflict solutions are rare, but they exist in so far as they guaranteed the further existence of systems with centrifugal tendencies such as Belgium or Canada. In most other cases only 'conflict management' seems to be possible.

An important contribution to conflict management is the capacity of federal systems not only to act as a brake on nation-wide innovation but to experiment with innovations on a regional level. Hawaii's health-care system had considerable influence on the Medicare solution in the USA in 1971 (Burgess and Gress 1999: 188) A cost–benefit analysis of federalism by no means remains as critical as Riker thought (1964: 145, 153). He called federalism a principle which is essentially anti-innovative. It can, however, hardly be denied that federalism occasionally promotes the 'tyranny of minorities'. It was Riker's historical achievement to have analysed who the actors are who receive most of the benefits from the federation. He found the whites in the southern states of the USA, Quebec in Canada, the landlords in the underdeveloped areas of India, and the non-Prussian Southwest in Germany. Even in the Australian context where no individual beneficiary could be named, trade interests were privileged because, via federal veto group politics, they were able to avoid central equalizing policies.

Leftists have always blamed federal autonomy as an instrument in the hands of rich veto groups. In the mean time Europeanization and globalization led to a situation in which the interests of capital owners no longer need federalism. On the contrary, the small basis of autonomous regional decisions is detrimental to their goals, exceeding regions and national states. Even in India the 'new regionalists' are no longer the agrarian oligarchy but rather mobile urban capitalists (Mitra 2000: 51).

Comparative democratic studies have the advantage that federal and central states are compared in their performance. The first result of such comparisons is that alleged centralized states are highly 'decentralized', as in Scandinavia. Socioeconomic performance proved to be superior only in federal systems which were decentralized below the state level (Keman 2000: 223). Federalism and centralism are no longer treated as fixed ontological entities, but are poles on a scale of varying degrees of decentralization. Moreover, decentralization on regional grounds has to be compared with the co-operation modes of functional groups. Fighting inflation, for instance, was more successful in federal states because they were more inclined to hand over control of inflation to an independent federal bank (Wachendorfer-Schmidt 2000: 243). But these experiences of comparative studies cannot be generalized. On the one hand, centralized systems have learned certain lessons; on the other hand, the EU generalizes certain experiences of the decentralists. The results of comparative studies are far from conveying a clear message: federalism has hampered central regulations in social policies in the USA, but not in Canada.

Symmetry in federalism used to be the undemocratic credo of smaller and weaker units. In the light of privileges given to ethnic minority areas in some federal states from Spain to Canada, democratic movements serve as centralizers in many respects. Asymmetric federalism and decentralism are, therefore, never the last word of history. The rise of the EU serves as a vehicle for continuing new balances between popular sovereignty of a not yet existing 'European people' and the 'states' rights/privileges' of regional majorities.

**Address for correspondence:** Klaus von Beyme, Institut für Politische Wissenschaft, Marstallstrasse 6, D-69117 Heidelberg, Germany. Tel: (+49) 6221 542860. Fax: (+49) 6221 542896. email: klaus.von.beyme@urz.uni-heidelberg.de

## REFERENCES

Agranoff, R. (ed.) (1999) *Accommodating Diversity: Asymmetry in Federal States*, Baden-Baden: Nomos.

Armingeon, K. (2000) 'Swiss federalism in comparative perspective', in U. Wachendorfer-Schmidt (ed.), *Federalism and Political Performance*, London: Routledge pp. 112–29.

Bell, D. (1988) 'The world in 2013', *Dialogue* 3: 2–9.

von Beyme, K. (1997) *Der Gesetzgeber. Der Bundestag als Entscheidungszentrum,* Opladen: Westdeutscher Verlag.
von Beyme, K. (2000) 'Federalism in Russia', in U. Wachendorfer-Schmidt (ed.), *Federalism and Political Performance,* London: Routledge, pp. 23–39.
Bowie, R.R. and Friedrich, C.J. (eds) (1954) *Studies in Federalism,* Boston: Little Brown.
Burgess, M. and Gagnon, A.-G. (eds) (1993) *Comparative Federalism and Federation,* London: Harvester Wheatsheaf.
Burgess, M. and Gress, F. (1999) 'Asymmetrical federalism in Canada, the United States and Germany: comparative perspectives', in R. Agranoff (ed.), *Accommodating Diversity: Asymmetry in Federal States,* Baden-Baden: Nomos, pp. 169–92.
Castles, F.G. (2000) 'Federalism, fiscal decentralization and economic performance', in U. Wachendorfer-Schmidt (ed.), *Federalism and Political Performance,* London: Routledge, pp. 177–95.
Delwit, P. *et al.* (1999) *Gouverner la Belgique,* Paris: PUF.
Deschouver, K. (2000) 'Belgien–Ein Föderalstaat auf der Suche nach Stabilität', in *Jahrbuch des Föderalismus,* Baden-Baden: Nomos, pp. 97–119.
Evers, T. (ed.) (1994) *Chancen des Föderalismus in Deutschland und Europa,* Baden-Baden: Nomos.
Germann, R.E. (1991) 'Die Europatauglichkeit der direktdemokratischen Institutionen der Schweiz', *Schweizerisches Jahrbuch für politische Wissenschaft,* Bd. 30: 257–69.
Görner, R. (1996) *Einheit durch Vielfalt. Föderalismus als politische Lebensform,* Opladen: Westdeutscher Verlag.
Grau i Creus, M. (2000) 'Spain: incomplete federalism', in U. Wachendorfer-Schmidt (ed.), *Federalism and Political Performance,* London: Routledge, pp. 58–77.
Keman, H. (2000) 'Federalism and policy performance', in U. Wachendorfer-Schmidt (ed.), *Federalism and Political Performance,* London: Routledge, pp. 196–227.
Knop, K. *et al.* (eds) (1995) *Rethinking Federalism,* Vancouver: UBC Press.
Kramer, J. (ed.) (1993) *Föderalismus zwischen Integration und Sezession,* Baden-Baden: Nomos.
Lehmbruch, G. (2000) 'Bundesstaatsreform als Sozialtechnologie? Pfadabhängigkeit und Veränderungsspiele im deutschen Föderalismus', in *Jahrbuch des Föderalismus,* Baden-Baden: Nomos, pp. 71–94.
Majone, G. (1996) *Regulating Europe,* London: Routledge.
Mayntz, R. (1989) *Föderalismus und die Gesellschaft der Gegenwart,* Köln: Max-Planck-Institut für Gesellschaftsforschung, Discussion Paper 3.
Mitra, S. (2000) 'The nation, state and the federal process in India', in U. Wachendorfer-Schmidt (ed.), *Federalism and Political Performance,* London: Routledge, pp. 40–57.
Moreno, L. (1999) 'Asymmetry in Spain: federalism in the making?', in R. Agranoff (ed.), *Accommodating Diversity: Asymmetry in Federal States,* Baden-Baden: Nomos, pp. 149–68.
Nohlen, D. and Kasapovic, M. (1996) *Wahlsysteme und Systemwechsel in Osteuropa,* Opladen: Leske & Budrich.
Painter, M. (2000) 'Conditional co-operation in Australia's arm's length federal polity', in U. Wachendorfer-Schmidt (ed.), *Federalism and Political Performance,* London: Routledge, pp. 130–45.
Peterson, P.E. (1995) *The Price of Federalism,* Washington, DC: Brookings Institution.
Rentzsch, W. (2000) 'Föderale Finanzverfassungen: Ein Vergleich Australiens, Deutschlands, Kanadas, der Schweiz und der USA aus institutioneller Perspektive', in *Jahrbuch des Föderalismus,* Baden-Baden: Nomos, pp. 42–54.
Riker, W. (1964) *Federalism. Origin, Operation, Significance,* Boston: Little Brown.
Scharpf, F.W. (1988) 'The joint-decision trap: lessons from German federalism and European integration', *Public Administration* 66: 239–78.

Schneider, H.-P. (1998) 'Nehmen ist seliger als Geben. Oder: Wieviel Föderalismus verträgt der Bundesstaat?', *Neue Juristische Wochenschrift* 51: 3757–59.

Sidjanski, D. (2001) 'The federal approach to the European Union or the quest for an unprecedented European federalism', Notre Europe, Research and Policy Paper, Nr. 14, Paris, July.

Smith, G. (ed.) (1995) *Federalism. The Multiethnic Challenge*, London: Longman.

Stepan, A. (1999) 'Federalism and democracy: beyond the US model', *Journal of Democracy* 10: 19–34.

Sturm, R. (2000) 'Aktuelle Entwicklungen und Schwerpunkte in der internationalen Föderalismus- und Regionalismusforschung', in *Jahrbuch des Föderalismus*, Baden-Baden: Nomos, pp. 29–41.

Tarlton, C.D. (1965) 'Symmetry and asymmetry as elements of federalism: a theoretical speculation', *Journal of Politics* 27: 861–74.

Traut, J.C. (ed.) (1995) *Verfassung und Föderalismus Russlands im internationalen Vegleich*, Baden-Baden: Nomos.

von Treitschke, H. (1921) *Bundesstaat und Einheitsstaat* (1864). In *Ders: Historische und politische Aufsätze*, Leipzig: Hirzel, Vol. II, 8. Edit., pp. 74–235.

Wachendorfer-Schmidt, U. (ed.) (2000) *Federalism and Political Performance*, London: Routledge.

Watts, R.L. (1999) 'The Canadian experience with asymmetrical federalism', in R. Agranoff (ed.), *Accommodating Diversity: Asymmetry in Federal States*, Baden-Baden: Nomos, pp. 118–36.

Wendland, K. (1997) *Spanien auf dem Weg zum Bundesstaat? Entstehung und Entwicklung der Autonomen Gemeinschaften*, Baden-Baden: Nomos.

Wheare, K.C. (1963) *Federal Government*, 4th edn, London: Oxford University Press. Originally published in 1946.

# Implementing (and radicalizing) art. I-47.4 of the Constitution: is the addition of some (semi-)direct democracy to the nascent consociational European federation just Swiss folklore?*

Yannis Papadopoulos

## IS THERE ANYTHING TO LEARN FROM THE SWISS MODEL?

Comparisons of the European (nascent, emerging, in the making, quasi-) federation (of nation-states) with federal countries are generally made with the United States or Germany (for recent exceptions see, however, McKay 2001; Benz 2003; Börzel and Hosli 2003). Yet the Swiss model of federalism is in several respects the one that is closer to the EU model. In Switzerland as in the European Union (EU) the strength of regional/state loyalties is on a par with a low degree of institutional centralization (McKay 2001: 16). For example, the structure and process of EU policy implementation is closer to the Swiss model, with a weak centre and a willingness to accept a dose of inter-state (respectively inter-cantonal) variation. Only in Switzerland can we find a combination similar to the one in the EU, of 'co-operative federalism'[1] – much dependent on the resources of the constituent units (unlike the United States) – and of a willingness to accept as a trade-off a good degree of heterogeneity in implementation, with widespread reluctance (unlike Germany) *vis-à-vis* 'unitarist' pressures. Further, the consociational style of EU decision-making – negotiated instead of competitive policy-making – resembles more the Swiss system than the bipolar German or American ones (notwithstanding bargaining occasionally induced by divided government in these countries). Even the Commission has been compared by its own officials with the (allegedly inefficient) Swiss federal executive.[2]

Hence there is indeed something to learn from the Swiss experience, as emphasized by McKay (2001: 153) who considers that Switzerland should be the major source of learning for the nascent European federation. Learning is, of course, not uncritical imitation.[3] The Swiss system has been presented as an export product by some, mainly inside this country (see also, however, Blondel 1998),[4] while being ignored by most proponents of institutional solutions for the EU (Switzerland's smallness and non-EU membership make it *quantité négligeable*). What then is to be learnt?

Democracy is the missing component in the EU system, which otherwise shares the two other major attributes which led to successful nation-building in Switzerland: federalism (although, of course, not all observers of the EU would agree to portray it as federalist) and consociational style politics (Armingeon 2000: 113; Benz 2003: 188). The Swiss model as a 'good governance' recipe for the management of heterogeneous polities cannot be considered without its participatory component (direct legislation along with representative institutions). Is there anything, then, that could be borrowed from Swiss participatory decision-making and adapted and transposed to the EU? Framing the question in such a manner implies acknowledging as indeed problematic the notorious democratic deficit of the EU,[5] and defining it primarily as an accountability problem.

## A SHORT NOTE ON THE ACCOUNTABILITY PROBLEM IN THE EU

Accountability in the EU is today partial and indirect. The European Parliament (EP) is directly elected but only in 'second-order' elections whose outcomes are weakly, if at all, determined by European issues. Further, the EP has a much weaker legislative role than its national counterparts (including the weakest among them). Ministers making decisions at Council meetings belong to governmental parties who are accountable to their national electorates,[6] but again European issues are not crucial for party competition within member states. Accountability linkages are weaker for the Commission or the European Court of Justice (ECJ). The influence of citizens is also essentially indirect, as it is primarily exerted through organized interests represented or lobbying in Brussels. And it is hard to derive from the 'Principle of Participatory Democracy' in art. I-47 of the draft Treaty (with the exception of I-47.4) any serious implications for sustained citizens' involvement. All this results in a normative problem: curiously, the EU resembles in several respects the 'mixed polities' (Majone 2002) of the pre-modern (i.e. pre-democratic) era. But it is also a problem of governability: although part of the opposition to European integration can be explained by the feeling that ordinary national citizens do not have much control over decisions in Brussels, nor much latitude to avoid them if they disagree with them, the lack of transparency also nourishes opposition to European integration. Dissatisfaction is probably generated more by the secrecy of procedures and by an excess of delegation than by outputs that would not be consistent with voters' preferences (Crombez 2003: 114). The argument that the EU specializes in those policy fields that are also delegated at the national level to non-participatory institutions, such as central banks, courts, or regulatory authorities (Moravcsik 2002: 606), is indeed problematic because this general shift seems to have nourished anti-establishment feelings at the national level too (Mény and Surel 2002). The same applies to network forms of governance whose sources of legitimacy lie in expertise and organizational representation, but which are at the origin of serious transparency and accountability problems (Papadopoulos 2003). This particularly applies to the EU not only because of the strong presence of networks there (Peterson and O'Toole 2001), but also because in the EU network governance does not cohabit with democratic government but takes place in the absence of it (Sbragia 2002).

The 'permissive consensus' on integration has now eroded and negative perceptions of the EU have increased: this is the reality we have to deal with. National referendums on European integration, held more and more frequently, are instructive in that respect, at least among the old EU member states. When their results are negative (as in Denmark or Ireland) they are labelled as inhibiting factors. It would, however, be more useful to identify why opposition to the integration process emerges in referendums. It is no accident, for example, that support for the EU is lower among groups with low educational skills.[7] Not only do they subjectively have good reasons to view 'negative integration' as a potential menace, they also have greater difficulty in understanding the complex decision-making process and thus come to develop growing feelings of alienation. There is clearly a cleavage on European integration with deep social roots, and it is indeed surprising that the overall weak identification of the mass public with the European project does not seem to preoccupy seriously its promoters. If we make a comparison, however, with previous nation-building processes there was in the past a more determinate will to enhance (even though it might be through coercion too) popular identification with the newly built polities. Hence, in the present context of European integration it comes as no surprise if the European issue is subject to increased politicization (Eijk and Franklin 2004; see also Mair 2004: 9).

Confronted with such a legitimacy problem, the EU cannot only be legitimized through output-legitimacy (Scharpf 1999b) or through its 'governance arrangements' (Schmitter 2002), assuming that the latter are sufficiently pluralist (Héritier 1999). In particular, the participatory mechanisms vaguely listed in the Commission's White Paper on Governance, limited to stakeholders and leaving ordinary citizens unaffected, remain underpinned by élitist and narrow functionalist assumptions and are very unlikely to become the appropriate answer to the problem of the democratic deficit (Magnette 2003; Trenz and Eder 2004).[8] Such an answer requires formal and transparent mechanisms ensuring the (possibly direct) accountability of European leadership, and thus inducing its responsive behaviour.

There are, of course, several paths to better accountability: more transparency and publicity in decision-making, but above all more ambitious measures leading to a 'parliamentarization' of the system.[9] They include a more prominent role for the EP, closer involvement of national parliaments, a more intimate connection between elections for the EP and the formation of a Europe-wide executive (European elections have no influence on the Council and only an indirect one on the Commision), a more clear division of labour between legislative competencies that would be attributed to the Council as a sort of senate of European states and the Commission as the European executive, etc. But one should not forget that the legitimacy problems of European integration occur within a more general framework of declining legitimacy of representative democracy (Hayward 1995), distrust with political élites (Norris 1999; Pharr and Putnam 2000; Dalton 2004), rising feelings of political alienation and 'Politikverdrossenheit'. The success of protest, anti-establishment, and populist parties (Mény and Surel 2002) – more often than not anti-European too – highlights that not only the EU but also 'pure' representative democracy in general suffers from declining legitimacy, especially among the least well-endowed social strata. Besides, European integration contributes to the decline of national representative democracy (Mair 2004). Hence, neither more 'good governance' (greater transparency, wider consultation, etc.), nor a reform of European institutions that would aim to strengthen their representative component, for example, through more pronounced competition for the formation of a European government or the election of a Head of the Union, would be likely to alleviate the democratic deficit.

Therefore, it is worth seeing if direct democracy mechanisms, as experienced in Switzerland, would be of any further help in solving this problem. These do not contradict any of the proposals designed to enhance accountability through mechanisms of representative democracy. According to Lord (2004: 195), an approach to accountability which rests mainly on the shadow of the replacement of governors ('throw the rascals out') is precluded by the dispersion of power in the EU. We find a similar horizontal and vertical power fragmentation in Switzerland, where accountability through direct democracy mechanisms in practice replaces accountability through (virtually non-competitive and deploying but indirect effects) parliamentary elections (Linder 1994).[10] Thus it is quite plausible that direct democracy provisions can be introduced irrespective of the success of any other attempts to reform the system in a more representative dimension.

I explore, then, how the Swiss approach to democratization, which not only combines representative with direct democracy, but also includes federalist provisions and implies consociational practices,[11] can be useful for the purpose of reducing the democratic deficit of the EU system. It would be naive to expect that merely copying institutions would automatically produce the effects experienced in the places from where these institutions are imported.[12] Institutional effects are context-related, and in modern polities single direct democracy provisions are always embedded in a more general framework of representative democracy. The latter is still missing in the EU (the composition and accountability of the Commission are not equivalent to those of national governments in their countries, and the same applies to the power balance between the Commission, the Council, and the EP). There are, however, enough similarities in the operation of the EU and the Swiss political systems (multi-level governance at the vertical level and consociational practices at the horizontal level) to expect that effects produced by direct democracy mechanisms in Switzerland would also probably occur in the EU. In particular, it can be expected that, given the similarities between the European and the Swiss political systems, direct democracy mechanisms in the EU would produce primarily – as in Switzerland – indirect integrative effects, reinforcing the negotiated aspect of policy-making instead of acting as majoritarian devices.

## THE REFERENDUM IN THE EU

There are increasing appeals for introducing referendums as legitimizing instruments of European integration. All but one (Cyprus) of the new member states held referendums on their accession to the EU, and national referendums will be held on the Treaty establishing a Constitution for Europe. Art I-47.4 of this document stipulates:

A significant number of citizens, no less than one million, coming from a significant number of Member States, may take the initiative of inviting the Commission within the framework of its power, to submit an appropriate proposal on matters where citizens consider that a legal act of the Union is required for the purpose of implementing this Constitution. A European law shall determine the provisions for the specific procedures and conditions required for such a citizens' initiative, including the minimum number of Member States from which they must come.

There is indeed a wide variety of referendum mechanisms. I propose here (as a way of implementing art. I-47.4) referendums that would be on ordinary EU legislation and initiated 'from below' by citizens' petition. A similar referendum right exists in Switzerland at the federal level: a petition with 50,000 signatures collected within 100 days forces the federal government to submit laws voted by the parliament to a popular referendum whose outcome is binding. In addition, a petition with 100,000 signatures collected in eighteen months allows novel issues to be put on the agenda. In the EU the Parliament has manifested in several resolutions and committee reports since the 1980s a wish to introduce these kinds of referendum elements, but these proposals have remained vague as to the exact content of referendum provisions (Auer 1997: 33).[13] The formulation of art. I-47.4 of the draft European Constitution is also vague and even ambiguous:[14]

- Curiously, the requirements regarding the regional distribution of signatures to be collected are delegated to a law, in a Treaty which contains several detailed rules about decision-making.
- The petition has no binding force; all the Commission would have to do is submit a proposal whose fate is uncertain, and even the binding force of such an 'invitation' to the Commission is not clear. The reform cannot be implemented through a referendum vote in case the EU institutions are unwilling to adopt it.
- It is unclear whether such a right would be possible not only in the spirit of implementing the Constitution but also for the purpose of abrogating existing European legislation.

Referendums by petition enable groups and interests which have no access to decision spheres, or are not well represented in them, to influence policy choice. They enhance the pluralism of the political system, and can be beneficial to a wide variety of groups, such as parties weakly represented in the EP or absent from national executives, unions, environmental or consumer interests, etc. Usually judgments on this kind of referendum are rather abrupt, and reflect the élitist or participatory leanings of their authors. Some believe that governing under the shadow of referendums is an impediment to governability, ignoring the fact that problems caused by élite remoteness from the citizenry can undermine it more seriously. Others praise the contribution of referendums to citizens' empowerment, without being seriously concerned about the 'steering' problems (risk of demagoguery, prevalence of short-term considerations, etc.) likely to be caused by them (Papadopoulos 1995).

What could referendums on ordinary European legislation look like? I do not propose an uncritical imitation of Swiss referendum mechanisms, and my proposal in several respects differs from them, as will be shown in the next section. Referendums by petition pursue different goals. As mentioned before, this is mirrored in Switzerland by two distinctive institutional procedures: that of the popular initiative and that of the optional referendum. The popular initiative enables a group of citizens to put on the agenda proposals for novel legislation, thus opening the policy-making process. The optional referendum, by contrast, enables a group of citizens to call a popular vote on decisions previously made by the political authorities, allowing the voters to veto them, and thus closing the policy-making process. In practice these two procedures can be combined, as is the case in California: popular initiatives can also be used for veto purposes, enabling citizens to propose novel legislation, but also to modify or abrogate the existing one. It is this form of direct legislation that I propose to introduce in the EU, and I have no problems in acknowledging that such an innovation may induce some other changes in the present institutional architecture. For example, today the Commission is unique as an executive in having an exclusive right to initiate legislation (under pillar one), and the EP in being a legislature without such a power (even though there is a general shift towards executive dominance). The popular initiative would represent such a dramatic shift in that it would be inconceivable for the EP not to obtain more initiative rights too. Of course, referendums by petition could be limited to a 'veto', consisting merely in abrogating or modifying legislation, but not in proposing new rules. But they would lose so much of their reason for being, and above all, they would then be used only to limit European integration, which is not suitable.

In more technical terms, I propose to introduce popular initiatives on European legislation ('laws' and 'framework laws' – in the new formulation of art. I-33 of the draft Constitution – not on European 'regulations' or 'decisions') on matters currently requiring qualified majority voting (QMV).[15] Such initiatives could be phrased as a general wish to introduce novel legislation, or to abrogate or modify the existing one. They should not necessarily contain detailed provisions, but should deal with one single issue at a time, and should be limited to the sphere of Union competencies. They would also be indirect; that is, they would not bypass the representative bodies of the EU. As a first step, the Commission should make a proposal to concretize them. This proposal would thereafter be discussed in the Council and the EP, and if it should be approved by the required majorities in these bodies, it would then become part of European legislation without a popular vote. Such a vote would be necessary only in case of rejection by the Council and the EP. Some advocates of direct democracy might consider that such a procedure leaves too much latitude to the European executive and to representative bodies. Yet one should not underestimate the refining role of élite deliberation (stressed as early as the eighteenth century by Burke and Madison), especially as a countervailing power to the risk of particularistic capture of the initiative right.[16]

## THE SUGGESTED DECISION-MAKING PROCEDURE FOR POPULAR INITIATIVES

The decision-making procedure for popular initiatives would be composed of the following phases:

- A **proportion of the European electorate** (under an initiative committee) would formulate a claim. This proportion could also be a percentage of the voters in the last EP election, which would be less demanding. In order to make sure that the initiative right is not captured by excessively narrow geographical or sectoral interests, those supporting the claim should come from several member states. A similar constraint for a wide cantonal representation does not exist in federal Switzerland which is, unlike the EU, more than a union of sovereign states. Of course, several variations are possible. The overall proportion of voters whose support would be required could be about 5 per cent of the total.[17] In addition, the same threshold should be reached in at least one-third of member states (or a lower threshold could be required in a larger number of states; Eurotopia proposes a threshold of only 1 per cent, but in all member states). Deadlines for the collection of signatures should be introduced, in order to avoid an overload of the agenda by problems which have lost their acuity for the public, save some tenacious minorities.

- There should be **judicial review** of the content of the claims, which could be performed by the ECJ. The Commission, the Council, the EP or any national parliament could ask the Court in case of doubt whether a proposal falls within the sphere of competence of the Union, or if it is in contradiction of the Constitution (see also Weiler 1997: 153). The Court could also verify that the principle of material unity is respected in the initiative proposal (only one issue at a time). Ex-ante checks seem to be more adequate than checks after a vote, as in several American states where initiative supporters who have won a popular vote consider that judges do not have the legitimacy to contradict the people's choice. If ex-ante control is not systematic (unlike in the Italian case) but takes place only on request, there is no risk of overload for the ECJ. Such a role for the Court does not exist in the Swiss federal Constitution where up to now the Parliament checked initiatives, having made sometimes politicized and thus controversial decisions on the matter. Recently, however, an additional procedure was introduced. For 'general popular initiatives' it is left to the discretion of the Federal Assembly to determine if they should be concretized as parts of the Constitution or of ordinary legislation. Should the initiative committee not be satisfied with the parliamentary decision, it can then appeal to the Federal Court. Anyway, given that this new form of initiative requires the same number of signatures (100,000) as the previous (and still in force) forms, while being subject to more stringent parliamentary filters, it is highly debatable whether they will be frequently used.

- The initiative being indirect, **representative institutions would play a filtering role**, on the model of several American states. In the present institutional configuration the most acceptable option would be for a proposal elaborated by the Commission, and thereafter a joint role of the Council and the Parliament. It would be in the interest of initiative committees to present precisely formulated propositions, thus 'binding' the Commission in its elaboration of the proposal, and the Council and EP on the content of the text they would eventually adopt (a typical 'principal–agent' problem).[18] Representative bodies would have deadlines for discussing the proposal, in order to avoid obstruction. A majority would be required in the EP, and qualified majority in the Council (see, for instance, its last version: a majority of 55 per cent of the member states representing at least 65 per cent of the total EU population). If the proposal is rejected by representative institutions, a Europe-wide referendum should be organized. This procedure differs from the Swiss one, where the legislature plays a less crucial role. In Switzerland, provided that the proposal contains specific statutory provisions, the parliament only issues recommendations to voters (generally followed by them), but a vote takes place regardless of the parliamentary majority being in favour or against.

– The referendum votes should be organized as a **'multipack'** of several issues to be decided by the citizenry on the same day. This would prevent voters from being overloaded and it would stimulate turnout because each proposition is likely to mobilize for and against it different segments of the electorate. Some of these votes should be organized parallel to the EP elections. That would not only stimulate participation, but it would above all constrain the European party federations to issue (as far as possible) common recommendations and conduct campaigns on salient European issues, instead of merely viewing elections for the EP as second-order elections (Lord 2004: 227–8). Not only would EP elections be revitalized by debates on referendums held in the public space, but they could also be a step towards the creation of a genuine Europe-wide party system.[19]

– Regarding the conditions for success, and for the reasons given about the procedure for the collection of signatures, a **double majority** should be achieved: majority of voters plus majority of member states. Considering that Europeans still feel each other to be foreigners, this requirement should be more stringent than in federal countries, in order to have effective safeguards against the risk of domination by a particular coalition of state interests.[20] Several variants can be envisaged, characterized by different degrees of deviation from the simple majority rule. Weiler (1997: 153), for instance, proposes a qualified majority of states or unanimity depending on the provisions of the Treaties regarding the legislation under consideration. Unanimity of states does not seem justified in the case of democratic consultations on ordinary legislation: it would be exaggerated if a majority of voters coming from a single small state would be endowed with a veto right against the will of the majority of voters in the Union.[21] For reasons of simplification I propose referendums only on matters decided by qualified majority, and for reasons of symmetry I propose to use the same formula as for QMV in the Council. One should consider that in Switzerland – true, a real federal state – a simple majority of states (the cantons) is required for constitutional issues. Hence, even if the EU is not exactly a federation, a form of qualified majority of states would suffice as a source of legitimacy for decisions concerning ordinary legislation: higher hurdles to majority 'tyranny' for formally less important decisions than in the Swiss federation. For reasons of simplicity (QMV being already sufficiently complicated in its present form!) one can use again the rule of a majority of 55 per cent of the states representing at least 65 per cent of the Union population.

- A **quorum of participation** is also suitable (such a requirement exists in Italy but not in Switzerland). Following the same logic as for the consent of concurrent majorities, Nentwich (1998: 137) proposes for constitutional referendums in the EU a double quorum: an overall turnout of 50 per cent plus a minimum of 30 per cent in each member state. A quorum seems, in fact, better justified for votes on popular initiatives than on amendments at the constitutional level proposed by public authorities. There is, indeed, in the case of popular initiatives a risk of the agenda being captured by active but marginal minority groups, or by futile issues. Although the rules for the collection of signatures and the necessity to achieve concurrent majorities should prevent this, the quorum requirement provides an additional safeguard. For ordinary legislation an overall turnout of 50 per cent plus at least 30 per cent in two-thirds (but not all) of the states should be sufficient. It would be paradoxical if, out of sheer disinterest on the part of its population, a small member state could veto a proposal approved by the majority of voters in a qualified majority of EU states.

- Ultimately, if the issue of the referendum is positive, the outcome would be **binding** and the content of the initiative should be incorporated into the body of European legislation.

One should note that, although inspired by Swiss legislation and practice, this proposal contains much more stringent and more sophisticated conditions for the adoption of direct legislation than in Switzerland. It contains material limits (only on ordinary legislation), stronger federalist checks at more levels (wide state representation in the collection of signatures, QMV in the Council, double majority plus QMV in the referendum, sufficient turnout in a number of states), judicial review and constitutional checks (role of the ECJ), checks by representative bodies (the Council and the EP), and specific requirements regarding participation thresholds. There is no doubt that this weakens the potential of referendum instruments but it should facilitate their incorporation into the complex political system of the EU.

## SOME LESSONS FROM THE SWISS EXPERIENCE ON THE PROBLEM OF THE MISSING 'DEMOS'

Referendums are binary majoritarian procedures that do not leave any other alternative but a 'yes' or 'no' choice. Hence, minorities must accept the legitimacy of majority decision. This requires that the distance between majority and minority preferences is not too wide, that vital interests of minorities are not endangered by majority decisions, and that no minorities are, for structural reasons, regularly losers in the democratic game. If these conditions are not met, there is a serious risk of the majority vote being delegitimized because it leads straight to majority tyranny. And, of course, the more heterogeneous the collectivity to which binding decisions taken by majority vote apply, the more such a risk is to be seriously considered.

In the EU we have the well-known problem of the lack of a common 'demos' which would be characterized by sufficient cultural homogeneity (as observed by the German Constitutional Court), or in other words by a 'Wir-Identität', as pointed out by Fritz W. Scharpf (1999b). Fragmentation of the public space along national and linguistic boundaries is the cause of a lack of feeling of common belonging among Europeans, and this problem has been aggravated by the recent enlargement. This can undermine the foundations of solidarity and can have negative consequences for redistributive policies, not least if some of them were to be decided by referendum. A plausible scenario is of populations with common interests coalescing against other segments of the EU considered as benefiting unduly from the system. Such a danger should not be underestimated in a period of widespread suspicion (including within national communities: see the rise of regional-populist parties such as the Lega Nord or the Vlaams Belang); where, owing to their structural character-istics, some groups are suspected to abuse others, so that the game is 'rigged' by the absence of 'fair play' (Levi 1998: 98–100). That is the reason why any provisions for referendums in the EU should be supplemented by higher obstacles to majority tyranny than in a federalist state such as Switzerland, although one should not forget that it is expected in general from federalist insti-tutions (and from consociational rules) to allow populations to live together even *in spite of* the lack of a common demos. The lack of a demos is not an argu-ment against direct democracy, but rather against majoritarian democracy in any of its forms (see Mair 2004: 15–16). One may, for instance, doubt whether the formation of a homogeneous European executive challenged by an equally homogeneous opposition in contrast to the 'Swiss-like' Commission would be an adequate solution, given the purely majoritarian flavour of the recipe.

It may also be, however, that the ties which united the populations of nation-states during the phase of nation-building have been overestimated (Abromeit 2000: 62). Cleavage theory teaches us that struggles between centres and peripheries have not only accompanied the nation-building process, but have also marked in the long run the partisan landscape in several countries. And this particularly applies to a country like Switzerland: not only is it still hetero-geneous today, but it is highly questionable whether anything like a common demos collectively exercising its *pouvoir constituant* existed in the nascent Swiss federation of 1848. Although the federal Constitution was a compromise on the crucial issue of the degree of centralization, there was no widely shared enthusiasm among the population to transform the old Confederation into a federal state, and it is instructive in that respect that in cantonal constitutional referendums majorities for the new Constitution were only achieved because abstainers were counted as 'yes' voters. Although federalism gradually reduced the salience of societal conflict in this country, deep animosity between centres and peripheries, Catholics and Protestants (*Kulturkampf*), progressives and conservatives persisted at least over half a century (supplemented by an acute cleavage between French and German speakers during the First World War). This did not prevent the development of direct democracy procedures at the federal level. The latter were set up as a result of power struggles and are not the natural outcome of any historical continuity or of any mythical Swiss exceptionalism (*Sonderfall*). Direct democracy was introduced in the federal Constitution (referendum as veto right in 1874, popular initiative for Constitutional amendments in 1891) as a result of pressure 'from below' and of successive waves of popular mobilizations against the authorities who were reluctant, fearing disorder.

Today, of course, the heterogeneity and size of the twenty-six Swiss cantons and half-cantons are not comparable to the heterogeneity and size of the twenty-five EU members. Nevertheless, a closer look at possible indicators of heterogeneity leads to more differentiated conclusions. In an article on the democratic deficit in the EU, Decker (2002: 263–4) presents the following indicators of a lack of a common demos in Europe:

– low turnout in elections for the EP;
– distinctiveness of national party systems;[22]
– and, above all, the strength of linguistic barriers and national identities.

Interestingly, all these characteristics can still be found in Switzerland too, although today no one would credibly argue that the Swiss should not enjoy democracy because they do not form a common demos:

– participation in federal elections is low because, in a similar way to European elections, they have no direct impact on the formation of the federal government (it is a grand coalition of the major parties and its composition did not vary between 1959 and 2003, probably the case best exemplifying the 'cartel-party' thesis: Katz and Mair 1995);
– there is considerable variation among cantonal party systems (Klöti 1997), depending on the presence of a Catholic population, the linguistic area, etc. (in other words, there is no nationalization of the party system equivalent to Germany or the US);
– linguistic barriers exist too (the media space is thoroughly segmented along linguistic lines, and more importantly the French- and German-speaking communities diverge on such crucial issues as EU membership),[23] and cantonal identities are still very strong (for example, a project to unify the neighbouring cantons of Geneva and Vaud was rejected by overwhelming popular majorities in both cantons).

The problem of linguistic barriers is the most serious, according to Dekker. This is a strange argument: for a common public space to be established, there is no necessity to speak the same language. Linguistic differences do not as such generate insurmountable cleavages: the latter are socially constructed by all sorts of entrepreneurs (politicians, the media, etc.) around these issues. On the other hand, for a common public space to be established it is necessary that the population debates about the same *issues*. That depends on the political agenda, and Europe-wide referendums would contribute much to the formation of an agenda of problems to be solved which would become common to the national public spaces. The members of the Convention who proposed a constitutional referendum did notice the possibility of such a virtuous effect. They maintain: 'While it is the case that a "European demos" does not exist, it is equally clear that a Europe-wide referendum would create a common political space. It would be a means of bringing the peoples of Europe closer politically; it would ensure that the people were more engaged with and had a greater knowledge of the project.' The history of modern Switzerland teaches us too – in accordance with 'neo-institutionalist' political theory – that institutions matter. The demos problem will remain unresolved if we do not opt for *demos-enhancing institutions*. In Switzerland it was precisely through the democratization of the political system via direct democracy in the second half of the nineteenth century that a common demos was established.

## NOT ONLY MORE EUROPEAN LEGITIMACY BUT ALSO MORE GOVERNABILITY THANKS TO THE REFERENDUM

Owing to the feeble Europeanization of the party system, campaigns for EP elections do not contribute to a debate on Europe-wide issues. Direct democracy campaigns on Europe-wide issues would by contrast stimulate and popularize the debate on integration. To be sure, safeguards for minority protection will not prevent the emergence in these campaigns (or at the moment of the interpretation of referendum outcomes) of various cleavages, including cleavages along state lines. To state it somewhat bluntly, there may be a certain price to pay in terms of European cohesion for the constitution of a public space. Yet it can be plausibly hypothesized that the salience of cleavages will gradually be attenuated. Although some observers see in direct democracy a source of ungovernability – either an additional veto point, or a source of overload – it can be reasonably argued that these are short-term problems. One should consider the contribution of such mechanisms more broadly and in the long run, and in general the more frequent and unexceptional the use of direct democracy instruments, the more routinized it becomes, and referendum campaigns gradually become immune from excessive dramatization.

As mentioned earlier, we tend to forget that the formation of national public spaces has not been immune either to deep social divisions, including along territorial lines. Such divisions cannot be credibly managed without some willingness to manifest openness to citizens' claims. Instead of keeping delicate issues off the agenda, it seems wiser to stimulate public debate and hence contribute to a feeling of integration instead of alienation among the citizenry. Referendum votes provide a good opportunity in that respect: according to a study on the German press (reported in Landfried 2002: 87), the number of newspaper articles on Europe significantly increased in the period covering the Danish, Irish, and French referendums on the Maastricht Treaty: *direct democracy produces public space and (re)vitalizes politics.*[24] Political competition and media coverage are in turn necessary for accountability because they simplify 'the complex set of actors, policy networks, institutions and procedures' (Magnette 2003: 153) that make decisions. In the EU this set is more complex and 'politics' is less developed than at the national level. Hence there is also a need for more coupling between the sphere of policy-making and the sphere of politics, and this indeed presupposes the revitalization of the latter on the EU level.[25] The interesting thing in the Swiss way is the coupling of competition in the arena of direct democracy with negotiation in the arena of representative democracy, and above all in the sphere of policy networks (Papadopoulos 2001b). Similar forms of coupling seem plausible in the EU.

In the EU where *consociational* decision-making is the rule (Bogaards 2002; Costa and Magnette 2003), the Damoclean sword of direct democracy would probably above all (like in Switzerland and unlike polities with more competitive-oriented politics such as Italy or the US) allow outsiders to gain better *negotiation* positions. Decision-makers would have to anticipate the risk of popular initiatives, and that would make them become more responsive either to opposition or to novel claims. As to the outsiders, experience from Switzerland teaches us that they would have to moderate their claims, either to obtain the consent of representative institutions of the Union and thus avoid expensive and time-consuming campaigns, or to achieve the required concurrent (super) majorities. The characteristics of the European political system make it plausible that the effects of direct democracy will be closer to the Swiss model: fragmentation, checks and balances, and multi-level govern-ance exert strong pressure to turn direct democracy instruments into negotiation devices that produce above all *indirect* effects. In a consociational polity they are largely incorporated into the overall consociational framework, and strengthen it instead of acting as majoritarian devices (Papadopoulos 2001b). On the other hand, their existence reduces accountability problems typical of consociational polities: direct democracy campaigns clarify political choices by their 'yes or no' logic, while remaining integrated in an overall framework of negotiation democracy.

As a result, it is likely that the initiative right itself would not be used frequently (in Switzerland no more than 7 per cent of federal legislation is challenged by petition), because it will be above all its 'shadow' that will count, acting as an incentive for negotiated policy-making. The risk of deadlock because of direct democracy would be diminished thanks to 'escape routes' (Héritier 2000) offered by bargaining and deliberation. Further, such a risk would in any case not be dramatic considering that referendums by petition would only be possible on ordinary legislation and not on major issues of a constitutional nature. And if negotiations in decision-making arenas fail and campaigns on popular initiatives are organized, that would oblige political actors to care more about providing information to the European public opinion on their preferences, and about justifying their action.[26] Therefore, we can anticipate that referendums would be integrated into the overall consociational framework. Their 'shadow' would induce a broader support for decisions (gains in governability), while at the same time strengthening the accountability of élites in the public space (gains in legitimacy), and thus alleviating the accountability deficits common in negotiation systems. To state it briefly, without idealizing direct democracy, it is worth specifying the conditions under which it is likely to produce virtuous effects. These are above all incentives for élite co-operation owing to power fragmentation and diffusion, accompanied by a well-established 'consociational' culture that allows élites to react to these incentives through deliberation and negotiation. Such conditions are particularly present at the EU level.

But gains in terms of legitimacy might be even larger. The Swiss example highlights the fact that the toolkit of direct democracy not only has an instrumental value, but also contributes to the formation of a common identity. Switzerland is portrayed as a paradigmatic case of political integration in spite of its heterogeneity (Deutsch 1976), and it is worth recalling that direct democracy played a significant role in that respect. With a more open opportunity structure, thanks to the availability of direct democracy institutions, the citizens increasingly viewed the newly established federal system as 'theirs'. Hence, direct (or other forms of participatory) democracy not only opens opportunities for a much more active 'specific' support of the citizenry for policy decisions, but it is also likely to generate a more robust 'diffuse' support for a political system that would as a whole be considered more 'citizen-friendly'.[27] European multi-level governance in particular is plagued by the problem of 'many hands'. In a period of declining confidence in national and European political élites, participatory institutions give to citizens a feeling of control over these many hands, a feeling of empowerment which legitimizes the system.

Today, according to Swiss Eurobarometer data (Christin and Trechsel 2002), neutrality, federalism, and direct democracy are considered as the three major pillars of Swiss identity. However, it is direct democracy that the Swiss consider to be the most important and of which they are most proud. Direct democracy is a major source, and today a component, of the Swiss variant of 'Verfassungspatriotismus' that compensates for a 'Wir-identität' still having to compete in this country with strong cantonal and even local loyalties. It does not seem unreasonable to think that similar evolutions would gradually take place at the European level too. Of course, introducing a Europe-wide popular initiative right by petition with binding effects would require the consent of member states which are unequally familiar with referendums (although at least in theory the new members are more familiar with them), and some frankly hostile. Hence, this proposal of citizens' empowerment à la Suisse should probably be considered as 'immodest' (Weiler 1997), notwithstanding its much attenuated formulation (so one should rather speak about semi-direct instead of direct legislation). But it would probably also be unfair to reject this proposal merely on the grounds that it is obsolete or misplaced Swiss folklore.

**Address for correspondence:** Yannis Papadopoulos, Institut d'Etudes Politiques et Internationales, Université de Lausanne, BFSH 2, CH-1015 Lausanne, Switzerland. Tel: (+41) 21 692 3143. Fax: (+41) 21 692 3145. email: ioannis.papadopoulos@unil.ch

## NOTES

* This article is a strongly revised version of Yannis Papadopoulos, 'Puet-on imaginer d'organiser des référendums à l'échelle européenne et à quelles conditions?', Groupement d'études et de recherches 'Notre Europe', Policy paper 2, November 2002.

1 Even authors emphasizing the dual aspects of Swiss federalism acknowledge its evolution towards a co-operative model (Börzel and Hosli 2003: 197 n.). For dissimilarities between forms of implementation in the EU and the US, see Halberstam (2001).

2 Pascal Lamy argued in *Le Monde*: 'Il faudra dépasser, pour assurer à la fois la cohérence de son action et l'intérêt des opinions publiques, le principe d'un exécutif à la manière suisse, où toutes les tendances "raisonnables" sont représentées et, se surveillant sans relâche, se paralysent souvent' (quoted by Magnette 2003: 155).

3 Although sheer mimetism can be justified on grounds of bounded rationality, uncertainty, high information costs, etc.; see the abundant body of work on institutional import, policy transfer, learning and emulation, and the subgroup of literature on Europeanization.

4 For a discussion of the 'export' possibilities of Swiss solutions, above all for stability and democratic consolidation in deeply segmented societies, see Linder (1994).

5 It seems fashionable now to underplay (and even to challenge the reality of) the problem of the democratic deficit not only in European technocratic circles but also in the academic community (Crombez 2003; Moravcsik 2002; Zweifel 2002). However, the problem is (as noted later in this paper) that the performative force of political discourses criticizing the deficit is by no means negligible. Hence the deficit causes governability and legitimacy problems too.

6 This may be a sufficient base of legitimacy for intergovernmentalists who logically consider that accountability is then a national matter. However, the limited accountability of European institutions is a broader problem, and even under the intergovernmentalist assumption, why should a government accountable to the citizenry A be authorized to influence decisions that are collectively binding for citizenries A + 24?

7 For a comparative analysis of citizens' behaviour in referendums on European issues, see Hug (2002).

8 See also several critical contributions in Joerges *et al.* (2001), and Follesdal (2003) on the contradictions of the White Paper.

9 See, for instance, the proposals made by Katharina Holzinger and Christoph Knill, 'Eine Verfassung für die Europäische Federation. Kontinuierliche Weiterentwicklung des Erreichten', European University Institute, Jean Monnet Working Paper 07/2000 (Responses to Joschka Fischer): http://www.jeanmonnetprogram.org/papers/00/00f1401.html.

10 Weiler (1997: 152) suggests that more direct forms of citizens' participation can be a substitute for the absence of governmental alternation at the EU level as an option for citizens dissatisfied with the performance of European authorities.

11 Federalism entails vertical power-sharing while consociation implies horizontal power-sharing, mostly as a result of rules for proportional political representation of the major social forces. This distinction roughly parallels that of the two dimensions of consensual democracies in Lijphart (1999).

12 For a comparison of diverging effects of largely similar direct democracy provisions in Switzerland, Italy and the United States, see Papadopoulos (1998: 37–81).

13 Proposals were made by academics too (Abromeit 2000: 186–7; Epiney 1997: 310; Nentwich 1998: 136; Weiler 1997: 152–3), and by some civil society circles (Eurotopia, the Initiative and Referendum Institute Europe, etc.).

14 For some proposals for clarification, see the contributions by Jürgen Meyer and Victor Cuesta in Filliez and Kaufmann (2004).

15 McKay (2001: 148ff.) recommends 'constitutionalizing' taxation issues and those necessitating a unanimous vote.

16 I return to this issue later with some suggestions about making capture more difficult. I would like to stress here that I consider opportunities for direct citizen involvement as necessary, without idealizing their virtues for policy-making. I have commented elsewhere in more detail on the 'broken promises' of direct democracy (Papadopoulos 2001a), but instead of throwing the baby out with the bathwater, one should look for those safeguards most likely to prevent perverse effects.

17 That is also the suggestion made by Eurotopia in its autumn 1995 theses (see Erne et al. 1995: 427). Nentwich suggests 3–4 per cent, while Epiney proposes 10 per cent. These proportions are much higher than the lower threshold in art I-47.4 of at least one million citizens, which roughly corresponds to 0.3 per cent of the European electorate.

18 On the other hand, it is known that in order to increase their chances of success popular initiatives should not be too detailed in their content.

19 See also on this subject Schmitter (2000: 36) who proposes popular initiatives including some on institutional matters, but only with a consultative role.

20 In Switzerland and Australia (where referendums are, however, less frequent) a majority of states suffices for the second majority requirement. It should be noted that over 150 years after it was established the double majority is challenged in Switzerland because it generates biases in representation (overrepresentation of small cantons) which can hardly be justified today. Population gaps between small and big cantons have increased a great deal, and new groups that claim protection of their interests by institutional mechanisms are not given consideration (Papadopoulos 2002). Representational privileges are hard to remove once awarded to minorities because they strengthen them in their role of veto players (Linder 1994). The same applies more strongly, of course, to unanimous voting.

21 Epiney (1997: 304 and 312) proposed a qualified majority of states for a vote on the Treaties, but a simple majority of states for ordinary legislation. Even on constitutional issues (including taxation as noted earlier) McKay (2001: 149) proposes a majority of two-thirds or three-fifths of all the member states accompanied by an opting-out clause for the states whose population would vote against.

22 However, the cohesiveness of transnational groups in terms of voting behaviour in the EP should not be underestimated (Lord 2004: 117).

23 See the detailed survey on this topic by Kriesi et al. (1996).

24 Warleigh (2003: 129) emphasizes the need to give priority 'to a process of political socialisation through which member state nationals can reinvent themselves as "European" citizens', but does not say much about the adequate instruments for that purpose. Lord (2004: 227) correctly notes that 'publics have historically been mobilised into political arenas in response to "concrete" experiences and problems'.

25 This is not to say that such a coupling between spheres functioning according to different logics is necessarily harmonious. There can be disjunctions such as those portrayed by Jean Leca (1996: 345–6) between the 'politique des problèmes' and 'politique d'opinion'. See also Gerhard Lehmbruch's (1999) work on German federalism, where he argues that the competitive logic of the party system cannot coexist without significant tensions with a logic of negotiation dictated by federalist

constraints. See also Grande (2000), according to whom the autonomization of a 'governance' sphere of 'problem-solving' is challenged in the public sphere by charismatic political entrepreneurs who reintroduce with support from the media a personalistic dimension in politics.

26 One could, for instance, take the opportunity to organize a Europe-wide 'deliberative opinion poll' for each issue on the agenda, bringing together a sample of European citizens from all member states (which would require simultaneous translation, but this is not a major problem). A 'deliberative opinion poll' was organized in Denmark on the euro, prior to the referendum on that issue. It was subject to extensive media coverage (Andersen and Hansen, forthcoming).

27 This argument presents some similarity with Trenz and Eder's (2004: 19) argument about the 'paradox of democracy' in the EU: 'intensified communication about the EU's multiple deficits has paradoxical effects: it might well become a self-help therapy that remedies the deficits it deplores'. I am afraid that I cannot agree on this point with Lord (2004: 73), who maintains that consensual decision-making within the EU reduces the need to identify in order to consent.

## REFERENCES

Abromeit, H. (2000) *Wozu braucht man Demokratie? Die postnationale Herausforderung der Demokratietheorie*, Opladen: Leske & Budrich.

Andersen, V.N. and Hansen, K. (forthcoming) 'How deliberation makes better citizens: the Danish deliberative poll on the euro', forthcoming in Y. Papadopoulos and P. Warin (eds), *Innovative, Participatory, and Deliberative Procedures in Policy-Making: Democratic and Effective?* (special issue of *European Journal of Political Research*, 2006).

Armingeon, K. (2000) 'Swiss federalism in comparative perspective', in U. Wachendorfer-Schmidt (ed.), *Federalism and Political Performance*, London and New York: Routledge, pp. 112–29.

Auer, A. (1997) 'Le référendum européen: définitions, repères historiques et jalons d'études', in A. Auer and J.-F. Flauss (eds), *Le référendum européen*, Brussels: Bruylant, pp. 23–47.

Benz, A. (2003) 'Demokratiereform durch Föderalisierung?', in C. Offe (ed.), *Demokratisierung der Demokratie. Diagnosen und Reformvorschläge*, Frankfurt and New York: Campus, pp. 169–92.

Blondel, J. (1998) 'Il modello svizzero: un futuro per l'Europa?', *Rivista italiana di scienza politica* XXVIII(2): 199–227.

Bogaards, M. (2002) 'Consociational interpretations of the European Union', *European Union Politics* 3(3): 357–81.

Börzel, T. and Hosli, M. (2003) 'Brussels between Bern and Berlin: comparative federalism meets the European Union', *Governance: An International Journal of Policy, Administration, and Institutions* 16(2): 179–202.

Christin, T. and Trechsel, A. (2002) 'Joining the EU? Explaining public opinion in Switzerland', *European Union Politics* 3(4): 415–43.

Costa, O. and Magnette, P. (2003) 'The European Union as a consociation? A methodological assessment', *West European Politics* 26(3): 1–18.

Crombez, C. (2003) 'The democratic deficit in the European Union. Much ado about nothing?', *European Union Politics* 4(1): 101–20.

Dalton, R.J. (2004) *Democratic Challenges. Democratic Choices*, Oxford: Oxford University Press.

Decker, F. (2002) 'Governance beyond the nation-state. Reflections on the democratic deficit of the European Union', *Journal of European Public Policy* 9(2): 256–72.

Deutsch, K.W. (1976) *Die Schweiz als paradigmatischer Fall politischer Integration*, Bern: P. Haupt.

Eijk, C. van der and Franklin, M. (2004) 'Potential for contestation on European matters at national elections in Europe', in G. Marks and M.R. Steenbergen (eds), *European Integration and Political Conflict*, Cambridge: Cambridge University Press, pp. 32–50.

Epiney, A. (1997) 'Le référendum européen', in A. Auer and J.-F. Flauss (eds), *Le référendum européen*, Brussels: Bruylant, pp. 287–315.

Erne, R. *et al.* (1995) *Transnationale Demokratie. Impulse für ein demokratisch verfasstes Europa*, Zurich: Realotopia.

Filliez, F. and Kaufmann, B. (eds) (2004) *The European Constitution. Bringing in the People*, Amsterdam and Bern: IRI Europe and Presence Suisse.

Follesdal, A. (2003) 'The political theory of the White Paper on Governance: hidden and fascinating', http://folk.uio.no/andreasf/ms/Wp-governance.rtf.

Grande, E. (2000) 'Charisma und Komplexität: Verhandlungsdemokratie, Mediende-mokratie und der Funktionswandel politischer Eliten', in R. Werle and U. Schimank (eds), *Gesellschaftliche Komplexität und kollektive Handlungsfähigkeit*, Frankfurt/Main: Campus, pp. 297–319.

Halberstam, D. (2001) 'Comparative federalism and the issue of commandeering', in K. Nicolaidis and R. Howse (eds), *The Federal Vision*, Oxford: Oxford University Press, pp. 213–51.

Hayward, J. (ed.) (1995) *The Crisis of Representation in Europe*, London: Frank Cass.

Héritier, A. (1999) 'Elements of democratic legitimation in Europe: an alternative perspective', *Journal of European Public Policy* 6(2): 269–82.

Héritier, A. (2000) *Policy-Making and Diversity in Europe. Escaping Deadlock*, Cambridge: Cambridge University Press.

Hug, S. (2002) *Voices of Europe. Citizens, Referendums and European Integration*, New York: Rowman & Littlefield.

Joerges, C., Mény, Y. and Weiler, J.H.H. (eds) (2001) *Mountain or Molehill?: A Critical Appraisal of the Commission White Paper on Governance*, Robert Schuman Centre of the European University Institute, Jean Monnet Working Paper 6/01.

Katz, R.S. and Mair, P. (1995) 'Changing models of party organization and party democracy: the emergence of the cartel party', *Party Politics* 1(1): 5–28.

Klöti, U. (1997) 'Kantonale Parteiensysteme. Die Bedeutung des Kantonalen Kontextes für die Positionierung der Parteien', in H. Kriesi *et al.* (eds), *Schweizer Wahlen 1995*, Bern: P. Haupt, pp. 45–72.

Kriesi, H. *et al.* (1996) *Le clivage linguistique. Problèmes de compréhension entre les communautés linguistiques en Suisse*, Bern: Federal Office of Statistics.

Landfried, C. (2002) 'Vers un etat constitutionnel européen', in R. Dehousse (ed.), *Une Constitution pour l'Europe?*, Paris: Presses de Sciences Po, pp. 79–113.

Leca, J. (1996) 'Ce que l'analyse des politiques publiques pourrait apprendre sur le gouvernement démocratique', *Revue française de science politique* 46(1): 122–33.

Lehmbruch, G. (1999) 'Verhandlungsdemokratie, Entscheidungsblockaden und Arenenverflechtung', in W. Merkel and A. Busch (eds), *Demokratie in Ost und West*, Frankfurt/Main: Suhrkamp, pp. 402–24.

Levi, M. (1998) 'A state of trust', in V. Braithwaite and M. Levi (eds), *Trust and Governance*, New York: Russell Sage Foundation, pp. 77–101.

Lijphart, A. (1999) *Patterns of Democracy*, New Haven and London: Yale University Press.

Linder, W. (1994) *Swiss Democracy. Possible Solutions to Conflict in Multicultural Societies*, London: Macmillan.

Lord, C. (2004) *A Democratic Audit of the European Union*, London: Palgrave.

Magnette, P. (2003) 'European governance and civic participation: beyond elitist citizenship?', *Political Studies* 51: 144–60.

Mair, P. (2004) 'Popular democracy and the construction of the European Union political system'. Paper presented at the workshop 'Sustainability and the European Union', ECPR Joint Sessions, Uppsala, April 2004.

Majone, G. (2002) 'Delegation of regulatory powers in a mixed polity', *European Law Journal* 8(3): 319–39.

McKay, D. (2001) *Designing Europe. Comparative Lessons from Federal Experiences*, Oxford: Oxford University Press.

Mény, Y. and Surel, Y. (eds) (2002) *Democracies and the Populist Challenge*, London: Palgrave.

Moravcsik, A. (2002) 'In defence of the "democratic deficit": reassessing legitimacy in the European Union', *Journal of Common Market Studies* 40(2): 603–24.

Nentwich, M. (1998) 'Opportunity structures for citizens' participation. The case of the European Union', in A. Weale and M. Nentwich (eds), *Political Theory and the European Union*, London: Routledge, pp. 125–40.

Norris, P. (1999) *Critical Citizens. Global Support for Democratic Governance*, Oxford: Oxford University Press.

Papadopoulos, Y. (1995) 'Analysis of functions and dysfunctions of direct democracy: top-down and bottom-up perspectives', *Politics and Society* 23(4): 421–48.

Papadopoulos, Y. (1998) *Démocratie directe*, Paris: Economica.

Papadopoulos, Y. (2001a) 'Citizenship through direct democracy? The "broken promises" of empowerment', in C. Crouch, K. Eder and D. Tambini (eds), *Citizenship, Markets, and the State*, Oxford: Oxford University Press, pp. 173–96.

Papadopoulos, Y. (2001b) 'How does direct democracy matter? The impact of referendum votes on politics and policy-making', *West European Politics* 24(2): 35–58.

Papadopoulos, Y. (2002) 'Connecting minorities to the Swiss federal system: a frozen conception of representation and the problem of "requisite variety"', *Publius: The Journal of Federalism* 32(3): 47–65.

Papadopoulos, Y. (2003) 'Cooperative forms of governance: problems of democratic accountability in complex environments', *European Journal of Political Research* 42(4): 473–501.

Peterson, J. and O'Toole, Jr., L. (2001) 'Federal governance in the United States and the European Union: a policy network perspective', in K. Nicolaidis and R. Howse (eds), *The Federal Vision*, Oxford: Oxford University Press, pp. 300–34.

Pharr, S.J. and Putnam, R.D. (2000) *Disaffected Democracies: What's Troubling the Trilateral Countries*, Princeton, NJ: Princeton University Press.

Sbragia, A. (2002) 'The dilemma of governance with government', Jean Monnet Working Paper 3/02, NYU School of Law.

Scharpf, F.W. (1999a) *Governing in Europe. Effective and Democratic?*, Oxford: Oxford University Press.

Scharpf, F.W. (1999b) 'Demokratieprobleme in der europäischen Mehrebenenpolitik', in W. Merkel and A. Busch (eds), *Demokratie in Ost und West*, Frankfurt/Main: Suhrkamp, pp. 672–94.

Schmitter, P.C. (2000) *How to Democratize the European Union . . . and Why Bother?*, New York: Rowman & Littlefield.

Schmitter, P.C. (2002) 'Participation in governance arrangements: is there any reason to expect it will achieve "sustainable and innovative policies in a multi-level context"?', in J.R. Grote and B. Gbikpi (eds), *Participatory Governance. Political and Societal Implications*, Opladen: Leske & Budrich, pp. 51–69.

Trenz, H.-J. and Eder, K. (2004) 'The democratizing dynamics of a European public sphere. Towards a theory of democratic functionalism', *European Journal of Social Theory* 7(1): 5–25.

Warleigh, A. (2003) *Democracy in the European Union*, London: Sage.

Weiler, J.H.H. (1997) 'The European Union belongs to its citizens: three immodest proposals', *European Law Review* 22: 150–6.

Zweifel, T.D. (2002) '. . . Who is without sin cast the first stone: the EU's democratic deficit in comparison', *Journal of European Public Policy* 9(5): 812–40.

# Federalism and the European party system

Lori Thorlakson

## INTRODUCTION

As an evolving party system, confederally constructed from national parties, the European party system faces much the same challenges for analysis as federations. Against a backdrop of increasing parliamentary powers and successive waves of enlargement, the European party system has developed through an aggregation of national parties and party systems. Despite the development of European parties and their organization into parliamentary party groups, national parties retain control over the crucial functions of campaigning and candidate selection and national political competition remains crucial for structuring vote choice. Federations, and particularly those created out of previously independent political units, have also faced this process. The question of aggregation is an important and timely one for the Union after the 2004 enlargement. How does a party system develop to incorporate twenty-five countries with distinct histories of national development, including regime discontinuities and varying levels of party system consolidation?

A comparative federalism approach can offer two important insights. First, it provides the analytic tools to assess the linkages between national and European party systems. Measures of party system congruence, the similarity of core party system structures, taken from comparative federalism research, can be used to assess the degree to which the party system of the European Parliament (EP) is structurally linked to national systems. Second, it raises important questions such as how different models of federalism aggregate political competition at the federal level, channel conflict, and balance partisan and territorial competition through the linkage or separation of party organizations and party systems. If the ideal construction of a European party system is one in which European parties cross-cut national divides (Thomassen *et al.* 2004: 114), what conditions may facilitate this?

Understanding the nature of linkages between the national and European party systems allows us to elaborate existing theoretical accounts of voter behaviour in EP elections – and predict the limits of such explanations. Reif and Schmidt have argued that as 'second order' elections, dwarfed in importance by national electoral competition, voting decisions for the EP are cognitively dependent upon the national electoral arena (1980: 8ff.). Depending on the national context, voters may use European elections to lodge protest votes against national governments, vote 'with the heart' for a party unlikely to win mandates nationally, support a newly installed government, or abstain altogether owing to a lack of interest (van der Eijk *et al.* 1996). Subsequent tests of European election results confirm these predictions (Marsh 1998) and confront us with normative concerns such as the sincerity of vote choice for EP elections and the potential for EP elections to provide meaningful representation.

This paper focuses on three main questions. First, what are the sociological and institutional drivers of party system development in multi-level systems, and can these processes of development be generalized to the European Union (EU) case? Second, in a party system confederally created from national parties, how well do national parties fit into the EP party system structure? Does the party family structure of the 2004 EP party system provide a meaningful framework of political contestation for parties and voters across the member states, or is it at odds with the party system structure in some member states? Finally, does the European party system resemble other models of multi-level party systems?

The first section of this paper defines multi-level aspects of electoral competition and presents sociological and institutional explanations of party system congruence and party organizational linkage. From the party system congruence and organizational patterns found in six federations, I propose four models of multi-level party systems. Section two draws upon data from the most recent national legislative elections in the twenty-five member states and the 2004 European parliamentary elections. While we find general congruence of core party system structures, some member states send a high proportion of Members of the European Parliament (MEPs) to the EP who are not aligned with the party groupings of the traditional Liberal, Social Democratic and Conservative/Christian Democratic party families.

# I. TYPES OF FEDERAL PARTY SYSTEMS

## Elements of multi-level competition

In a multi-level party system, we are not only interested in features of the party system such as its dimensionality or core components, but also in the competitive linkages – whether parties serve as integrative linkages between the two levels of competition, and the congruence of party systems. Party system congruence refers to the similarity of the core structures and competitive dynamics of party systems in a multi-level system. Measured horizontally, it refers to the similarity of the number of effective parties and party electoral strength across the constituent units of a federation or other multi-level system. It serves as a measure of the overall heterogeneity of the multi-level party system. High congruence can reflect the organizational presence and electoral success of national parties that cross-cut territorial divisions. Measured vertically, congruence refers to the similarity of party systems at the state and federal (or national and European) levels. It tells us the extent to which political contestation at the state and federal level is similar owing to the presence of the same parties at each level. Party system congruence can signal a high degree of linkage of issues, parties and voter behaviour, owing perhaps to the cognitive dependence of voters on the 'first order' arena. Incongruence, meanwhile, can signal the evolution of arenas of competition with distinct issue spaces and different parties, because of heterogeneity of the underlying social cleavage basis or differences in the way these cleavages have been mobilized and institutionalized.

Competition across levels of government in a multi-level system can be linked through integrated party organizations, where parties of the same name compete at each level of government, united by common membership, governance structures, and sharing a common ideological position. Integrated parties, such as those in Germany, maintain strong integrative linkages between state and federal organizations and a balance of power toward the federal 'centre' so that it is meaningful to consider the party as a single political actor. Integrated parties can serve as a channel for party co-ordination or control across levels of the party system.

Party competition can also be waged relatively independently at each level of government when split parties, those with no organizational linkages to parties at another level of government, compete. Split systems can provide an institutional basis for differential mobilization of cleavages in the federal and state party systems, increasing the potential for party system incongruence. We find this in Canada, where political parties in some provinces either have no federal counterpart, or are organizationally divorced from the federal party. These organizational differences affect whether parties have the ability and interest to represent state interests at the risk of conflict with federal party interests, and whether we can consider parties in federations to be one actor, or several actors which sometimes serve as an additional form of political opposition.

**Explaining party system linkage**

Both sociological and institutional accounts of politics offer explanations for the development of party system congruence and party organizational linkages. In sociological accounts, party system incongruence can be explained by a social cleavage basis that differs from one constituent unit to another. When federations are created to accommodate social cleavages by creating territorial units that coincide with the linguistic, religious or ethnic cleavage lines that give rise to distinct societies, the result can be patterns of relevant social cleavage that vary from one federal unit to another. In Switzerland, territorial cleavages coincide with, rather than cross-cut, linguistic and religious cleavages, producing cantons that are more homogeneous than the country as a whole (Lijphart 1977: 89–94). We would therefore expect the social cleavage basis of party competition to have a high degree of inter-cantonal variation. In Austria, another plural society, territorial divisions cross-cut social cleavages, yielding a similar social cleavage pattern across *Länder* (Lijphart 1977: 98). In Canada and Germany, by contrast, federal territorial boundaries generally cross-cut religious or linguistic cleavages with some exceptions. The boundaries of Quebec coincide with a linguistic cleavage, and the boundaries of Bavaria create a homogeneously Catholic *Land*. In addition, the legacy of communism and democratic transition has left its imprint on the new *Länder* in the form of the Party of Democratic Socialism (PDS). A heterogeneous social cleavage basis and differences in the mobilization and politicization of cleavages at each level of government can also indirectly lead to parties that are organizationally split. When cleavages emerge that are unique to one arena of competition, split parties may follow.

Political cleavages are important to the extent that they are mobilized and institutionalized. However, they are not strictly endogenous. The institutional structure, such as the constitutional allocation of power and legislative decision rules, may also exert slow and steady pressure that shapes the evolution of party systems, affecting patterns of congruence and party organizational linkages. First, the relative power of the level of government affects the congruence of the party system and the organizational linkages that develop between them. This follows the logic of Reif and Schmidt's argument that how much is 'at stake' at each electoral arena affects the behaviour of voters and parties. Voters respond to the location of power in a general sense by directing their political demands to the arena they perceive to be the most effective; this in turn can affect the orientation of parties (Thorlakson 2002; Chhibber and Kollman 2004). As the rewards of gaining public office increase at the state level, state parties will be more likely to develop campaigns that respond to local concerns – even if this means diverging from the federal-level party platform. This can also affect party organization, as state parties value increased autonomy and flexibility – difficult to achieve within an integrated and centralized party structure. This creates an incentive for parties to adapt over time by developing (or maintaining) weak integrative linkages, or even split organizations. The index of federal power, presented in Table 1, provides an indicator of the relative

*Table 1* Resource allocation, joint federalism and party system congruence

| Country | Index of federal power | Joint federalism | Mean SD of electoral support 1990–2000 | Mean SD of effective number of parties, 1990–2000 |
|---|---|---|---|---|
| Canada | 0.58 | Absent | 0.12 | 0.43 |
| United States | 0.65 | Absent | 0.11 | 0.28 |
| Switzerland | 0.66 | Absent | 0.10 | 1.13 |
| Germany | 0.73 | Strong | 0.06 | 0.51 |
| Australia | 0.73 | Absent | 0.07 | 0.31 |
| Austria | 0.79 | Moderate | 0.06 | 0.26 |

*Notes*: Mean standard deviation of electoral support and standard deviation of effective number of parties calculated by author using data from official national and state, provincial cantonal and *Land* electoral agencies and statistical offices. See Thorlakson (2002). See appendix for calculation of index of federal power and party system congruence measures.

power of the federal level of government derived from its taxing power, spending power and jurisdictional reach. Its range approaches 0 (complete decentralization) and 1 (complete centralization). See appendix for details of the calculation.

The method of power division in a federation – whether levels of government exercise their powers jointly, in the same arena, or independently, in separate arenas – can affect the organization of conflict in federal party systems. Joint federalism is characterized by a high degree of co-operation of state governments in federal policy-making, and the representation of state-level governments in federal policy-making (Thorlakson 2003: 16–18; Scharpf 1995: 32). This creates an incentive for federal parties to cultivate integrative linkages with state-level parties as a means of influencing state governments, and restricts the freedom of governing parties to stake out distinctive policies, thus limiting the potential for divergent issue space to develop in each electoral arena. Vertical integration of the party organization is a desirable outcome for the party at the federal level, as it enhances the governmental party's policy efficiency and the ability of the opposition party to block policy (see Scharpf 1995: 32; Chandler 1987: 157–8).

Table 1 classifies joint federalism as strong, moderate and absent. Only Germany is a case of strong joint federalism. The *Länder* governments are represented in the Bundesrat and have veto power over legislation that affects *Länder* interests. Austria is classified as a case of moderate joint federalism. While representatives of *Länder* legislatures sit in the Austrian upper house, it enjoys only weak legislative powers. We may find co-ordination, but not joint federalism in the remaining cases. In Switzerland, a high degree of co-ordination between the federal and cantonal governments occurs outside the formal legislative process. Cantonal voters, and not cantonal governments, are represented in the Council of States. While this may encourage the development of structures of intergovernmental co-operation, it may not necessarily foster stronger integrative linkages within parties. In Canada, Australia and the United States, the institutional structure does not create a joint site of political competition. None of these upper houses represent state or provincial governments in federal decision-making.[1]

Table 1 presents measures of party system congruence in six federations. The mean standard deviation of electoral support measures the standardized variation in electoral support for parties across units of the federation, aggregated across parties, during the 1990s. A lower value means that parties tend to have a similar level of electoral support across all party systems in the federation, while a higher value means that the electoral fortunes of parties tend to have greater variation across the state party systems. The mean standard deviation of the effective number of parties provides a measure of structural incongruence – standardized variance of the effective number of parties across all party systems in each federation in the 1990s. For details of the calculation, see the appendix.

Incongruence – both in terms of the variation in the level of a party's electoral support and variation in the number of effective parties in the system – is generally highest among the most decentralized federations. This is consistent with the findings of Chhibber and Kollman (2004), who argue that party systems are shaped by the location of political and economic authority. Structural congruence (column 5) is less predictable in response to the institutional factors of power allocation and joint federalism. In this case we also see the imprint of sociological factors, including Switzerland's inter-cantonal variation in social cleavage basis and Germany's post-communist transition in the eastern *Länder*.

Party system congruence accompanies strong organizational linkages between the state and federal parties. In Austria and Germany, both cases of joint federalism and relatively centralized federations, parties maintain strong organizational linkages between the state and federal organizations. This means that the same parties compete at the federal and state level, the *Land*-level parties are organizational sub-units of the federal parties, and ultimate power in the party rests with the federal organization. In Australia, linkages between the state and federal parties are strong, although the state branches of the National Party have more autonomy than is typical of German or Austrian parties – according to the 2000 National Party constitution, in the event of a breach of rules, the federal party can expel, but not internally interfere with the state party. Canadian, Swiss and American parties maintain the weakest integrative linkages between the state and federal parties. In the American case, this is because of the overall low degree of organization in its political parties. In Canada, where the same parties by label compete at the provincial and federal levels, many have developed completely separate organizations at each level (see Dyck 1991). In the confederally organized Swiss parties, power is weighted firmly toward the cantonal parties. With the exception of the Social Democrats, which have a top-down organizational structure, the federal parties, or '*landesparteien*', are chiefly umbrella organizations for the cantonal parties. Autonomy for the cantonal parties is 'sacrosanct', and cantonal sections have a high degree of autonomy in the consideration of federal policy (Linder 1999: 89).

Research from comparative federalism suggests several different drivers to party system development. These include not only the heterogeneity of the social cleavage basis (and the extent to which cleavages cross-cut territorial divisions), but also the relative (and perceived) power of each level of government and the institutional incentives for intra-party co-operation. These federal examples also yield several models of multi-level party systems, each with a different mode of multi-level linkage and method of managing territorial conflict. In the Canadian model, high party system incongruence, fuelled by decentralization, is accompanied by split party organizations, yielding separate political worlds for both parties and voters, and a high degree of autonomy for parties. In the Swiss model, party system incongruence is coupled with confederal parties, whose loose organizational structure and high cantonal party autonomy accommodates inter-cantonal diversity. Consociational devices and direct democracy reduce the amount of conflict that is channelled through the party system. In the German and Austrian model, relatively congruent party systems are accompanied with parties that organizationally and competitively link the land and federal levels of competition. A fourth possibility – typified by the newer federal and quasi-federal cases of Belgium and Spain – is a regional party model, with a high degree of party system incongruence because of the presence of different regional parties across the state party systems, which form loose coalitions at the federal level.

## II. THE EUROPEAN PARTY SYSTEM

The European parliamentary party system can be described in terms of the party groupings that structure its political competition. The seven party groupings in the EP generally correspond to the traditional party families in party systems in Western Europe. The European People's Party and European Democrats (EPP-ED) include parties from the traditional party families of Christian Democrats and conservatives, the Group of the Party of European Socialists (PES) contains parties from the social democratic party family and the Group of the Liberal, Democratic and Reform Party includes parties from the liberal party family. On the far left of the European party system, the Confederal Group of the European United Left/Nordic Green Left (EUL/NGL) includes parties from the communist and socialist party families. The Group of the Greens and the European Free Alliance (Greens/EFA) includes parties from two families, greens and regional/ethnic parties. The nationalist grouping Union for a Europe of the Nations Group (UEN) contains conservative nationalist and populist parties, and the Group for a Europe of Democracies and Diversities (EDD), now named the Independence/Democracy group (I/D), contains Euro-sceptic parties. In addition, there are a number of non-aligned parties.

Three party groups – the EPP-ED, the PES and the Group of the European Liberal, Democrat and Reform Party (ELDR) – form the core of this party system as the strongest, most enduring and most effective parliamentary party groups.[2] Analysis of party manifesto data reveals that party competition at the European level is principally structured along a left–right dimension (Gabel and Hix 2002: 953), with pro- and anti-integration positions providing only a secondary axis of competition. This leaves a triangular party system in the EP, where party competition occurs between the two core blocs of the EPP-ED on the centre-right, and the PES on the left. Together with the often-pivotal ELDR, these parties are able to form stable and winning coalitions that effectively shut out the smaller party groupings in the parliament (Hix 1999: 91). The degree of competitiveness of the European party system depends upon both the issue area and the stage of the legislative process. 'Grand coalitions' between the PES, EPP and ELDR tend to form on external relations and foreign and security policy, ELDR–PES coalitions on environmental issues and ELDR–EPP coalitions on social policy (Hix 2001: 680). Competition between party groups has increased in the parliament over time on legislative amendments and internal matters. On whole legislative proposals, however, co-operation between the PES and EPP has increased over time (Hix et al. 2003: 92). This collusive behaviour of the core parties, along with the low cohesion of the UEN or EDD (Hix and Lord 1997: 150), reduces the chances of these smaller parties gaining power as a pivotal actor.

Table 2 presents each party grouping's share of seats in the parliament from 1994 to 2004. Over time, the share of mandates for the major party groupings (EPP-ED, PES and ELDR) has remained relatively stable. The combined seat share of the three parties has increased slightly over time, from 73 per cent to over 74 per cent (column 11), and despite the entry of parties from ten new member states, overall, the effective number of party groupings has decreased slightly from 4.23 in 1994 to 4.13 in 2004. Over the past decade, the composition of all party groups with the exception of the Independence/Democracy group has become increasingly transnational.[3]

Does this three-party concentration in the EP party system reflect a similar pattern in the national party systems? A high degree of incongruence may signify a European party system in which some national parties – the organizational basis of the European parties – are not integrated as effectively as others.

Table 3 presents an indicator of the congruence of the EP party system and the EU twenty-five national party systems. It is a standardized measure of the variance in the effective number of parliamentary parties (n) across party systems, calculated using the percentage of seats won by each party in the last national legislative elections, and each party group in the last EP elections. Comparing seats provides a measure of governmental power.

Table 2 Core structure measures of the European party system, 1994–2004

| | | | | | Seat share in the EP, in % | | | | | | |
| | (1) EPP-ED | (2) PES | (3) ELDR | (4) EUL/NGL | (5) Greens/EFA | (6) UEN | (7) EDD | (8) Others | (9) N | (10) Three-party concentration |
|---|---|---|---|---|---|---|---|---|---|---|
| 1994 | 0.321 | 0.342 | 0.067 | 0.054 | 0.043 | 0.054 | 0.024 | 0.061 | 4.23 | 73.0% |
| 1999 | 0.358 | 0.288 | 0.069 | 0.056 | 0.061 | 0.027 | 0.034 | 0.088 | 4.31 | 71.4% |
| 2004a | 0.374 | 0.295 | 0.085 | 0.070 | 0.060 | 0.038 | 0.022 | 0.056 | 4.04 | 75.4% |
| 2004b | 0.380 | 0.272 | 0.092 | 0.053 | 0.056 | 0.037 | 0.020 | 0.090 | 4.13 | 74.3% |

Sources: European Parliament website: http://www.elections2004.eu.int/results/en/ep_parties.html accessed 25 June 2004; Cracknell and Morgan (1999); European Parliament (1999).

Notes: 2004a refers to the composition of the EP after enlargement on 1 May 2004. 2004b refers to the composition of the EP after the elections of June 2004.

Three-party concentration measures the combined seat share of the EPP-ED, PES and ELDR.

EPP-ED  Group of the European People's Party and European Democrats.

PES  Group of the Party of the European Socialists.

ELDR  Group of the European Liberal, Democrat and Reform Party.

EUL/NGL  Confederal Group of the European United Left/Nordic Green Left.

Greens/SEFA  Greens/European Free Alliance.

UEN  Union for a Europe of the Nations Group.

EDD  Group for a Europe of Democracies and Diversities.

*Table 3* Structural congruence in the European party system and selected federations

| Country | Standard deviation of the effective number of parties (n) |
|---|---|
| EU 25, all parties | 1.57 |
| EU 25, grouped by party family | 0.84 |
| Switzerland | 0.84 |
| Germany | 0.48 |
| Australia | 0.43 |
| Canada | 0.40 |
| Austria | 0.26 |

*Sources*: Calculated by author, based upon author's data. EU party system measures based upon the EP composition after the 2004 elections; national party system measures based upon most recent legislative election. Party system measures in the five federations based upon the parliamentary composition in 2000.

With a standard deviation of the effective number of parties of 1.57, the structural incongruence of the European party system is markedly higher than the other federations measured here. This is not surprising. First, because we are comparing the proportion of parliamentary mandates won by parties, the outcomes will be affected by the differences in the proportionality of national electoral systems across the EU twenty-five. The 'mechanical effect' of a high electoral threshold will tend to reduce the number of parties in the party system, contributing to a high structural incongruence. The least pro-portional electoral systems, found in Malta, the UK, France, Greece, Hungary and Spain, produce party systems with fewer than 2.5 effective parties.

High variation in the effective number of parties across the EU twenty-five party systems is also due to the tendency of parties to fragment into separate parties or loose coalitions. Belgium is the most extreme outlier. Its federal party system has 9.05 effective parties owing to the split of party organization along linguistic lines. When the Belgian parties are grouped into party families, the score remains a relatively high 5.23 owing to the populist mobilization of ethnic and linguistic cleavages. France and Lithuania also stand out for their national party organizations characterized by fluid and shifting party organi-zations and party coalitions.

A more meaningful way to assess congruence across national and EP systems is to compare the number of party families in party systems, to assess the simi-larity of the ideological cleavages that structure party systems across the EU twenty-five. This can give us better insight into how national party competition can be aggregated into a European party system. When structural congruence is measured by the party families in the system, the result for the EU twenty-five party systems is a high degree of incongruence, equal to that found in Switzerland, with a value of 0.84. Incongruence of party family strength across national party systems and the EP suggests a high variation in the number of relevant cleavages expressed in national party systems.

Party family incongruence across national party systems can affect the effectiveness of the aggregation of national party systems into a European party system in the parliament. Recent research has demonstrated the ability of national political cleavage structures to absorb the European integration conflict and the general coherence of party families across the EU fifteen on the right–left issue dimension and pro- and anti-integration stances (Marks and Wilson 2000; Marks *et al.* 2002; Hooghe *et al.* 2002). However, this does not tell us the extent to which we find a congruence of core party families – the extent to which the triangular core structure of the EP party system, consisting of parties in the EPP, PES and the ELDR party groups, is replicated in the party systems of the EU twenty-five. If the core cleavages of national party systems are not reflected in the main dimensions of EP party competition, this could limit the effectiveness of the EP party system for providing a meaningful structure for party competition for some member states.

In the 2004 EP, 24 per cent of parliamentary seats are held by MEPs from what is here termed 'non-core' party groups – MEPs outside of the EPP-ED, PES and ELDR party groups, the three most powerful party groupings in the parliament. The non-core party groupings are marginalized in the EP and so are less important for the purposes of predicting legislative outcomes. However, they constitute a sizeable minority of what we may consider to be ineffectively channelled mandates. It can tell us whether some national party systems emerge at a greater disadvantage than others.

Table 4 presents measures of non-core party strength in the EP, as well as in the national legislatures of the member states. In 12 member states, voters are sending MEPs to the EP representing non-core parties in a greater proportion than the EP average – more than 25 per cent of MEPs are from parties outside of the PES, ELDR and EPP-ED party groups. There are two different reasons for this. The first reason is a high incidence of 'non-core power' in national party systems. In national party systems, non-core power is defined as the percentage of mandates held by parties who are not members of the EPP-ED, PES and ELDR EP party groups, or their corresponding party federations.

For Poland, Latvia, Ireland and Cyprus, non-core party strength in the EP reflects a correspondingly high level of populist, communist and conservative nationalist political forces in the national legislatures.[4] Ireland tops the scale, with 64.2 per cent of mandates in the 2002 elections to the Dáil drawn from parties outside these party family groups. Fianna Fáil, which sits with the nationalist UEN party grouping in the EP, accounts for 49 per cent of these mandates. Green party seats and independents (8 per cent of seats) make up the difference. Non-core party strength is due to the national power of populist or ethnic nationalist parties in Slovakia, Poland, Belgium, communist and radical left parties in Cyprus and Slovakia, Greens and civil rights parties in

*Table 4* Non-core party strength and split parties in the European party system, 2004

| Country | Non-core power | | | Split parties | |
| | % of national EP mandates | % of domestic mandates | Code | % of national EP mandates | Party name |
| --- | --- | --- | --- | --- | --- |
| Ireland | 46.2 | *64.2 | | | |
| Latvia | 44.4 | *53.0 | | | |
| Poland | 42.6 | *29.8 | | | |
| Cyprus | 33.3 | *42.9 | 2 | 16.7 | Rally for Europe |
| Italy | 33.3 | 5.7 | | | |
| Czech | 33.3 | 20.5 | | | |
| Sweden | 31.6 | 13.5 | 2 | 15.8 | Junilisten |
| Netherlands | 29.6 | 20.0 | 2 | 7.4 | EuropaTransparant |
| Denmark | 28.6 | 21.7 | 2 | 14.3 | Junibevaegelsen, Folkebevaegelsen Mod |
| Austria | 27.8 | 19.1 | 2 | 11.1 | Martin List |
| UK | 24.4 | 4.4 | 1 | 17.9 | UKIP, Green Party |
| France | 24.4 | 9.0 | 2 | 3.8 | Mouvement Pour La France |
| EU | 24.0 | | | | |
| Slovakia | 21.4 | *31.5 | | | |
| Greece | 20.8 | 6.0 | | | |
| Belgium | 20.8 | *29.3 | | | |
| Germany | 20.2 | 9.5 | | | |
| Luxembourg | 16.7 | 20.0 | | | |
| Lithuania | 15.4 | 11.3 | | | |
| Finland | 14.3 | 18.5 | | | |
| Portugal | 12.5 | 12.8 | | | |
| Spain | 7.4 | 6.0 | | | |
| Estonia | 0.0 | 12.9 | | | |
| Slovenia | 0.0 | 11.1 | | | |
| Hungary | 0.0 | 0 | | | |
| Malta | 0.0 | 0 | | | |

Notes: * indicates that domestic non-core party strength is higher than the EP average. Split parties are coded as 1 or 2. 1 = nationally insignificant parties (won no seats in the last national elections) that compete and win mandates in EP elections. 2 = system contains parties that compete only at the European level. Domestic mandates are those from the last national elections to the lower house preceding the 2004 EP election.

Latvia and Belgium and conservative nationalists in Ireland. This means that political forces that are significant at the national level in these states may remain ineffectively represented in the EP. While non-aligned parties and non-core parties may be a marginal political force in the EP party system, they are of central importance in certain member state party systems. In these systems, the structures of national party competition are not easily aggregated into the triangular structure of the European party system.

## Split parties

The second explanation for high non-core party strength in national mandates to the EP is the rise of split parties – when new parties form to contest elections to the EP. We find this in Sweden, the Netherlands, Denmark, Austria, France and (again) Cyprus. These parties emerge primarily to compete in the European arena on a European integration issue dimension, and are either absent or unsuccessful at national political competition. They differ from split parties that we find in multi-level systems because their organizational base remains at the national level, even if their activity is directed at the European arena. New parties are making a strategic decision to target the European, and not the domestic, arena. This signals politicization of the EU arena, albeit by a legislatively marginal group of parties.

## Party organization

Christopher Lord's description of the European party system as a 'split level' party system where 'national parties structure voter choice whilst representatives only join transnational party groups once they arrive in the Parliament' (Lord 2004: 116) can also be applied to the party organizations. The national parties are the most important actors in both the extra-parliamentary party federations and the party groups in the parliament. In the absence of a uniform European electoral procedure, they control the vital functions of managing campaigns and selecting candidates. No sanction that the European party federations or EP party groups possess can compare to the power of candidate re-selection.

European party federations are confederally organized. National parties are the most important units. They possess a monopoly over party lists and campaigning and the leaders of national party organizations are represented in the most influential decision-making bodies in European party federations, the Party Leaders' Conference (PES), the Summit (EPP) and the Political Leaders' Meeting (ELDR). There is no constituency-level representation to integrate individual party members and grassroots organization with the European organizations. This structure makes the European party federations similar to the organization of Swiss parties, where the federal parties are organized as loose associations of cantonal parties.

The confederal organization preserves the autonomy of the national parties, but provides the co-ordination that facilitates the cohesion needed in EP party groups. Party groups created from parties that do not have a corresponding party federation (such as the UEN and the Independence/Democracy group) or out of more than one party federation provide ideologically heterogeneous coalitions with the flexibility they need. The group of the Greens and the European Free Alliance brings together ecology and regional parties in the parliament in pursuit of common policy objectives including sustainable development, subsidiarity, cultural and democratic rights, and regional recognition. Their protocol of understanding commits the group to building a consensus within the Parliamentary group, but emphasizes the ultimate right of member parties to pursue their own manifesto commitments in the case of a disagreement.

## III. EVALUATING EXPLANATIONS OF PARTY SYSTEM LINKAGE

### How much is 'at stake'?: why the power of the arena is subjective

The evidence from federations suggests that when state governments are more important in the lives of their citizens, through broader taxing and spending powers and wider jurisdictional power, we are more likely to see patterns of political competition at the state level that diverge from those at the federal level. Continuous treaty revisions have increased the power of the EP. However, this has not generally translated into increases in perceived power, and we have seen increasing voter apathy rather than voter mobilization. Voter turnout in the European parliamentary elections has fallen steadily since the first direct elections to the EP in 1979.

One of the explanations for this is that the Union's power is derived from regulatory activities, with rather low public visibility, rather than from taxing and spending power. The Union share of revenues and expenditures is miniscule – the EU levies no direct taxes on individuals, and its budget ceiling is capped at 1.25 per cent of Gross National Income (GNI) of the EU fifteen. (OJ L53, 2004: 11). Second, the Union has few areas of exclusive competence, relying instead primarily on shared competences with the member states. This further reduces the visibility and therefore the perceived importance of the supranational sphere. Finally, the influence of the EU does not necessarily translate into influence of the EP, which must compete with the European Commission and Council of Ministers. The parliament is a co-legislator with the Council of Ministers and its budgetary powers are shared with the Council.

While the constitutional treaty increases the influence of the supranational arena, this is unlikely to significantly affect voters' perception of Union power, as it still lacks direct control over taxing and spending. The lack of overt distributional conflict in the supranational arena limits the ability of parties to mobilize issues. Short of levying a direct tax on citizens, as was once suggested by German finance minister Hans Eichel, it is difficult to imagine voters altering their assessment of the importance of the EU and of the impact of the EP on their lives.

However, 'how much is at stake' at the European level can be subjective. For some parties, European integration has been an important factor that has affected their strategic decisions to target the EP as an important electoral arena in its own right. For Green parties, early integration which gave the EP an influential role in environmental regulation, and a sympathetic public willing to vote Green in 'second order' European elections, has meant that much is to be gained for Green parties in European parliamentary elections. The Greens responded by becoming the first European political party to contest EP elections using a European-wide campaign. Similarly, euro-sceptic parties such as the UK Independence Party (UKIP) and Junilisten (June List) in Sweden, Junibevaegelsen and Folkebevaegelsen in Denmark, and the Mouvement pour la France have mobilized on anti-integration issues and have found electoral success at the European, rather than the national, level. For some parties which compete on an anti-integration dimension of conflict, the European arena may not be where their ultimate policy goals may be achieved, but it is an arena that offers opportunities for publicity while they await an electoral foothold nationally or at least locally – in the words of the UKIP, the EP is the 'platform we use to reveal the truth about the EU' (UKIP 2004). For other anti-integration parties, such as Denmark's Junibevaegelsen and Folkebevaegelsen, the EP arena offers strategic opportunities unavailable at the national level. At the European level, they are able to disregard the left–right dimension of political conflict and operate as a cross-partisan coalition of anti-European forces.

## Joint federalism: the need for alliances

Policy-making in the EU is characterized by a high degree of joint decision-making between the member states in the Council and the supranational institutions, the Parliament and the Commission (Scharpf 1988). Similar to the European federations, a functional division of power predominates in the EU, and the member states are generally responsible for implementing Union legislation, creating a requirement for co-ordination through the comitology committees. Member state participation in policy-making at the supranational level occurs in the EU through the Council of Ministers, which represents the member state governments. The role of the member states in the Council can be compared to the representation of *Länder* governments in the German Bundesrat.

Joint federalism has not led to the development of strong integrative linkages between parties at the member state and Union level. Development of common positions in the Council has, generally, been achieved through an institutional framework (the Committee of Permanent Representatives – COREPER) designed to co-ordinate in an intergovernmental, rather than partisan, framework. However, joint decision-making in the EU may explain why national parties have retained an important means of control over parties in the EP – veto power over MEP re-selection. In the EU, joint federalism has encouraged the development of linkages between the parties in government, rather than between national and European party organizations. As a result of party leaders' meetings, integrative linkages in the European party federation are strongest not between parties in central office, but the parties in government (see Hix and Lord 1997: 183); the development of linkages between Europarties and national executives is especially strong where national parties are electorally strong (Delwit *et al.* 2004: 13).

Interinstitutional competition between the EP, Commission and Council rivals partisan competition in the Parliament and so alters the incentives of EP party groups, with the result that they do not seek influence through forging co-ordinating linkages with national parties. While the EP is experiencing increased partisan competition over legislative amendments, the 1999 Parliament still saw a high degree of collusion over whole legislative proposals. Amie Kreppel argues that in order for the Parliament to be influential, it needs to be pragmatic and to compromise, because legislative proposals must be acceptable to the Commission, the Council and the Parliament. She finds that policy areas of environment and public health are particularly non-ideological. Grand coalitions of the PES and EPP tend to form, because the goal of EP party élites is EP success *vis-à-vis* the Council and Commission, rather than partisan success (Kreppel 2002: 169–74).

## CONCLUSIONS

As a supranational aggregation of political competition in twenty-five member states, the party system in the EP is remarkably stable, with increasing system concentration on three core party groupings. Generally, the traditional party families found across the national party systems of Europe underpin the structure of its party competition. Approximately 75 per cent of MEP seats belong to the core PES, ELDR and EPP-ED groupings based on the Social Democratic, Liberal and Conservative/Christian Democratic parties. This proportion has been growing over the past decade.

However, like Swiss federalism, the party systems across the EU twenty-five and the EP have a high degree of incongruence, both in terms of the number of parties in the system and the degree of electoral support for the three core EP parties. This heterogeneity is to be expected as the result of twenty-five party systems which, despite facing similar historical crises, experienced different historical paths of party system development. It is accommodated by a loose party organizational structure which preserves the maximum amount of autonomy demanded by parties that must respond first and foremost to a national electoral base. This party system incongruence also points to some of the difficulties – and inherent limitations – of party system aggregation, especially after an enlargement which introduces party systems that are fluid, not fully consolidated, and shaped by the cleavages arising from market transition.

An examination of party system congruence highlights two developments. Vertically, it highlights the emergence of split parties, and horizontally, it highlights incongruence in 'core power' among national party systems. One form of party system incongruence is development of split parties, often because of the mobilization of anti-integration issues. This may signal the emergence of a distinct European issue space and European party competition. The rise, to some extent, of separate political worlds at the national and European levels is similar to the Canadian model of federalism. This occurs in rare instances where there is more 'at stake' for a party in the European than in the national arena. For some parties, such as anti-European parties and some green parties, the EP represents an opportunity for electoral success that is difficult to attain in national systems. The second order election thesis emphasizes the role of the voter willing to 'waste' a vote on these parties; this perspective considers the strategic decisions that parties make to concentrate their efforts at the European level, as some anti-European parties do. It is not only the relative power of each level of government, but also a party's opportunities for electoral success relative to the national level that shape a party's incentives and strategies for competing in each arena.

Second, while party groups in the EP maintain a broad territorial base, we still find horizontal incongruence. Approximately a quarter of EP seats are held by MEPs from 'non-core' party groups. One of the reasons for this is that for a minority of member states, including several from the 2004 enlargement, there is a high incidence of non-core party strength in their national party systems in which conservative nationalist and populist parties are electorally strong. This is also a by-product of the fluidity of many party systems, and party organizations, in post-communist systems.

For stability, this is good news. It creates a party system based around three traditional party families which anchor many party systems across Europe. Moderate and with pro-European credentials, they pose no threat of either polarizing or anti-system behaviour. If our normative concern is representation, however, it raises some concerns. First, owing to the collusive behaviour of parliamentary groups, non-core groups in the EP exercise limited parliamentary influence. This leaves conflict over European integration, the secondary dimension of European parliamentary competition, ineffectively expressed in the parliament. Second, this type of incongruence may signal a 'poor fit' between the political cleavage basis in some national party systems and the political cleavages structuring the European parliamentary party system.

These observations hint at the limits of our ability to construct a common party system and political community out of twenty-five member states. The stable (and collusive) EP party system core comes at a price of leaving some member states with ineffectively channelled mandates. Perhaps a saving grace of the European party system is another feature which it shares with Swiss federalism. The conflict arising from its heterogeneous composition is not channelled through the party system alone. Where a common structure for partisan competition does not sufficiently exist for some member states, intergovernmental competition in the Council of Ministers provides a valuable alternative channel. The weakness of the parliament preserves a strength of the system.

## APPENDIX

The index of federal power presents the average of measures of revenue and expenditure centralization and range of federal jurisdiction. It ranges from 0 (least centralized) to 1 (most centralized). Revenue centralization is measured as total federal revenues compared to total revenues of all levels of government. Only revenues that accrue automatically and unconditionally to lower levels of government are counted as non-federal. Expenditure centralization is measured as total federal expenditures (including transfers) compared to total revenues of all levels of government combined. Public finance data from International Monetary Fund, *Government Finance Statistics Yearbook*, volumes from 1978, 1985 and 2001, covering the period 1974–1999 (1975–1999 for the US). Swiss data for 1985–1990 are unavailable. The range of federal jurisdiction ranges from 0 (least centralized) to 1 (most centralized) and is calculated as the inverse of the proportion of policy areas of exclusive state jurisdiction compared to areas of concurrent, dual and exclusive jurisdiction, based upon jurisdiction data compiled by Ron Watts (1996: 68).

The structural congruence of the party system is measured by standard deviation of the effective number of parties (N) across party systems in each federation. The effective number of parties is calculated by taking the inverse of the sum of the fractional vote share of each party, expressed in the following equation:

$$N = 1/\Sigma p_i^2$$

where $p_i$ is the fractional vote share of the $i$th party (Taagepera and Shugart 1989: 79).

**Address for correspondence:** Lori Thorlakson, School of Politics, University of Nottingham, University Park, Nottingham NG7 2RD, UK. Tel: (+44) 115 951 4862. Fax: (+44) 115 951 4859. email: lori.thorlakson@nottingham.ac.uk

## NOTES

1 Senators in Australia and the United States are directly elected and so do not create a linkage between state and federal governments (although before the 17th amendment of the US constitution in 1913 mandated the popular election of senators, they were chosen by state legislatures). In Canada and Australia the upper houses have weak powers.

2 This is similar to Smith's 'system core' concept (Smith 1990: 161), which refers to the most enduring structural features of the party system. The system core concept is useful for measuring party system change, as well as measuring party system congruence.

3 This is based upon Raunio's index of transnationality (Thomassen *et al.* 2004: 145), a fractionalization index that ranges from 0 (when party group composition is maximally concentrated in a single country) to 1 (party group composition is maximally dispersed across member states). In the 1994–1999 parliament, the values for the EPP, PES and ELDR were 0.87, 0.85 and 0.86 respectively. In the 2004 parliament, these values increased to 0.92 for all parties. Calculated by author with data from Cracknell and Morgan (1999) and the EP website, 2004.

4 Slovakia and Belgium also have national party systems with a higher proportion of mandates from parties that fall outside of the liberal, social democratic and Christian Democratic party families than the EU twenty-five average. However, less than 25 per cent of their mandates in the EP are from non-core parties and so are not included here.

## REFERENCES

Chandler, W. (1987) 'Federalism and political parties', in H. Bakvis and W. Chandler (eds), *Federalism and the Role of the State*, Toronto: University of Toronto Press.

Chhibber, P. and Kollman, K. (2004) *The Formation of National Party Systems*, Princeton and Oxford: Princeton University Press.

Cracknell, R. and Morgan, B. (1999) *European Parliament Elections 1979 to 1994*, Research Paper 99/57, London: House of Commons Library, Social and General Statistics Section.

Delwit, P., Külahci, E. and van de Walle, C. (eds) (2004) *The Europarties: Organization and Influence*, Brussels: Centre d'étude de la vie politique of the Free University of Brussels.

Dyck, R. (1991) 'Links between federal and provincial parties and party systems', in H. Bakvis (ed.), *Representation, Integration and Political Parties in Canada*, Toronto: Dundern Press.

van der Eijk, C., Franklin, M. and Marsh, M. (1996) 'What voters teach us about Europe-wide elections: what Europe-wide elections teach us about voters', *Electoral Studies* 15(2): 149–66.

European Parliament (1999) *EP Elections – June 1999 Results and Elected Members*, Brussels: Directorate General for Information and Public Relations.

Gabel, M. and Hix, S. (2002) 'Defining the EU political space: an empirical study of the European elections manifestos, 1979–1999', *Comparative Political Studies* 35(8): 934–64.

Hix, S. (1999) 'Dimensions and alignments in European Union politics: cognitive constraints and partisan responses', *European Journal of Political Research* 35(2): 69–106.

Hix, S. (2001) 'Legislative behaviour and party competition in the European Parliament: an application of nominate to the EU', *Journal of Common Market Studies* 39(4): 663–88.

Hix, S. and Lord, C. (1997) *Political Parties in the European Union*, London: Macmillan.

Hix, S., Kreppel, A. and Noury, A. (2003) 'The party system of the European Parliament: collusive or competitive?', *Journal of Common Market Studies* 41(2): 309–31.

Hooghe, L., Marks, G. and Wilson, C. (2002) 'Does left–right structure party positions on European integration?', *Comparative Political Studies* 35(8):965–89.

Kreppel, A. (2002) *The European Parliament and Supranational Party System: A Study in Institutional Development*, Cambridge: Cambridge University Press.

Lijphart, A. (1977) *Democracy in Plural Societies: A Comparative Exploration*, New Haven and London: Yale University Press.

Linder, W. (1999), *Schweizerische Demokratie*, Bern: Verlag Paul Haupt.

Lord, C. (2004) *A Democratic Audit of the European Union*, Basingstoke: Palgrave Macmillan.

Marks, G. and Wilson, C. (2000) 'The past in the present: a cleavage theory of party response to European integration', *British Journal of Political Science* 30: 433–59.

Marks, G., Wilson, C. and Ray, L. (2002) 'National political parties and European integration', *American Journal of Political Science* 46(3): 585–94.

Marsh, M. (1998) 'Testing the second-order election model after four European elections', *British Journal of Political Science* 18(3): 591–607.

*Official Journal of the European Union*, L53, vol. 47, 23 February 2004.

Reif, K. and Schmidt, H. (1980) 'Nine second order national elections: a conceptual framework for the analysis of European election results', *European Journal of Political Research* 8: 3–44.

Scharpf, F. (1988) 'The joint-decision trap: lessons from German federalism and European integration', *Public Administration* 66: 239–78.

Scharpf, F. (1995) 'Federal arrangements and multi-party systems', *Australian Journal of Political Science* 30: 27–39.

Smith, G. (1990) 'Core persistence: change and the "People's Party"', in P. Mair and G. Smith (eds), *Understanding Party System Change in Western Europe*, London: Frank Cass.

Taagepera, R. and Shugart, M. (1989) *Seats and Votes: The Effects and Determinants of Electoral Systems*, London: Yale University Press.

Thomassen, J., Noury, A. and Voeten, E. (2004) 'Political competition in the European Parliament: evidence from roll call and survey analyses', in G. Marks and M. Steenbergen (eds), *European Integration and Political Conflict*, Cambridge: Cambridge University Press.

Thorlakson, L. (2002) 'Federalism and party competition: a comparative analysis of Canada, Australia, Switzerland, Austria, Germany and the United States'. Unpublished Ph.D. thesis, University of London.

Thorlakson, L. (2003) 'Comparing federal institutions: power and representation in six federations', *West European Politics* 26(2): 1–22.

United Kingdom Independence Party official website: http://www.ukip.co.uk, accessed 18 October 2004.

Watts, R. (1996) *Comparing Federal Systems in the 1990s*, Kingston, Ontario: Queen's University Institute of Intergovernmental Relations.

# Federalism in the European Union: the view from below (if there is such a thing)[1]

Thomas Christin, Simon Hug and Tobias Schulz

## 1. INTRODUCTION

According to most definitions the European Union (EU) is a federal political system. Riker's (1964) classic definition clearly applies, since in particular policy domains the member states still have the power to make final decisions, while in others the institutions of the EU have the final say. Similarly, the definitions by Elazar (1991),[2] Watts (1999) and many others apply as well.

Thus, it can hardly surprise us that the EU, as any federal system, struggles with the appropriate division of authority between the central level (the EU) and its constituent units (the member states). In this regard the EU has undergone important changes and the new constitution adopted in June 2004 comprises additional innovations. Some of these changes are not uncontroversial and might become of relevance in the ratification stage of the constitution. In this stage the views of the citizens of the member countries may come to play a role, mostly in those countries scheduled to hold a referendum. Thus, in this paper we assess to what degree the voters in the current EU member countries have well-established ideas about the domains in which authority should be delegated to the EU, and in which it should be kept at the national level.

This assessment of the voters' views on the location of authority in various policy fields has to be embedded in the larger context of how the distribution of competencies in federal systems interacts with political accountability, an issue looming large in the EU's current institutional make-up.

Thus, we start in the next section to place the question of the assignment of authorities in the broader context of federal arrangements. Based on this we highlight the trade-off that exists between federal arrangements which, at least theoretically, might be more stable, and those which ensure a high degree of political accountability. In section three we assess, based on this framework, the ways in which the EU's citizens have formed their opinion on the delegation of authority to the EU's institutions. We find some evidence that respondents in surveys in all member countries appear to respond to some degree haphazardly. This suggests that opinions on the appropriate amount of delegation to the EU's institutions are still not formed in the electorate. At the same time it also supports the view that the less than crystal-clear assignment of authority in the EU makes a clear assessment of the appropriate distribution of powers in the EU difficult for the citizens. We also find that federalism fails to affect opinions on the distribution of competencies. We elaborate on these insights in our conclusion where we link them to the basic trade-off between flexible assignments of competencies and strengthened political accountability.

## 2. THE FEDERAL PROBLEM IN THE EU

Given the federal character of the EU, the distribution of competencies between the EU institutions and the member states is of great importance. Several scholars have attempted to study this thorny issue both empirically and theoretically. Hooghe (2003), for instance, notes that in some policy domains there seems to be agreement between élites and citizens on whether issues in these domains should be dealt with by the EU or not. In other domains, however, the desired assignment of powers diverges between these two groups of political actors. Alesina *et al.* (2004, forthcoming) assess the assignment of competencies from the angle of three criteria. These concern the degree to which externalities are created by various government activities, whether preferences are likely to be heterogeneous, and whether there are economies of scale in the production of certain public goods. Based on these criteria, the authors compile a list of activities to be kept at the national level, while others should be dealt with by the EU institutions. Compared to an assessment of the involvement by the EU in these areas, they note a mismatch in the area of agriculture, citizen and social protection, the environment and to some degree international relations. The other areas, namely international trade, the common market, money and finance, education, research and culture, and non-sectoral business relations seem to be adequately assigned.[3] Swenden (2004), on the other hand, attempts to evaluate the changes introduced in the constitution from a theoretical perspective. He argues that a catalogue of competencies is not advisable, since there hardly exists a consensus about the degree of integration sought.

Behind these assessments of whether the EU is engaged in the right policy domains, one finds the implicit view that the assignment of authority across the different levels in a federal system should be kept fixed.

An advantage of such a fixed distribution of competencies is that it enhances political accountability (e.g. Manin *et al.* 1999; Przeworski *et al.* 1999), since voters have a better understanding about who is responsible in particular policy domains.[4] Thus, if the assignment of powers is rigid, holding to account elected officials is often easier.

The opposing view suggests that some flexibility in the assignment of competencies is likely to foster political stability. At least since Riker's (1964) classic book on federalism, most scholars and observers agree that federal institutions are delicate. Thus, in the EU context many politicians, observers, and scholars alike fear a centralizing tendency similar to the one Riker (1964) had observed for the United States. It is hardly surprising that in one of his last writings he expressed his scepticism regarding the feasibility of a federal EU.[5]

This has also been highlighted in the more recent theoretical literature on federalism. Filippov *et al.* (2004), for example, argue that the assignments of competencies should be part of an open-ended bargain among the N + 1 players in a federal system. Building up on Riker's (1964) seminal work many authors attempted to determine what elements might make federal arrangements stable. Some scholars emphasize the way in which powers are assigned across different levels, while others stress the importance of other institutional factors, like consociationalism (e.g. McGarry and O'Leary 2003), judicial review (e.g. Lijphart 1999; Bednar 2004), party systems (e.g. Riker 1964; Filippov *et al.* 2004), etc.

Of course, fixed distributions of competencies combined with considerable hurdles to change them (as envisioned in the US constitution, but largely disabled by the Supreme Court (Riker 1964)) make renegotiations particularly difficult and might make a federal system unstable. Further, additional institutions often lengthen and weaken the chain of accountability (e.g. Müller 2000; Strøm 2003). Hence, consociational arrangements or a strong judiciary often blur political accountability. Similarly, party systems which ensure that parties are 'imperfect agents' of their local constituents, as suggested by Filippov *et al.* (2004), hardly contribute to political accountability.[6]

Thus, what scholars suggest should enhance the stability of a federal system like the EU are often elements which diminish political accountability.[7] If we look at the current state in the EU, according to many scholars (e.g. Mair 2000) political accountability is a major problem in the EU's institutional architecture, especially because the assignment of competencies is far from transparent from a voter's perspective.[8] The proposed constitution attempts to address this point by dividing policy domains into three categories, namely those with exclusive competence for the EU, those with shared competence, and finally those with complementary actions by the EU. By listing these various competencies, the constitution introduces a certain element of rigidity. At the same time, however, the constitution strengthens the subsidiarity principle by envisioning an 'early warning system', which allows national parliaments to signal that a particular decision does not comply with this principle. Obviously, the subsidiarity principle and the safeguards wish to ensure that the EU does not experience a centralizing tendency. This implies, however, also that changes in the distribution of competencies will be less transparent for citizens.

Thus, the trade-off is clearly visible: on the one hand, the assignment of powers is supposed to become more transparent with a categorization of competencies into the categories exclusive, shared and complementary. At the same time, however, the possible safeguards exercised by national parliaments, if used effectively, are likely to blur the assignment of authorities. And even though these safeguards are supposed to ensure that the EU does not encroach on the competencies of the member states, this is likely to reduce political accountability.

On the other hand, the EU institutions also undergo reforms to ensure greater accountability. The draft Constitution addresses this through an extension of the codecision procedure which strengthens the role of the European Parliament and other elements. These changes are potentially of considerable importance.

First of all, they may address to some degree the problems that Mair (2000) nicely illustrates. He shows the difficulties European citizens face when trying to untangle the various chains of accountability. Second, in some countries the new draft treaty will have to be ratified in referendums,[9] and both the distribution of powers and the reforms of the institutions might be of importance in the voters' decision. However, we know very little about the ways in which voters perceive the issues related to the assignment of powers. Alesina *et al.* (2004, forthcoming) provide some illustrations demonstrating that voters appear to prefer EU involvement in those policy domains where this seems normatively to make sense, while Hooghe (2003) notes some disagreements between élites and citizens.

## 3. EU FEDERALISM FROM THE CITIZENS' PERSPECTIVE

The voters' views on the ways in which competencies are assigned in the EU are of importance in two regards. First, since the Convention on the Future of the Union delivered its draft of a constitution and the Intergovernmental Conference (IGC) adopted a revised version in June 2004, it is likely that the discussion about competencies will move to the centre stage, possibly also in the public realm. The latter is likely to occur in countries which will hold referendums on the proposed constitution. Second, since the assignment of authority is quite convoluted today, it is important to assess whether this state of affairs makes the voters' assessment difficult when trying to decide where authority should be located.

Thus, the question arises as to what degree voters have clear views with respect to the vertical distribution of powers in the EU. We attempt to assess this based on information stemming from Eurobarometer surveys, covering both old and new members of the EU. Respondents in these surveys are asked to indicate whether decisions in twenty-five policy domains[10] should be made at the national or EU level.[11] The first interesting piece of information appears with the distribution of response patterns across the twenty-five policies. For this we counted the number of times respondents indicated that the national governments should decide jointly within the EU in these policy areas, instead of keeping the competency at the national level. Thus, 0 corresponds to a complete EU-phobic person (all policy decisions should be made at the national level), while 25 corresponds to a EU-phil (all policies should be decided jointly within the EU).[12]

In Figure 1 an interesting tri-modal distribution appears for the total population (solid line): on the one hand, more than 11 per cent of the respondents want the decisions in all twenty-five policy areas to be made 'jointly' within the EU (right-hand peak in Figure 1). On the opposite side, a little less than 6 per cent of the respondents want the decision-making powers to reside in all twenty-five policy areas at the national level (left-hand peak in Figure 1). Finally, in between is a third peak formed by respondents wanting national governments to remain responsible in close to half of all twenty-five policy areas (to be precise in thirteen policy areas).[13] This distribution seems to suggest that apart from the extreme 'euro-phobes' and 'euro-phils' there might also be some respondents who average out their responses over the twenty-five categories. Consequently, it is important to determine which part of the hump in the middle of the distribution is made up of individuals who have no – or

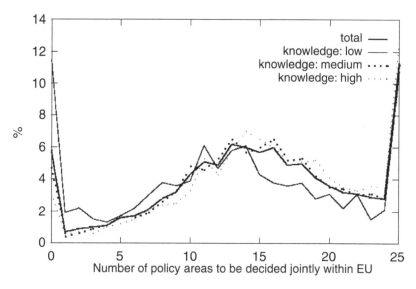

*Figure 1* Response pattern for question on level of decision-making (national or jointly within EU) in twenty-five policy areas (2003), EU twenty-five members

no particularly strong – opinion about the distribution of competencies across the different levels of government in the EU.

To assess whether some interviewed individuals responded haphazardly we would need ideally observations over time to assess the stability of their opinions. In the absence of such data, we rely on the individuals' self-assessment about their knowledge on the EU. We depict in Figure 1 the response patterns for three groups distinguished by the subjective perception of their knowledge about the EU (low, middle, high).[14] The response patterns across the twenty-five policies for the different groups of subjective knowledge are presented in Figure 1. This analysis indicates essentially that the proportion of EU-phobics is much smaller among individuals with a high level of knowledge about the EU. EU-phobics represent 11.5 per cent of the lowest subjective knowledge group, less than 5 per cent of the middle subjective knowledge and a small proportion of 3 per cent for the individuals with high subjective knowledge of the EU. There is no such tendency for the EU-phils. Whatever the level of subjective knowledge the proportion of EU-phils is high. The proportion of EU-phils is even higher for the group with the highest level of subjective knowledge (13 per cent) than for groups with lower levels of subjective knowledge (about 11 per cent for both groups). Moving from a low level of knowledge to a mid or high level of subjective competence increases the proportion of individuals on the right-hand side of the distribution. In short, systematic EU-phobic answers appear essentially for less informed respondents.

The tri-modal distribution in the response pattern for the twenty-five policy areas still raises the question of how people perceive the vertical distribution of competencies from the national to the European level for each policy. The third column of Table 1 presents the percentage of respondents who are in favour of decisions taken jointly within the EU for each policy area. In the first column we list the policy areas covered by the questions and in column 2 the question number is given.[15] What clearly appears in this table is that the percentage of respondents favouring decisions taken jointly within the EU is rather important. It varies between 31.4 per cent (b4, *Police*) and 84.1 per cent (b10, *The fight against the trade in, and exploitation of, human beings*). Apart from this last category we find the following policy areas where voters strongly prefer decisions to be made jointly within the EU: *Information about the EU, its policies and institutions* (a13, 81.1 per cent), *Foreign policy towards countries outside the EU* (a14, 78.0 per cent), *The fight against organized crime* (b3, 77.1 per cent) and *Humanitarian aid* (a4, 75.6 per cent). After *Police*, the policies that citizens would like to see least in joint hands with the EU are *Justice* (b5, 31.4 per cent), *Education* (a11, 37.4 per cent), *Health and social welfare* (a5, 37.8 per cent), *Urban crime prevention* (b8, 38.4 per cent) and *Basic rules for broadcasting and press* (a6, 38.5 per cent). This order of responses seems rather persistent, since similar analyses based on surveys carried out in 2001 yield very similar, but slightly more polarized results.[16]

Therefore, policies which are favoured to be taken at the national level are those which are traditionally taken at the local or national level, which have a

Table 1 Explaining responses on decision-making in EU twenty-five members (EB 59.1 and CCEB 2003.2)

| Policy area | Question number | % jointly within the EU | % correct | Items predictors | | | | |
|---|---|---|---|---|---|---|---|---|
| | | | | All cases | | Knowledge | | |
| | | | | | Low | Middle | High |
| Defence | a1 | 55.3 | 74.4 | a3 a2 a14 | a2 a14 a3 b1 | a3 a2 | a14 a2 a3 b1 |
| Protection of the environment | a2 | 67.3 | 79.7 | a1 a4 | a1 a4 b9 | a1 a4 | a1 a5 a3 a4 |
| Currency | a3 | 71.3 | 81.6 | a1 | a4 a9 a1 a11 | a1 | a2 a14 a1 |
| Humanitarian aid | a4 | 75.6 | 84.3 | a5 a2 a7 b10 | a5 b10 a3 a2 | a5 a2 | a5 a7 a2 |
| Health and social welfare | a5 | 37.8 | 80.8 | a4 a11 a6 a8 | a4 a6 a11 b5 a8 | a4 a11 a6 a8 | a11 a4 b5 a8 |
| Basic rules for broadcasting and press | a6 | 38.5 | 76.1 | a5 a7 | a5 a7 a11 b2 a9 | a5 | a7 a15 |
| Fight against poverty/ social exclusion | a7 | 65.3 | 81.3 | a8 a4 a6 a10 | a8 a10 a6 | a8 a4 | a8 a4 a6 |
| The fight against unemployment | a8 | 54.1 | 79.7 | a7 a5 a9 | a7 a9 a5 b5 | a7 a5 a9 | a7 a5 |
| Agriculture and fishing policy | a9 | 55.7 | 74.3 | a10 | a3 a8 a10 a6 | a10 a8 | a10 b10 |
| Supporting regions which are experiencing economic difficulties | a10 | 66.5 | 77.3 | a9 | a7 a11 a9 a13 | a9 | a9 |
| Education | a11 | 37.4 | 80.6 | a12 a5 a15 | a12 b8 a6 a10 a5 a3 | a12 a5 a15 a8 | a12 a5 a15 |

| | | | | | | | |
|---|---|---|---|---|---|---|---|
| Scientific and technological research | a12 | 73.1 | 81.2 | a11 a13 | a11 a14 a13 b10 | a11 a13 | a11 a13 |
| Information about the EU, its policies and institutions | a13 | 81.1 | 87.5 | a14 a12 | a14 | a14 a12 | a14 a12 |
| Foreign policy towards countries outside the EU | a14 | 78.0 | 85.3 | a13 a15 | a13 a15 a1 b1 a3 a12 | a13 a15 | a13 a15 a1 a3 |
| Cultural policy | a15 | 45.4 | 72.1 | a14 a11 | a14 b7 | a14 a11 | a14 a11 a6 |
| Immigration policy | b1 | 55.2 | 85.5 | b2 b6 | b2 b6 a14 a1 | b2 b6 | b2 b6 a1 |
| Rules for political asylum | b2 | 56.7 | 85.3 | b1 b6 b3 | b1 b6 b3 | b1 b6 b3 | b1 b6 |
| The fight against organized crime | b3 | 77.1 | 87.0 | b4 b9 b10 b7 b2 | b4 b9 b7 b10 b2 | b4 b9 b10 b7 b2 | b10 b4 b9 b8 |
| Police | b4 | 31.4 | 88.5 | b5 b3 b8 | b5 b3 b8 | b5 b3 b8 | b5 |
| Justice | b5 | 35.5 | 87.9 | b4 b6 | b4 b6 b9 a5 b10 a8 | b4 b6 | b4 b6 a5 |
| Accepting refugees | b6 | 55.8 | 78.9 | b2 b1 b5 | b2 b1 b5 b7 | b2 b1 b5 | b2 b5 b1 b7 |
| Juvenile crime prevention | b7 | 42.4 | 88.9 | b8 b3 b9 b6 | b8 b3 b9 a15 b6 | b8 b3 b9 | b8 b6 b9 |
| Urban crime prevention | b8 | 38.4 | 88.7 | b7 b9 b4 | b7 b9 b4 a11 | b7 b9 b4 | b7 b9 |
| The fight against drugs | b9 | 72.8 | 86.1 | b10 b8 b3 b7 | b10 b8 b3 b7 a2 | b10 b8 b3 b7 | b10 b8 b3 |
| The fight against the trade in, and exploitation of, human beings | b10 | 84.1 | 91.8 | b9 b3 a4 | b9 a4 b5 b3 | b9 b3 | b9 b3 |
| weighted n | | | | 16061 | 2880 | 10186 | 2798 |
| % missing | | | | 25.8 | 41.4 24.0 | | 16.7 |
| Average number of predictors (pro item) | | | | 2.7 | 4.1 2.4 | | 2.8 |

direct impact on individuals, like health or education policies, and those which potentially restrict national sovereignty, such as *press, justice* and *police*. Policies preferred to be taken jointly within the EU are those which do not have direct effects on individuals and, in a globalizing world, cannot be resolved by national governments. These are, for example, *trade in, and exploitation of, human beings, organized crime* or *foreign policy towards non-EU countries*. At the other end of the scale we find policies normally associated with national competencies.[17]

Apart the indication from the tri-modal distribution, another way to assess whether the responses are well informed is to try to explain the responses on one particular item, by using the responses given by an individual on the other twenty-four items. Table 1 depicts the corresponding results.[18] In the fourth column, we list the percentage of correctly predicted responses based on a logit model, where the response on one item is the dependent[19] variable and all the others are used as independent variables. Then in column 5 we list the items which are strong predictors for the relevant item.[20]

Two conclusions follow quite directly from Table 1. First, the responses of individuals are highly predictable, independent of the modal response. Even though the modal response is chosen in the various items by 50–84 per cent of the respondents, the percentage of correctly predicted responses never falls below 74 per cent and approaches 90 per cent for some items. Second, the responses fail to follow perfect patterns, but groups of items explain each other mutually. On the one hand, this suggests that at least some individuals used the responses to these questions for nuanced evaluations about the appropriate level of decision-making. On the other hand, given that most of the policies in these groups followed each other in the questionnaire, this may also be indicative of contagion from one question to the other. Support for this view appears in Figure 1, which suggests that there is also quite the same random noise in the responses provided by individuals.

In order to assess the importance of this random noise we control for the subjective knowledge of the individuals. Columns 6, 7 and 8 display the strongest predictors for each level of subjective knowledge. The last row presents the number of cases, the percentage of missing data, and the average number of strong predictors per item for each group. We notice that the average number of predictors fulfilling our criterion is drastically reduced for the category of respondents with mid (2.4 factors pro item) and high (2.8 factors pro item) level of knowledge, compared to the low knowledge category (4.1 factors pro item).

One can also argue that, especially for the group with a low knowledge level, individuals tend to reduce their effort when evaluating the policies by systematically assigning policies to the national or the European level of competencies. Therefore, when respondents systematically attribute competencies to the national or European level, the number of predictors per item is inflated but it does not necessarily reflect a sophisticated reasoning. We therefore control for this potential effect by suppressing all the individuals who always assigned the competencies to the national or European level. In other words we suppressed the euro-phobes and euro-phils from the analysis. These results are presented in Table 2, columns 2 to 5. The second column displays the results for all cases, while columns 3 to 5 present the results within sub-groups of knowledge. Considering first the average number of predictors per item for the whole set of individuals or within sub-groups of subjective competencies, we clearly see a smaller number of predictors per item than in the previous analyses which included the extremes. This is particularly remarkable for the low competencies sub-category, where the average number of strong predictors decreases from 4.1 to 2.7 per item (compared to 2.4–2.2 for the mid category and 2.8–2.4 for the high category). In other words the structure of responses is rather stable for respondents with mid or high competencies with or without the euro-phobes and euro-phils. These results tend to support the view that respondents with low levels of knowledge are more likely to assign competencies at the national or at the EU level at random. The main predictors for each knowledge sub-groups are often the same, sometimes in a different order. Nonetheless, we notice some differences. For example, responses to the *Currency* policy domain (a3) are strongly explained by responses on the *Humanitarian aid* item (a4), *Agriculture and fishing policy* (a9) and *Defence* (a1) for the group with a low level of knowledge. Apart from this last item which also taps into national sovereignty, this seems hardly consistent. *Defence* (a1) is the only strong predictor for the mid knowledge group, while respondents with a high level of knowledge also add the *Foreign policy towards countries outside the EU* (a14) item. This is clearly more consistent.

It can be argued that the number of predictors shown in Table 1 reflects also a lack of control in the analyses and that the introduction of some other factors might reduce the weight of some random factors. As it is often done in analyses which explain support for European integration, we have to take into account national traditions (Eichenberg and Dalton 1993) by introducing country dummies.[21] Finally, we also add an individual level variable which measures the support for European integration, namely whether people consider that being a member of the EU is or would be a good thing.[22] The results are presented in columns 6, 7 and 8 (Table 2). Again, as in the previous analyses without the extremes, the analysis with country dummies and 'EU as a good thing' reduces the number of strong predictors per item. This effect is rather strong for the low knowledge sub-group. Turning to the country dummies, we summarized the single effects by grouping federal states and other countries. One might argue that citizens from federal states are more used to federalist arrangements and therefore much more in favour of delegating competencies to a higher level.[23] The results, however, are very unsystematic. First, over twenty-five policies, in ten policies (a2, a4, a6, a7, a10, a13, a15, b5, b9, b10), federal states and other countries are less pro-European than the UK.[24] It is worth noting that the strongest difference between the UK and all countries (federal and others) concerns the currency. In this area, the UK is much less pro-European. Concerning the difference between federal states and the others, over these twenty-five policies, it appears that federalist states and other countries

Table 2 Explaining responses on decision-making in EU twenty-five members (EB 59.1 and CCEB 2003.2), with controls

| Policy area | Question number | Items predictors without extremes | | | | Items predictors with control variables | | | |
| | | | Knowledge | | | | | Knowledge | |
| | | All cases | Low | Middle | Low | All cases | Low | Middle | Low |
|---|---|---|---|---|---|---|---|---|---|
| Defence | a1 | a3 a2 | a2 a14 a3 | a3 a2 | a14 a2 a3 | a2 a3 | a2 a14 | a3 a2 | a2 |
| Protection of the environment | a2 | a1 a4 | a1 b9 a4 | a1 a4 | a1 a3 a5 a4 | a1 a3 | a1 a3 | a1 a3 | a1 a3 |
| Currency | a3 | a1 | a4 a9 a1 | a1 | a1 a14 | a1 a4 a2 | a4 | a1 a2 | a4 a2 |
| Humanitarian aid | a4 | a5 a2 | a5 b10 a3 | a5 a2 | a5 a7 a2 | a5 a3 | a3 a5 14 | a5 | a5 a3 |
| Health and social welfare | a5 | a4 a11 a8 a6 | a4 a6 | a4 a11 a8 a6 | a11 a4 b5 a2 a8 | a4 a6 a11 | a4 a6 a7 a11 | a4 a6 a6 a8 a11 | a4 a6 a11 |
| Basic rules for broadcasting and press | a6 | a5 | a5 a7 | a5 | a7 | a5 | a7 a11 | a5 | a5 a7 |
| Fight against poverty/ social exclusion | a7 | a8 a4 | a8 a10 a6 | a8 | a8 a4 a6 | a8 a6 | a8 a5 a6 a10 | a8 | a8 a6 |
| The fight against unemployment | a8 | a7 a5 | a7 a9 a5 | a7 a5 | a7 a5 | a7 a5 | a7 a11 a9 b5 | a7 a5 | a7 a9 |
| Agriculture and fishing policy | a9 | a10 | a3 a8 | a10 | a10 | a10 | a10 a8 | a10 | a10 a8 |
| Supporting regions which are experiencing economic difficulties | a10 | a9 | a7 | a9 | a9 | a9 | a9 a12 | a9 | a9 |
| Education | a11 | a12 a5 a15 | a12 b8 a6 | a12 a5 a15 | a12 a5 a15 | a12 a15 a5 | a12 a6 a5 a15 a8 | a12 a15 a5 | a12 a15 a5 |
| Scientific and technological research | a12 | a11 a13 | a11 | a11 a13 | a11 a13 | a11 a13 | a11 a13 b10 | a11 a13 | a11 b10 a13 |
| Information about the EU, its policies and institutions | a13 | a14 a12 | a14 | A14 a12 | a14 | a12 a14 | a14 a12 | a14 a12 | a14 b10 |

| | | | | | | | | |
|---|---|---|---|---|---|---|---|---|
| Foreign policy towards countries outside the EU | a14 | a13 a15 | a13 a15 a1 | a13 a15 | a13 a15 a1 a3 | a13 a15 | a13 a15 a1 a4 | a13 a15 | a13 a15 |
| Cultural policy | a15 | a14 | a14 b7 | a14 a11 | a14 a11 | a14 a11 | a14 a11 | a14 a11 | a11 a14 |
| Immigration policy | b1 | b2 b6 | b2 b6 | b2 b6 | b2 b6 | b2 b6 | b2 b6 | b2 b6 | b2 b6 |
| Rules for political asylum | b2 | b1 b6 | b1 b6 b3 | b1 b6 | b1 b6 | b1 b6 | b1 b6 | b1 b6 b3 | b1 b6 |
| The fight against organized crime | b3 | b4 b9 b10 b7 | b4 b9 b7 b2 | b4 b9 b7 b10 | b10 b9 | b4 b9 b10 b7 | b4 b9 b10 b7 | b9 b4 b10 b7 | b10 b4 b9 b7 |
| Police | b4 | b5 b3 b8 | b5 b3 b8 | b5 b3 b8 | b5 | b5 b3 b8 | b5 b3 b8 a6 | b5 b3 b8 | b5 b3 |
| Justice | b5 | b4 b6 | b4 b6 | b4 | b4 b6 a5 | b4 | b4 b6 b7 | b4 | b4 b6 a11 |
| Accepting refugees | b6 | b2 b1 b5 | b2 b1 b5 b7 | b2 b1 | b2 b5 b1 b7 | b2 b1 | b2 b1 b5 b7 b10 | b2 b1 | b2 b1 b5 |
| Juvenile crime prevention | b7 | b8 b3 b9 | b8 b3 b9 a15 b6 | b8 b3 b9 | b8 b6 b9 | b8 b9 b3 | b8 b9 b3 b6 b5 a15 | b8 b9 b3 | b8 b9 |
| Urban crime prevention | b8 | b7 b9 b4 | b7 b9 b4 a11 | b7 b9 b4 | b7 b9 | b7 b9 b4 | b7 b9 b4 | b7 b9 b4 | b7 b9 |
| The fight against drugs | b9 | b10 b8 b3 b7 | b10 b8 b3 b7 | b10 b8 b3 b7 | b10 b8 b3 | b10 b3 b8 b7 | b10 b8 b3 b7 | b10 b3 b8 b7 | b10 b8 b7 b3 |
| The fight against the trade in, and exploitation of, human beings | b10 | b9 b3 | b9 a4 | b9 b3 | b9 b3 | b9 b3 | b9 b3 a12 | b9 b3 | b9 b3 a13 |
| weighted n | | 13312 | 2242 | 8567 | 2351 | 18741 | 2987 | 11918 | 3611 |
| Average number of predictors (pro item) | | 2.2 | 2.7 | 2.2 | 2.4 | 2.2 | 3.2 | 2.2 | 2.3 |

have very similar views on delegating authority (coefficients differ at most by 0.2). Over the twelve remaining policies, in six policies, the federalists are more pro-European than other countries (a1, a3, a9, a14, a15, b6); in six policies, the federalists are less pro-European (a5, a8, a11, a12, b5, b9) than other countries.[25]

Thus, in our analyses we find some indications that voters have not yet formed very well-established views about the appropriate way to assign authority between the EU and the member states. While those respondents with a high subjective knowledge of the EU appear to have quite nuanced views with respect to the distribution of powers, those with less knowledge appear to respond either much more haphazardly or systematically by choosing the option of national competencies.

## 4. CONCLUSION

The EU will have to tackle one way or another how competencies are assigned across the different levels of government. In this paper we emphasized how this distribution is related to the problem of political accountability. Currently, the rather 'opaque' way in which competencies are assigned, combined with the complicated decision-making procedures, make it difficult for citizens to determine the relevant channel for political accountability. Thus, it is certainly not surprising that respondents in *Eurobarometer* surveys in part chose haphazard answers when asked to assign competencies to the EU or the national governments. This tendency is all the more marked among individuals with a low degree of knowledge about the EU. Obviously, such a state of affairs is barely congenial to ensure political accountability in the EU.

Thus, it can hardly surprise us that the constitution adopted in June 2004 attempts to strengthen political accountability by making the assignment of competencies more transparent and by simplifying the decision-making procedures. But as many scholars of federalism suggest, this requirement from the perspective of political accountability may be counterproductive for enhancing the stability of a federal arrangement. Hence, the safeguard measures introduced to give the subsidiarity principle more of a bite, by rendering the assignments of competencies possibly less transparent, might address in part the issue of how federal systems may remain stable. Some degree of flexibility in the assignment of competencies appears to be an important prerequisite.

These countervailing tendencies to be found in the proposed constitution will not necessarily make the assessment by citizens easier. Clear views about the assignment of competencies are likely to be indicative of a better understanding of the location of authority in particular policy domains. Our empirical analyses presented in this paper give at least suggested evidence for this link. And given that, on the one hand, a major objective of the constitution was a simplification of the treaties and, on the other, citizens in many countries will vote on the constitution, their views will be of considerable importance. The analyses presented here give evidence for still quite unclear opinions about the competencies to be assigned to the EU or national governments. It is likely, however, that owing to the upcoming ratification debates in the twenty-five national arenas the voters' views will be sharpened. For instance, it is likely that the referendum campaign in Great Britain will emphasize the government's 'red-line issues'. Thus, the voters' opinions will probably become more nuanced as the ratification stage is reached. In the absence of this, political accountability is less likely to be strengthened.

**Addresses for correspondence:** Thomas Christin, Institut für Politikwissenschaft (IPZ), Universität Zürich, Hirschengraben 56, CH-8001 Zürich, Switzerland. Tel: (+41) 44 634 5091. email: christin@pwi.unizh.ch/Simon Hug, Institut für Politikwissenschaft (IPZ), Universität Zürich. Tel: (+41) 44 634 5090. email: hug@pwi.unizh.ch/Tobias Schulz, Institut für Politikwissenschaft (IPZ), Universität Zürich. Tel: (+41) 44 634 5092. email: schulz@pwi.unizh.ch

## APPENDIX

In this appendix we present the logit analyses with only the fifteen current member states in 2003 (Table 3) or with the ten new members (Table 4) as well as replications based on data from 2001 (Table 5).

*Table 3* Explaining responses on decision-making in EU fifteen members (EB 59.1)

| Policy area | Question number | % jointly within the EU | % correct | Items predictors |
|---|---|---|---|---|
| Defence | a1 | 52.3 | 74.5 | a3 a2 a14 |
| Protection of the environment | a2 | 66.0 | 79.4 | a1 a4 |
| Currency | a3 | 70.8 | 81.6 | a1 |
| Humanitarian aid | a4 | 74.9 | 84.1 | a5 a2 |
| Health and social welfare | a5 | 32.7 | 81.7 | a4 a6 a11 b5 |
| Basic rules for broadcasting and press | a6 | 37.9 | 76.7 | a5 |
| Fight against poverty/ social exclusion | a7 | 63.4 | 80.7 | a8 a10 a4 a6 |
| The fight against unemployment | a8 | 49.1 | 78.6 | a7 a5 |
| Agriculture and fishing policy | a9 | 53.4 | 73.0 | a10 |
| Supporting regions which are experiencing economic difficulties | a10 | 63.2 | 75.3 | a9 a7 |
| Education | a11 | 32.9 | 81.5 | a12 a15 a5 |
| Scientific and technological research | a12 | 71.1 | 79.9 | a11 a13 b10 |
| Information about the EU, its policies and institutions | a13 | 80.0 | 86.9 | a14 a12 |
| Foreign policy towards countries outside the EU | a14 | 78.6 | 86.1 | a13 a15 a1 |
| Cultural policy | a15 | 46.0 | 72.3 | a14 a11 |
| Immigration policy | b1 | 54.2 | 85.5 | b2 b6 |
| Rules for political asylum | b2 | 56.7 | 85.3 | b1 b6 b3 |
| The fight against organized crime | b3 | 74.5 | 85.7 | b4 b10 b9 b7 b2 |
| Police | b4 | 27.3 | 89.9 | b5 b3 b8 |
| Justice | b5 | 32.0 | 88.8 | b4 b6 a5 |
| Accepting refugees | b6 | 56.6 | 79.3 | b2 b1 b5 b7 |
| Juvenile crime prevention | b7 | 38.4 | 88.8 | b8 b3 b9 b6 |
| Urban crime prevention | b8 | 34.3 | 88.5 | b7 b9 b4 |
| The fight against drugs | b9 | 69.8 | 84.8 | b10 b8 b3 b7 |
| The fight against the trade in, and exploitation of, human beings | b10 | 82.7 | 91.3 | b9 b3 a4 |
| weighted n | | | | 12272 |
| % missing | | | | 25.2 |
| Average number of predictors (pro item) | | | | 2.8 |

*Table 4* Explaining responses on decision-making in EU ten new members (CCEB 2003.2)

| Policy area | Question number | % jointly within the EU | % correct | Items predictors |
|---|---|---|---|---|
| Defence | a1 | 71.1 | 77.7 | a2 |
| Protection of the environment | a2 | 74.5 | 82.9 | a1 b3 a12 a3 |
| Currency | a3 | 74.4 | 80.8 | a2 |
| Humanitarian aid | a4 | 79.5 | 84.7 | a5 a7 a10 |
| Health and social welfare | a5 | 64.4 | 79.7 | a4 a8 a11 b10 |
| Basic rules for broadcasting and press | a6 | 41.7 | 74.6 | a15 a7 |
| Fight against poverty/social exclusion | a7 | 75.5 | 87.3 | a8 a6 a4 |
| The fight against unemployment | a8 | 80.1 | 88.6 | a7 a5 b7 a9 a10 |
| Agriculture and fishing policy | a9 | 67.9 | 80.0 | a10 a15 a8 |
| Supporting regions which are experiencing economic difficulties | a10 | 83.1 | 88.3 | a9 b10 a4 |
| Education | a11 | 60.8 | 77.2 | a12 a5 a15 b5 |
| Scientific and technological research | a12 | 83.6 | 88.0 | a11 b3 a13 |
| Information about the EU, its policies and institutions | a13 | 86.9 | 90.8 | a14 a12 |
| Foreign policy towards countries outside the EU | a14 | 75.3 | 82.3 | a13 a15 |
| Cultural policy | a15 | 42.3 | 77.1 | a14 a11 a6 b8 a9 |
| Immigration policy | b1 | 60.6 | 85.3 | b2 b6 |
| Rules for political asylum | b2 | 57.1 | 85.1 | b1 b6 |
| The fight against organized crime | b3 | 90.9 | 93.6 | b9 b4 b7 a12 a2 b10 |
| Police | b4 | 52.8 | 83.1 | b5 b3 b8 |
| Justice | b5 | 54.1 | 83.0 | b4 b7 b6 |
| Accepting refugees | b6 | 51.9 | 80.3 | b2 b1 b7 |
| Juvenile crime prevention | b7 | 63.0 | 89.4 | b8 b10 b5 b3 a8 |
| Urban crime prevention | b8 | 60.1 | 89.7 | b7 b9 b4 a15 |
| The fight against drugs | b9 | 88.6 | 93.6 | b10 b3 b8 |
| The fight against the trade in, and exploitation of, human beings | b10 | 91.0 | 94.3 | b9 b7 a10 b3 a5 |
| weighted n | | | 3733 | |
| % missing | | | 28.6 | |
| Average number of predictors (pro item) | | | 3.2 | |

*Table 5* Explaining responses on decision-making in EU twenty-five members (EB 56.2 and CCEB 2001.1)

| Policy area | Question number | % jointly within the EU | % correct | Items predictors |
|---|---|---|---|---|
| Defence | a1 | 56.2 | 76.0 | a2 a3 |
| Protection of the environment | a2 | 66.7 | 80.0 | a1 b3 |
| Currency | a3 | 68.3 | 80.0 | (a1) |
| Humanitarian aid | a4 | 76.3 | 85.7 | a5 a7 |
| Health and social welfare | a5 | 41.8 | 80.6 | a4 a6 a11 |
| Basic rules for broadcasting and press | a6 | 40.7 | 77.0 | a5 |
| Fight against poverty/social exclusion | a7 | 70.1 | 83.5 | a8 a4 |
| The fight against unemployment | a8 | 58.4 | 81.5 | a7 a11 a9 a5 |
| Agriculture and fishing policy | a9 | 57.7 | 75.2 | a10 a8 |
| Supporting regions which are experiencing economic difficulties | a10 | 68.6 | 78.9 | a9 |
| Education | a11 | 40.0 | 80.6 | a12 a15 a5 a8 |
| Scientific and technological research | a12 | 73.7 | 83.1 | a11 a13 |
| Information about the EU, its policies and institutions | a13 | 80.0 | 87.6 | a14 a12 |
| Foreign policy towards countries outside the EU | a14 | 76.8 | 86.1 | a13 a15 |
| Cultural policy | a15 | 46.2 | 74.8 | a14 a11 |
| Immigration policy | b1 | 52.3 | 86.0 | b2 b6 |
| Rules for political asylum | b2 | 54.4 | 85.7 | b1 b6 |
| The fight against organized crime | b3 | 76.9 | 86.6 | b4 b10 b9 b7 a2 |
| Police | b4 | 38.1 | 87.5 | b5 b3 b8 |
| Justice | b5 | 41.6 | 86.3 | b4 b6 |
| Accepting refugees | b6 | 55.3 | 81.3 | b2 b1 b7 |
| Juvenile crime prevention | b7 | 49.9 | 87.8 | b8 b3 b6 |
| Urban crime prevention | b8 | 44.7 | 88.1 | b7 b9 b4 |
| The fight against drugs | b9 | 75.9 | 87.3 | b10 b8 b3 |
| The fight against the trade in, and exploitation of, human beings | b10 | 84.2 | 91.8 | b9 b3 |
| weighted n | | | | 16193 |
| % missing | | | | 24.7 |
| Average number of predictors (pro item) | | | | 2.4 |

# NOTES

1  This paper relies in part on a joint research project financed by the European Commission in the Fifth Framework Programme entitled 'Domestic Structures and European Integration. A multistage two-level analysis of the constitution building in the European Union'. Financial support by the Swiss Bundesamt für Bildung und Wissenschaft (Grant number BBW Nr 02.0313) and the Grundlagenforschungsfonds of the University of St Gallen (Grant number G12161103) is gratefully acknowledged. Earlier versions of the paper were presented at the 'Authority Migration' conference, Ann Arbor, 30–31 May 2003, and at a conference in Geneva. Extremely helpful comments from the participants at this conference as well as an anonymous reviewer are gratefully acknowledged. Data used in the paper were made available through the ICPSR.

2  The treaties might be considered as some sort of 'covenant', even though they do not contain an explicit reference to federalism.

3  Interestingly, however, citizens favour the delegation of authority to the EU in those domains where this is appropriate from Alesina et al.'s (2004, forthcoming) theoretical perspective. An explanation for the mismatch with the current distribution of competencies may be found in Hooghe's (2003) work, since she finds some divergence between élite and voter preferences.

4  This point is highlighted by Strøm (2003). Maskin and Tirole (2001) argue, however, that perfect accountability is not necessarily desirable, since it might lead politicians to pander to the electorate.

5  Riker (1996) saw in the lack of a military threat to the EU an element which made all other federal systems hold together. Filippov (2004), however, demonstrates that this factor contributing to federal stability is overstated.

6  Interestingly, Filippov et al. (2004) suggest that the way in which the political parties in the EU operate, makes them 'imperfect agents' of their local constituents, namely the member states of the EU.

7  A different view appears in Schwartz (2004), who argues that all power should be vested at the central level. Through dual representation (the federal parliament would be composed of members of parliament of the lower levels), he expects that devolution would naturally occur.

8  Some authors go as far as arguing that this leads to a game of EU governments against their voters (e.g. Franklin and McGillivray 1999).

9  At the time of writing eight countries are certain to vote on the Constitution, namely Denmark, France, Ireland, Luxembourg, the Netherlands, Portugal, Spain and the United Kingdom. Belgium, the Czech Republic and Poland might join these eight countries (*Financial Times*, 15 July 2004, p. 2).

10  The policies covered appear in Tables 1 and 2. For the analyses presented here we rely on the Eurobarometer 59.1, carried out in Spring 2003, and the Candidate Countries Eurobarometer 2003.2 for the newest EU members. The questions used contain relatively few non-responses (varying between 3.2 per cent (b9) and 8.3 per cent (a9) in the two datafiles combined), while the percentage of missing cases for the whole set of items is 25.8 per cent. We carried out our analyses also on datasets imputed with EMis ('Expectation-Maximization with importance resampling'), where the missing responses for the twenty-five items were estimated with the responses to the other items and in addition to information on the survey (Standard EB or candidate countries), country, knowledge and EU as a good thing variable). We used the multiple imputation technique proposed by King et al. (2001) in order to estimate the missing categories with the AMELIA 2.1 software (Honaker et al. 2001). The analyses of the EMis model were done with the help of the CLARIFY software (Tomz et al. 2003) suggested by King et al. (2000), which allows us to analyse simultaneously multiply imputed datasets. Compared

to the results reported in Table 1 the estimated coefficients based on the imputed datasets are slightly smaller and the standard errors a bit larger. For this reason we refrained from reporting these analyses. In all analyses we used the weights provided in the two datafiles and adjusted them to make the sample representative for the enlarged EU.

11  The exact question wording is as follows in the Standard Eurobarometer: 'For each of the following areas, do you think that decisions should be made solely by the (NATIONALITY) government, or made jointly within the European Union?' The question for the Candidate Countries Eurobarometer adds: '(...), once (COUNTRY) becomes a member?'

12  Obviously these responses concerning attributed internationalization may be influenced by the satisfaction or salience of particular policies in the views of the respondents (Sinnott 1995). This issue, however, is tangential to our research question.

13  Very similar distributions, with some exceptions, obtain for most of the current fifteen member states. Separate analyses for the fifteen current members together and the ten candidates show that the distribution is negatively skewed for candidate countries.

14  We have recoded a ten-categories scale in three categories (1,2 = low) (3 to 6 = mid) (7 to 10 = high). The question is: 'Using this scale, how much do you feel you know about the European Union, its policies, its institutions?'

15  The question numbers refer to the Standard Eurobarometer questionnaires (e.g. a3 = q22a1, b5 = q22b5). The corresponding questions for the Candidate Countries Eurobarometer (q36.1 to q37.10) are easily found in the respective questionnaires.

16  The policies which, it is thought, should be handled at the EU level are (after *The fight against the trade in, and exploitation of, human beings*) for the 2001 datafiles: *Information about the EU, its policies and institutions* (a13, 80 per cent), *The fight against organized crime* (b3, 76.9 per cent), *Foreign policy towards countries outside the EU* (a14, 76.8 per cent) and *Humanitarian aid* (a4, 76.3 per cent). After *Police*, the policies that citizens would like to see least in joint hands with the EU are *Education* (a11, 40 per cent), *Basic rules for broadcasting and press* (a6, 40.7 per cent), *Justice* (b5, 41.6 per cent) and *Health and social welfare* (a5, 41.8 per cent). Previous analyses on these questions also appear in Dalton and Eichenberg (1998).

17  In other words, these issues are those that are supposed to be satisfactorily handled at the national level. This seems to be coherent with the conditions that sustain the principle of subsidiarity, particularly the necessity condition (Follesdal 1998).

18  Almost identical results are obtained if we conduct separate analyses for current members or candidates in 2001. Furthermore, similar results can be obtained if in addition country controls are introduced. The results of these analyses appear in the Appendix.

19  Strictly speaking, this would suggest that we have a set of twenty-five related equations. Thus, the coefficients of interest should be estimated jointly, for instance with multinomial probit. Given the exploratory character of this paper and the estimation difficulties of multinomial probit models, we refrain from presenting these more complicated results.

20  The criterion we used was that the estimated coefficient b had to fulfil the following criterion: $e^b \geq 2$. If no coefficient fulfilled this criterion we list in parenthesis the item with the largest coefficient in absolute values. The criterion might appear as odd, since negative effects are not taken into account. But since the responses are systematically positively correlated, if at all, this odd criterion performs well enough. In addition, given the sample size, the coefficients fulfilling this criterion almost automatically also reach statistical significance.

21  The reference category is the United Kingdom. This is convenient because its citizens are typically euro-sceptics. The country dummies are not shown in the table.

22  The question in the Standard Eurobarometer is: 'Generally speaking, do you think that (OUR COUNTRY)'s membership of the European Union is [for Candidate Countries: would be]: a good thing, a bad thing, neither good nor bad, don't know.' We recoded this variable as follows: [0] A bad thing, [0.5] neither good nor bad and don't know, [1] A good thing.
23  For the following analyses we considered Austria, Belgium, Germany and Spain as federal countries.
24  For two policies only federal states (a5, *Health and social welfare*) or only other countries (b6, *Accepting refugees*) are less pro-European than the UK.
25  For a8 and a12, federal states are very close to the United Kingdom.


## REFERENCES

Alesina, A., Angeloni, I. and Schuknecht, L. (2004, forthcoming) 'What does the European Union do?', *Public Choice*.

Bednar, J. (2004) 'Judicial predictability and federal stability: strategic consequences of institutional imperfection', *Journal of Theoretical Politics* 16(4): 423–46.

Dalton, R. and Eichenberg, R. (1998) 'Citizen support for policy integration', in W. Sandholtz and A. Stone Sweet (eds), *Supranational Governance: The Institutionalization of the European Union*, New York: Oxford University Press.

Eichenberg, R.C. and Dalton, R. (1993) 'Europeans and the European Community. The dynamics of public support for European integration', *International Organization* 47(4): 507–34.

Elazar, D.J. (ed.) (1991) *Constitutional Design and Power-sharing in the Post-modern Epoch*, Lanham, MD: University Press of America.

Filippov, M. (2004) 'Riker and federalism'. Paper prepared for presentation at the conference 'Micro-Foundations of Federal Institutional Stability', Durham, 30 April–1 May 2004.

Filippov, M., Ordeshook, P. and Shvetsova, O. (2004) *Designing Federalism: A Theory of Self-Sustainable Federal Institutions*, Cambridge: Cambridge University Press.

Follesdal, A. (1998) 'Subsidiarity', *The Journal of Political Philosophy* 6(2): 231–59.

Franklin, M. and McGillivray, F. (1999) 'European Union politics as a multi-level game against voters'. Paper presented at the APSA Annual Meeting, Atlanta, GA, 2–5 September.

Honaker, J., Joseph, A., King, G., Scheve, K. and Singh, N. (2001) 'Amelia: a program for missing data (Windows version)', Cambridge: Harvard University. http:// gkingharvard.edu/.

Hooghe, L. (2003) 'Europe divided?: elites vs. public opinion on European integration', *European Union Politics* 4(3): 281–304.

King, G., Tomz, M. and Wittenberg, J. (2000) 'Making the most of statistical analyses: improving interpretation and presentation', *American Journal of Political Science* 44(2): 347–61.

King, G., Honaker, J., Joseph, A. and Scheve, K. (2001) 'Analyzing incomplete political science data: an alternative algorithm for multiple imputation', *American Political Science Review* 95(1): 49–69.

Lijphart, A. (1999) *Patterns of Democracy: Government Forms and Performance in Thirty-Six Countries*, New Haven: Yale University Press.

Mair, P. (2000) 'The limited impact of Europe on national party systems', *West European Politics* 23(4): 27–51.

Manin, B., Przeworski, A. and Stokes, S.C. (1999) 'Introduction', in A. Przeworski, S.C. Stokes and B. Manin (eds), *Democracy, Accountability, and Representation*, New York: Cambridge University Press, pp. 1–26.

Maskin, E. and Tirole, J. (2001) 'The politician and the judge: accountability in government'. Prepared for presentation at the Annual Meeting of the European Public Choice Society, Paris, 18–22 April 2001.

McGarry, J. and O'Leary, B. (2003) 'Federation, conflict regulation and national and ethnic power-sharing'. Paper presented at the APSA Annual Meeting, Philadelphia, PA, 27 August–5 September.

Müller, W.C. (2000) 'Political parties in parliamentary democracies: making delegation and accountability work', *European Journal of Political Research* 37(3): 309–33.

Przeworski, A., Stokes, S.C. and Manin, B. (eds) (1999) *Democracy, Accountability, and Representation*, New York: Cambridge University Press.

Riker, W.H. (1964) *Federalism: Origin, Operation, Significance*, Boston: Little, Brown.

Riker, W.H. (1996) 'European federalism. The lessons of past experience', in J.J. Hesse and V. Wright (eds), *Federalizing Europe? The Costs, Benefits, and Preconditions of Federal Political Systems*, Oxford: Oxford University Press, pp. 9–24.

Schwartz, T. (2004) 'Design of federal constitutions: varieties, problems, and incentives'. Paper prepared for presentation at the conference 'Micro-Foundations of Federal Institutional Stability', Durham, 30 April–1 May 2004.

Sinnott, R. (1995) 'Policy, solidarity, and legitimacy', in O. Niedermayer and R. Sinnott (eds), *Public Opinion and Internationalized Governance*, Oxford: Oxford University Press, pp. 246–76.

Strøm, K. (2003) 'Parliamentary democracy and delegation', in K. Strøm, W.C. Müller and T. Bergman (eds), *Delegation and Accountability in Parliamentary Democracies*, Oxford: Oxford University Press, pp. 55–106.

Swenden, W. (2004) 'Is the European Union in need of a competence catalogue? Insights from comparative federalism', *Journal of Common Market Studies* 42(2): 371–92.

Tomz, M., Wittenberg, J. and King, G. (2003) 'CLARIFY: software for interpreting and presenting statistical results. Version 2.1', Stanford University, University of Wisconsin, and Harvard University, http://gking.harvard.edu/, 5 January.

Watts, R.L. (1999) *Comparing Federal Systems*, 2nd edn, Montreal: McGill-Queen's University Press.

# The European Union and cybercrime: insights from comparative federalism

Fernando Mendez

## INTRODUCTION

Approaches applying a comparative federalism lens to the European Union (EU) have been a regular, though not necessarily prominent, feature of the burgeoning European integration literature (Cappelletti *et al.* 1986; Scharpf 1988; Sbragia 1992). In recent years, however, a more explicitly theory-driven literature has appeared seeking to explain the effects of the EU's federal structures on policy outcomes and performance by drawing comparisons with other federal polities (see especially McKay 1999, 2001; Nicolaidis and Howse 2001; Kelemen 2000, 2003). This article takes its theoretical cue from this latest literature and asks whether a comparative federalism perspective can shed light on the dynamics surrounding a newly emerging and politically salient issue, that of criminality on the internet. Whether it is in the form of distributing computer viruses, defacing corporate websites, facilitating cyber attacks on critical information infrastructures or disseminating child pornography, the internet is seen as a threat to certain aspects of the established order. How lawmakers in the US, Switzerland and the EU have responded to this challenge, and the insights gained from adopting a comparative perspective on the EU, are the focus of this article.

## A COMPARATIVE FEDERALISM FRAMEWORK

Federalism is a theory of government that uses a system of checks and balances to curb power and, according to William Riker, one of the prominent scholars of federalism, offers an alternative to empire (Riker 1964). The key to Riker's understanding of the institution of federalism is that there are two sets of government, one of the federation and one of the member units, and that each has authority to make some decisions independently of the other. Building on these insights, Follesdal (2003) offers a useful working definition which will be followed in this article. According to Follesdal, a federal arrangement refers to a political order where 'final authority is divided between sub-units and a center' and in which 'sovereignty is constitutionally split between at least two territorial levels so that units at each level have final authority and can act independently of the others in some area'. Thus, whatever the structural differences that may exist between the EU, the US and Switzerland, they all possess a federal arrangement which disperses power among various jurisdictional units and typically generates high levels of 'constitutional politics' over the appropriate vertical allocation of authority (Bermann and Nicolaidis 2001; Donahue and Pollack 2001; Follesdal 2003; Filippov *et al.* 2004). Still, as noted by Riker (1964), there is considerable variation among federal polities. To this end he distinguished between systems with centralized federal constitutions and those with more decentralized federal constitutions. The US, Switzerland and the EU constitute examples of decentralized federal polities, although from a Rikerian perspective, the EU is clearly the more 'peripheralized' of the three.

Yet Riker (1993) has also argued that the US has become a 'centralized federation'. Thus, when it comes to the powers vested in the centre both Berne and Brussels are significantly weaker than Washington. Nonetheless, most comparisons of the EU's federal arrangement are usually made in relation to the US (e.g. Nicolaidis and Howse 2001; Fabbrini and Sicurelli 2004) although, in many respects, it is the Swiss model that comes closest to the EU model of federalism (see Papadopolous 2005). In fact, when it comes to policy implementation, and the centre's dependence on the sub-units to carry out its policies, the differences between Switzerland and the EU, on the one hand, and the US, on the other, are quite striking. As Halberstam (2001) has pointed out, the US federal government can draw on a more fully developed federal bureaucracy and judiciary for implementing federal laws as well as the financial resources to create new bureaucracies and, crucially, is able to do so without the consent of the sub-units. The US's model of federalism is usually referred to as 'dual federalism' owing to its tendency to replicate the entire machinery of government at both the federal and state levels (Börzel and

Hosli 2003). Recently, however, the centre has managed to acquire a stronger capacity to take independent policy action, especially since the New Deal era (Dye 1990). Indeed, Kincaid (1993) has identified a growing 'coercive federalism' in the US based around presidential ascendancy while Fabbrini and Sicurelli (2004) have noted that a century of congressional government has been followed by a long period of presidential government. On the other hand, among the effects generated by the Swiss and the EU's more 'co-operative model of federalism' has been a stronger presence of the sub-units during the decision-making process and, because the centre is weaker and more fragmented, a higher degree of heterogeneity with regard to policy implementation (see Papadopolous 2005).

Nonetheless, the literature on federalism is more than simply concerned with the identification of particular models of federalism and certainly harbours theory-building aspirations. Broadly speaking, this literature falls more or less into two categories. The first frames federalism as an independent variable, i.e. an institutional structure, which helps to explain particular policy outcomes. A second strand focuses on federalism more as a dependent variable, where, for instance, the stability (or instability) of federal institutions is the object of investigation. The approach in this article is of the former type. Scholars working within this frame have recently begun to (re)apply institutionalist insights to their subject matter (McKay 2001; Kelemen 2000; Filippov et al. 2004). In doing so they tend to focus on institutional variables, such as the basic structural configuration of the federal polities under investigation, and proceed to study the way in which these help to define and regulate interactions among political actors. A similar institutionalist understanding of federalism will be followed here. With regard to the case at hand, the internet has altered the perceptions of a whole series of actors, presenting them with new opportunities or risks, and mobilizing them into seeking political action. But it is not sufficient that new demands are simply placed on political systems. What is essential is that the competing demands between the different political actors require authoritative political resolution. In federal polities this usually takes the form of disputes over the appropriate allocation of authority among the various levels of government (Kelemen 2000; Bermann and Nicolaidis 2001). However, as Easton (1957) recognized, for them to be transformed into policy issues it is necessary that, first, there should be sufficient conflict among political actors and that, second, lawmakers are sufficiently concerned with the issues to place them on the policy agenda. As we shall see, both these conditions are operative. In fact, federal political actors may even seize the opportunity to supply centralizing solutions in order to increase their respective competencies, especially where the policy field has cross-border effects (Coglianese and Nicolaidis 2001). Part of the motivation may be attributed to the need to reduce some of the inefficiencies generated from capability and resource asymmetries among the sub-units, or to prevent the emergence of potential distortions if the sub-units adopt divergent responses. One of the consequences of increased federal activity, however, is that the centre can potentially expand the scope of its authority into new areas and, if successful policies are pursued, its support among the general public (Kelemen 2000).

In this article two claims are put forward. The first relates to vertical inter-actions, which refers to the relations between central/federal level authorities and the sub-units or, in some cases, even lower units (e.g. regions, communes, local authorities, depending on the polity in question). The second claim con-cerns the capabilities of central level institutions. While vertical dynamics can be expected to be similar in the three units of analyses, the same does not hold for the implementation or enforcement capabilities of the centre. A strong centre is able to implement autonomous policy actions by drawing on its own resources or bureaucracy without the necessary consent or assistance of the sub-units. The opposite is the case for a weak centre. These insights lead to the formulation of two hypotheses:

*Hypothesis 1*: Increased vertical interactions among the various levels of public authority around a specific policy field could potentially lead to upward/downward shifts in legal competencies. Moreover, where the policy field has significant cross-border effects there will be greater opportunities for centraliza-tion and the more likely federal actors will be mobilized to offer centralizing solutions.

*Hypothesis 2*: Where a weak centre is dependent on the resources or consent of the sub-units we would expect the sub-units to retain important powers while delegating only co-ordinating functions to the central level. The inverse is the case for a stronger centre which would be able to pursue and implement policy measures independently.

## CYBERCRIME AS A POLICY CHALLENGE

Before probing these hypotheses it is important to note certain features of the policy challenge itself. Cybercrime merges two little understood spheres – technology and crime – which most lawmakers, officials and the public at large do not fully understand and therefore tend to fear. Furthermore, defining the many types of criminality on the internet has been notoriously difficult (exceptions include Sieber 1998; Brenner 2004). For the purposes of this inquiry internet crimes and abuses will be broken down into two major (and overlapping) areas. The first relates to the regulation of content. The internet has facilitated, to an unprecedented degree, the dissemination of potentially illegal and harmful content such as child pornography, obscene and xenophobic material as well as offering new possibilities for the abuse of content, e.g. copy-right infringement or the unlawful collection of personal data. The second issue area relates to the security of information systems and could be more accurately described as computer crime or cybersecurity. The policy challenge is how to protect the information systems that modern advanced societies increasingly rely upon. There is concern, for instance, that this reliance on computers and computer networks makes countries' 'critical information infrastructures' vulnerable to cyber attacks from terrorists and disgruntled hackers. Further down the danger scale, but certainly more real for the individual user or for the business organization, are the spread of computer viruses and worms and, for some corporations, having to deal with high profile denial of service attacks.

There are three overlapping issues that preoccupy policy-makers and, in particular, law enforcement agencies. First, there is the assumption that, based on current trends, cybercrimes will continue to increase and that in the near future most crimes will have a cyber component.[1] Second, getting access to data, i.e. through the electronic interception of communication or the search and seizure of computer evidence, will become increasingly important for crime-fighting purposes and not just for hi-tech crimes, but also for ordinary crimes. Third, these problems are exacerbated by the fact that the internet is an international communication medium that transcends territorial and jurisdictional borders. These challenges are putting pressure on the neat compartmentalization of criminal justice systems in the three multi-tiered polities. Three case studies are presented below, followed by a comparative review section bringing together some of the central findings.

## THE US CASE

The dual federalism model of the US has, through deliberate constitutional design, set up a criminal justice system that operates on various levels: the federal, state and local. Historically, there has been a deeply engrained belief that general law enforcement powers reside with the states and are administered locally. This has been upheld by a very strict delineation of competencies which has placed fundamental restrictions on the expansion of federal law enforcement powers. The result is that the US dual federalism model is characterized by significant variation among the sub-units with regard to criminal laws and it is quite common to find that state prohibitions and punishment differ markedly (e.g. on the death penalty).

This careful decentralization of criminal law authority is, however, being undermined by a wave of federalization. According to the American Bar Association (ABA 1998) nearly half of all the federal crimes enacted since 1865 have been passed since 1970. The reasons for this wave of federalization are manifold but one significant factor is the perceived need, on the part of the federal authorities, to be seen to be addressing high-profile criminal incidents and other social ills by passing federal legislation. There is, of course, a rational self-interest to passing federal criminal legislation even though, in practice, only 5 per cent of prosecutions are federal (Stuntz 2001). Essentially, it confers new powers on federal entities (prosecutors, administrative agencies, courts, etc.) and to executive departments, such as the Department of Justice (DOJ), which assume broad supervisory responsibilities over the new federalized crime, as well as extending the power of federal investigatory agencies, such as the Federal Bureau of Investigation (FBI) (ABA 1998).

It is appropriate to view current debates concerning internet criminality in the light of this increasing trend towards the federalization of competencies that were traditionally the prerogative of the states. Copyright laws, which among other things deal with online piracy, have been a source of great controversy in the US, pitting powerful interest groups such as the music and movie industry against telecommunication operators and internet service providers. Yet, in terms of the vertical dimension (i.e. federal versus state) the issue is relatively straightforward: copyright law in the US is derived from the constitution and is an exclusive federal competence (Brenner 2004). Instead, most controversies have centred on the mode of regulation rather than the level and, in relation to the former, what for some analysts has been the development of a particularly repressive copyright regime in the form of the 1998 Digital Millennium Copyright Act (DMCA) (see especially Lessig 1999; Samuelson 1999). On the other hand, when it comes to data protection the US has opted for a self-regulatory approach and, as a consequence, no statutory provisions exist at the federal or at the state level. This does not mean that there is no privacy regime in the US, but rather that it is geared towards privacy violations by the state instead of what is believed by analysts to be the growing threat to privacy – that posed by non-governmental private parties (Brenner 2004).

As far as illegal and harmful content is concerned, the starting point for any discussion in the US is the constitution and, in particular, the core First Amendment freedom of speech provision. It prohibits federal or state legislatures from criminalizing speech on the basis of content and has therefore been the focal point of most debates. Federal efforts to regulate internet content can be traced back to the mid-1990s when a number of organizations began lobbying for federal legislation to protect minors from sexually explicit material (Sutter 2000). Various federal proposals were put forward and enacted by Congress to address the problem. Two of the most controversial have been the Communications Decency Act of 1995 and the Child Pornography Prevention Act of 1996. Both these federal acts, and more recent follow-up laws,[2] have provoked much constitutional controversy and helped to mobilize civil liberties groups and industry organizations to mount successful constitutional challenges through the courts.[3] Limited in their ability to implement statutory measures to pursue their policy objectives, US policy-makers have resorted to increasing law enforcement agencies' powers. On the one hand, internet service providers have been encouraged to report incidents to law enforcement agencies through hotlines while, on the other, enhanced investigatory approaches such as the FBI's Innocent Images National Initiative (IINI) have been developed. The IINI has used undercover investigative methods with agents posing as children or as adults with an interest in child pornography. This investigatory mode of regulation is, for obvious reasons, more costly than simply imposing liability on content or access providers (the object of earlier legislation).

When it came to addressing computer crimes, the FBI was able to build upon its work during the 1980s[4] when it acquired particular expertise in investigating hacker intrusions and data theft. It was thus well placed to acquire a prominent role in dealing with cybersecurity issues (Bendrath 2001). Nonetheless, from a legal perspective federal activity was restricted to computers used by the federal government – consistent with the traditional dual criminal justice system under which federal crimes were narrowly defined and limited to protecting special federal interests. With computer crimes and cybercrimes on the rise, it was increasingly felt by the DOJ that new centralizing legislation was required.[5] The result was the 1996 National Information Infrastructure Protection Act (the title is instructive and gives a sense of urgency with strong national security overtones to a problem that is not limited to individual computers but to a *national* infrastructure). Cybercrimes were now federalized under one statute and this was achieved by introducing the term of a 'protected computer' instead of the more restrictive 'federal interest computer'. The new definition, based on an expansive reading of the interstate commerce clause, increased the federal scope of the laws to encompass any computer connected to the internet (Brenner 2004).

Following the attacks of 9/11 Congressional interest in the area of cybersecurity was renewed. Shortly after the attacks the Bush Administration released two Executive Orders, creating the Office for Homeland Security and establishing a new cybersecurity organization (the President's Critical Infrastructure Protection Board) to be chaired by a newly appointed Cyberspace Czar.[6] The attacks of 9/11 provided new opportunities for centralization in the cybersecurity domain although, in many respects, these built on the earlier efforts of the Clinton Administration.[7] With the creation of the Department of Homeland Security (DHS) in January 2003, a consolidation of efforts in the area of cybersecurity after almost a decade of activity was achieved. The other major component of the Bush Administration's cybersecurity strategy was the passage, just one month after the 9/11 attacks, of controversial legislation known as the Patriot Act. It significantly expanded government, and in particular law enforcement's, surveillance and investigatory capabilities in cyberspace by making it easier for law enforcement agencies to obtain information from internet service providers while also increasing the penalties for cybercrimes. Although the Act was framed in terms of fighting terrorism, by enhancing the electronic investigatory capabilities of law enforcement agencies, the result is that their general crime-fighting capacity has been strengthened (see especially Kerr 2003).

With the passing of the Patriot Act the issue of federalism and internal security has been dramatically raised. Although the word 'federalism' may not be mentioned, the tensions between the sub-units and central government are familiar to students of comparative federalism. One of the problems concerns the Act's expansion of federal powers by requiring, in some instances, state and local authorities to assist federal agencies in their investigatory efforts. Recently, many state and local authorities are resisting, claiming that co-operation will force them to violate civil liberties. As with the controversial illegal and harmful content laws, grassroots civil rights movements have been mobilized and have successfully lobbied local and state authorities to pass anti-Patriot Act Resolutions.[8] Two years following the enactment of the Patriot Act, more than 300 cities and four states (Alaska, Hawaii, Maine and Vermont) have passed resolutions calling on Congress to repeal or change parts of the controversial law which, according to activists, violates constitutional rights. Although such resolutions have no legally binding force, they do, nonetheless, send a powerful message to federal lawmakers, especially since the Act's sunset provisions will need to be renewed.

## THE SWISS CASE

Switzerland is considered to be not only one of the classic federal systems but also probably the most decentralized, in terms of the autonomy enjoyed by the sub-units (Elazar 1991). The operation of its criminal justice system neatly illustrates the constraints of Switzerland's model of co-operative federalism. The Swiss Constitution of 1848, which set up the first (modern) federal constitution to be ratified on European soil, left responsibility for criminal legislation to the cantons. It was to take almost a century, however, before a Swiss penal code came into effect. During this time various efforts to craft a federal penal code were attempted, most notably in 1898 when the revised Constitution of 1874 was amended to make criminal legislation a federal competence (Trechsel and Killias 2004a). Only after half a century of preparatory work, including comparative studies on existing cantonal criminal legislation, various expert committees and a referendum vote passed by a narrow majority, did the Swiss penal code come into force in 1942. Since then, the Swiss penal code has been amended numerous times to include crimes such as money laundering, organized crime and racism and xenophobia.

While the substantive law aspects of what actually constitutes a crime were federalized, the same cannot be said for procedural law, which determines the procedures for investigating crimes and collecting evidence. Criminal procedural laws were left to the twenty-six cantons (see Article 64-bis of the Swiss Constitution) and this has led to significant variations among the cantons, a situation not entirely unrelated to the fact that the cantons drew inspiration from French, German/Austrian and Italian codes of criminal procedure (Trechsel and Killias 2004b). However, with the second total revision of the Swiss Constitution in 1999 the federal level has been vested with new powers to harmonize procedural criminal law (Kalin 2004; Trechsel and Killias 2004a). In sum, this rather unique constitutional set-up, in which the centre (subject to the considerable constraints of the Swiss policy process) defines substantive criminal law while the sub-units enjoy autonomy for the investigation and prosecution of crimes, helps to explain another Swiss peculiarity – a federal police force which resembles an administrative unit rather than an actual field force and which has only recently (in 2002) acquired investigative powers and (until 2004) had no federal-level criminal court.

Over the past decade the increasing internationalization of crime has, however, put considerable strain on this extremely decentralized set-up. In response, the investigation of certain areas of criminal activity – namely organized crime – has been centralized. Thus, although a federal police office has been created, its remit is strictly limited to investigating organized crime. The strict and very narrow definition of organized crime contained in the Swiss penal code effectively ensures that most instances of these crimes are, in any case, investigated by the cantons.[9] In view of the constitutional constraints and the extremely decentralized nature of the Swiss law enforcement and justice system, it comes as no surprise that cybercrime, given the intensive resources required to mount successful investigations and prosecutions, would pose problems for a system characterized by significant variation among the twenty-six investigative authorities (one for each canton). Recognizing this, a 2001 parliamentary initiative called for further centralization in view of the fact that the 'investigation of crimes committed on the internet is laborious ... and there are a number of cantons lacking the human resources and an adequate infrastructure for effectively investigating these crimes. The fact that there are 26 different criminal procedural codes and police forces is an obstacle for conducting effective investigations.'[10] The initiative, which was framed in terms of the evils of child pornography and protecting children's rights, called for a centralization, at the federal level, of the investigation and prosecution of cybercrimes.

The Federal Assembly rejected certain parts of the initiative, which would have made the investigation of cybercrime, especially hard pornography, a federal competence (i.e. giving it the same status as organized crime). These attempts have failed mainly because, as noted by the Federal Assembly, 'a centralization of investigative competences of these crimes would represent a fundamental mutation of the penal system of our country.'[11] In policy-making circles, and among the investigative authorities, it was felt that in the near future the majority of crimes would be committed over the internet, federalization therefore would signal 'the beginning of the end of cantonal investigative crime fighting, and you would get an FBI instead of the current cantonal police'.[12] Moreover, even if broad political and legislative agreement could be fostered, the proposal would be subject to the referendum process, and it is here that the cantons would be mobilized.

In view of these serious institutional constraints, other mechanisms would have to be developed. In 2000 an InterCantonal Working Group on cybercrime, which included police chiefs, legal specialists and other interested parties, was created to study the problem.[13] They formulated a series of proposals, mainly centred on harmonizing law enforcement techniques, but also recommended the creation of a 'cybercrime unit'. The difficulty was in trying to set up a unit which did not infringe upon the investigative authority of the cantons, but at the same time reduced the inefficiencies resulting from information and investigative asymmetries among the twenty-six different authorities.[14] The result was the creation of a cybercrime co-ordination unit, CYCOS, which would deal with reports of misuse, and act as a legal clearing house (i.e. check whether the subject matter was illegal or not and conduct nationwide analyses). By delegating some of the costly manpower and specialized activities to the new unit, the cantons, and in particular those which are smaller and less well resourced, have been able to free up resources while still maintaining their full investigative authority. The cantons decide whether they wish to initiate a prosecution on the basis of the file presented to them by the federal unit.

But the role of the cantons has also been strengthened in further ways. As the principal paymaster – the cantons provide two-thirds of the finance for CYCOS – they are able to wield significant influence in dictating what the unit should focus on.[15] Thus, although the unit's website mentions a variety of cybercrimes (including unlawful entry into IT systems, violation of copyright and the spreading of computer viruses), its *de facto* focus has been on hard (mostly child) pornography, given that this is politically the most salient issue and is what the cantons are most concerned about.

Concerning some of the other issue areas relevant to internet criminality in general, the trend is somewhat less ambiguous although progress is typically slow. Switzerland is in the process of updating its current copyright laws, and the legislation is making its way through Switzerland's lengthy consociational policy process. Having started proceedings in 2000, involving several working groups, draft legislation was expected in late 2004 and even then this will have to be followed by a further consultation process.[16] On the data protection front, however, progress has been more rapid and Switzerland has adopted a multi-tiered system consisting of a Federal Data Protection Commissioner, Cantonal Data Protection Commissioners and there are even some municipal Data Protection Commissioners (Berne and Zurich). With regard to the security of information infrastructures, various federal level units have been created to share information among the public and private sector (Dunn and Wigert 2004). The most important will be a new agency, the Reporting and Analysis Centre for Information Assurance (known as Melani), which will perform a role similar to CYCOS, i.e. information sharing with no investigative authority.

In sum, various initiatives (Watermann and Pfisterer[17]) and expert committees (expert commission on cybercrime and the Genesis working group[18]) have called for an enhanced federal role. While there has certainly been a mobilization of actors favouring further centralization, and many of these proposals are still making their way through the policy process, the latest report by the Federal Council makes for some pessimistic reading for advocates of centralization. It states that the 'Federal Council wishes to stop short of establishing a new federal competency or area of federal jurisdiction' and, moreover, 'that the federal role should be restricted to coordination functions only while cantonal prosecuting and investigative competencies are to be retained'.[19]

## THE EU CASE

To understand the EU's growing involvement in the area of internet criminality one has to take account of the major treaty modifications, all of which have had far-reaching implications for the conduct of police and judicial co-operation.

Within the space of little over a decade the policy area of justice and home affairs, which did not even figure within the scope of the treaties and was characterized by limited intergovernmental co-operation, has advanced to the top of the political agenda to become an integral component of the EU treaties (Monar 2001; Walker 2003). Co-operation in policing and judicial affairs at the European level can be traced back to the 1970s when a special working group (Trevi) was created to enhance co-operation between law enforcement agencies in the area of internal security. Nonetheless, these activities were firmly outside the European Community framework and it was not until the Maastricht Treaty of 1991 that police and judicial co-operation was brought into the treaty structure. With the Treaty of Amsterdam in 1997 another turning point was initiated with the creation of new legal instruments known as 'Decisions' and 'Framework Decisions'. Both these legal instruments strengthened the capacity for the 'harmonization' of criminal laws as well as facilitating co-operation among member state justice systems. By the time of the entry into force of the Amsterdam Treaty in 1999, the small task force for justice and home affairs created by the Maastricht Treaty was expanded into a full Directorate General (DG). It has since become the driving force behind initiatives in the area of organized crime and cybercrime.[20] The EU Constitution takes these developments even further and Article III-271 provides for the harmonization of criminal laws in areas of serious crime with cross-border dimensions. It lists ten crimes including cybercrime (although it is referred to as computer crime) as well as organized crime, terrorism, and the sexual exploitation of women and children.

With regard to cyber piracy and copyright infringement, the EU has played a major role in fostering a European approach with the adoption in 2001 of a copyright directive.[21] In many respects, the copyright wars that surrounded the most 'lobbied directive' in the Community's history were a rerun of what had occurred earlier in the US with the 1998 DMCA (Hargreaves 2001). As this was an internal market issue, the Commission was to play a pivotal role. What is interesting to note are some of the controversies surrounding the EU's latest weapon in the fight against cyber piracy, the Intellectual Property Rights Enforcement Directive[22] where the Commission's attempts to introduce mandatory criminal sanctions for copyright violations were resisted by the member states.[23]

On the question of illegal and harmful content the constitutional battles that were unfolding in the US during the mid-1990s did not go unnoticed across the Atlantic. When in 1997 German prosecutors held the general manager of *Compuserve* (an American internet service provider) responsible for trafficking in pornography and neo-Nazi propaganda, policy-makers at the Commission took note. Events in Europe had potentially grave implications for the internal market. If member states adopted diverging approaches to the regulation of internet content, distortions to the internal market could be created (Goldsmith 2000a; Mayer 2000). Further unilateral member state attempts at internet content regulation appeared in 2000 when three anti-racist and

Jewish associations successfully filed a complaint against *Yahoo!* before a French court for hosting online auctions of Nazi memorabilia (for a discussion, see Goldsmith 2000b).

In any event, the Commission had already given much thought to the issue of illegal and harmful content, and the dangers posed by unilateral member state regulation of information services, well before the French *Yahoo!* and German *Compuserve* cases. Two major policy statements, a Communication on Illegal and Harmful Content and a Green Paper on the Protection of Minors, had already been adopted in 1996. These were followed up by a Council Recommendation and the disbursement of research funds via the 1999 Safer Internet Action Plan for funding the development of a European system of hotlines where users could report content they considered to be illegal. Of course, responsibility for the prosecution and investigation would remain with the member state law enforcement authorities. By 2001, and under the responsibility of the new DG Justice and Home Affairs, the Commission published its Communication on Cybercrime.[24] This document signalled a new approach to cybercrime which differed markedly from the more self-regulatory rhetoric of the mid-1990s and inaugurated a new trend towards closer police and judicial co-operation as well as a greater harmonization of penal laws. Thus, in the same month as the publication of the Cybercrime Communication, a proposal for a Framework Decision on Child Pornography,[25] harmonizing penal laws in this area, was published and took effect in 2004. The issue of racism and xenophobia has, however, been more controversial given the wider divergences in this area among the member states. Nonetheless, a proposal for a Framework Decision was published in 2001 which states that 'the Commission's approach on this issue is to ensure that racist and xenophobic content on the Internet is criminalized in all Member States.'[26] At the time of writing the proposal has yet to be adopted by the Council.

The 2001 Communication on Cybercrime also addressed the issue of cyber-security. Computer crime and information security issues had already been advancing on the European policy agenda from the early 1990s. At the same time data protection issues were acquiring a heightened importance as a result of fears that a lack of consistency among the member states with regard to privacy could constitute a serious impediment to the emerging single market of the information age. This led to the development of a multi-tiered data protection regime which, despite its defensive economic background, provides evidence of the EU's desire to intervene in commercial activity to protect the rights of the 'data subject' (Charlesworth 2000). The problem with the EU's data protection laws,[27] however, is that they impose constraints on member states' and law enforcement agencies' ability to acquire information on citizens' electronic communications for general crime fighting and anti-terrorist purposes. This has provoked significant battles between data protection authorities and law enforcement agencies over 'data retention'. The most recent development in this area is a member state driven proposal for a framework decision on data retention.[28]

As in the US, the attacks of 9/11 were to alter the political climate surrounding security as well as police and judicial co-operation, especially with regard to the fledgling organizations of Europol and Eurojust (Gilmore 2003). Just before the attacks the Commission had published its first policy statement specifically addressing the issue of cybersecurity (the Communication on Network and Information Security). Although much attention has focused on the two Framework Decisions leading to a European arrest warrant and a common definition of terrorism, a proposal for a Framework Decision specifically dealing with the security of cyberspace and attacks against information systems[29] was also adopted following the 9/11 attacks. These measures to harmonize criminal laws related to cybercrimes have been further supplemented by the decision to create a specialized European Network and Information Security Agency (NISA). Its aim is to co-ordinate efforts relating to network and information security and provide assistance to the national regulatory authorities, which are at very different stages and levels of preparation. In sum, the Commission, with the Council's support, has managed to successfully articulate the case that cybercrime is an issue which needs to be addressed at the EU level.

## COMPARATIVE REVIEW

Some of the main findings will now be reviewed in light of the initial hypotheses. First, with regard to the strategic vertical interactions, attempts by the centre to offer federal solutions to internet criminality and internet governance problems in all three polities can clearly be identified. The Swiss case has been the most straightforward concerning legal competencies given that penal laws, as well as those that relate to copyright and data protection, are a federal competence. In the area of copyright the centre's regulatory capacity has been enhanced in all three units of analysis, with particularly intense controversies concerning the mode of regulation generated in the US and the EU. Legal competencies regarding data protection rules have moved to the centre in the EU and in Switzerland although in the US a self-regulatory model has been pursued. On the question of illegal and harmful content, although there have been considerable difficulties in criminalizing certain types of content and imposing liability on third parties in the US, federal law is explicit with regard to prohibiting child pornography and material that is obscene.[30] When it comes to federalizing computer crimes and dealing with issues related to cybersecurity at the federal level, there have been relatively fewer difficulties in the US. This upward shift in legal competencies has been especially notable with the passing of the Patriot Act. Similarly, in the EU a growing trend towards the approximation of criminal laws can be detected. Framework Decisions have been put to effective use in various internet crime related areas, including child pornography, attacks on information systems, racism and xenophobia, and data retention (the last two have yet to be approved). The result has been a creeping approximation of criminal laws at the EU level, although this process is still at an embryonic stage. Thus, in all three systems we have witnessed shifts in legal competencies towards the centre, with federal policy-makers offering centralizing solutions to problems with obvious cross-border effects among the sub-units.

Although there are similarities among the units with regard to the vertical dimension, this is less so with regard to the specificity of the policy outputs. A comparative federalism lens has drawn attention to how differences in federal structures can impact on outcomes. In all three polities constitutional constraints impose important limitations on the centralizing mechanisms available to the centre. This is particularly the case in relation to the policy enforcement dimension. With regard to data protection, both the EU and Switzerland have adopted multi-tiered regimes in which enforcement is primarily the responsibility of the sub-units, or even lower units such as the *Länder* in Germany or city data protection commissioners in Switzerland. In the US by contrast the absence of a specific data protection authority means that conflicts are largely enforced by the courts or by the Federal Communications Commission. With regard to copyright, although most cases are mainly brought about by private parties in all three units, policy-makers in the US have not solely relied on the private sector to police violations. Significant resources have been directed to creating federal agencies specialized in the investigation of copyright infringement, and these have achieved some notable successes over the last few years.[31] The same applies to computer crimes and investigating the distribution of illegal content where the FBI's investigative powers, in terms of its capacity to monitor and analyse internet traffic and its ability to use undercover investigative methods in the fight against child pornography, have been notably increased.

These options are simply *not* available in the EU or even in the Swiss context where enforcement is carried out exclusively by the sub-units and where any attempts to centralize policing would be firmly resisted. In the Swiss case the federal police force's remit is narrowly restricted to organized crime and cantonal competence over the investigation and prosecution of crimes is exclusive. Moreover, a strict delineation of competencies concerning cybercrime has imposed serious constraints on the federal level's ability to frame cybercrime as a national security issue. Therefore, the investigation and prosecution of cybercrime remains an exclusive cantonal competence. Under such conditions, the cantons have been careful to delegate only co-ordination functions to a central organization (e.g. CYCOS). This is not dissimilar to the EU where there have been successful attempts at approximating cybercrime related penal laws in combination with the development of new co-operation and monitoring mechanisms at the centre. The creation of new agencies such as NISA is an example. Yet the member states have been careful not to endow it with any regulatory or investigative powers and its main function is to collect and analyse data with the aim of also assisting the member states. The same holds for the network of EU-funded European hotlines. Just as in the Swiss case, the investigation and prosecution aspects are dominated by the sub-units. In sum, where a weak centre has been dependent on the resources or the consent of the sub-units as in Switzerland and the EU only co-ordination functions have been delegated at this initial stage to the central level. Where a stronger centre has been able to draw on its own resources and has not been constrained by the sub-units, as in the US, it has been easier either to create new federal agencies with autonomous investigatory powers or to empower existing agencies.

## CONCLUSIONS

The case studies have highlighted how developments in the wider domain of police and judicial affairs in the EU share certain similarities with earlier experiences in decentralized federal polities such as the US and Switzerland. Of course, the sheer scale and complexity of the exercise, as well as the heterogeneity among the sub-units, make the EU's experiment the most daring to date (Walker 2003). Yet this does not mean that policy dynamics cannot be profitably compared to those experienced in other federal systems. Thus, the increasing politicization of the internet and the regulatory dilemmas that surround its governance have generated typical centre–periphery conflicts over policy outputs. Allocational shifts in authority towards the central level have occurred in all three units of analysis. At the same time, however, variations in capabilities at the central level have influenced the specificity of policy outputs, especially in relation to the investigation of cybercrimes. Whereas in the US the centre has been able to enhance the role of federal agencies or create new investigative agencies, in Switzerland and the EU the absence of powerful federal investigative agencies help to explain the co-ordination and monitoring mechanisms which have been developed to address internet criminality issues. To this end, Swiss insights, such as extremely weak federal investigative agencies and a propensity towards legal harmonization at the centre with the sub-units controlling the implementation process, could be especially pertinent to the future trajectory of current EU policies in the domain of police and judicial co-operation.

**Address for correspondence:** Fernando Mendez, E-Democracy Centre, University of Geneva, Faculté de droit, 40, bd. du Pont-d'Arve, 1211 Geneva 4, Switzerland. Tel: (+41) 22 379 85 56. Fax: (+41) 22 379 85 36. email: Fernando.Mendez@droit.unige.ch

## NOTES

1 Interview with Swiss official 23/06/04 at Berne.
2 For example, the 1998 Child Online Protection Act.
3 In relation to the Communications Decency Act, see *Reno* v. *ACLU*, no. 96–511. For the Child Pornography Prevention Act, see *Ashcroft* v. *Free Speech Coalition*, no. 00–795.
4 The FBI was able to set up a specialized computer squad on the basis of the Computer Fraud and Abuse Act 1986.
5 See the National Information Infrastructure Protection Act 1996: Legislative Analysis by the Computer Crime and Intellectual Property Section of the US Department of Justice. Available at: http://www.cybercrime.gov/1030_anal.html

6　Executive Order 13228 set up the Office for Homeland Security while Executive Order 13231 set up the President's Critical Infrastructure Protection Board.

7　The most important development was Clinton's Presidential Decision Directive 63 (PDD-63) on Critical Infrastructure Protection which set out a national strategy. See the Presidential Decision Directive 63, White Paper, May 1998. Available at: http://www.mipt.org/pdf/ClintonPolicyCIP_PDD63.pdf

8　The most influential civil liberties group has been the Bill of Rights Defense Committee; see their website: http://www.bordc.org/

9　Interview with crime analyst 22/05/04 in Geneva.

10　Author's translation. See Parliamentary initiative 01.3196 *Améliorer la procédure de lutte contre la cybercriminalité*, déposé par Aeppli Wartmann Regine.

11　Author's translation. See the position of Federal Council 12-09-2001 in Parliamentary initiative 01.3196 *Améliorer la procédure de lutte contre la cybercriminalité*, déposé par Aeppli Wartmann Regine.

12　Interview with Swiss Federal official 23/06/04 at Berne.

13　For an overview, see the website of the Swiss Co-ordination Unit for Cybercrime Control: http://www.cybercrime.admin.ch/

14　Interview with official at the Swiss Co-ordination Unit for Cybercrime Control 23/06/04 at Berne.

15　Interview with official at the Swiss Co-ordination Unit for Cybercrime Control 23/06/04 at Berne.

16　See the 6th Report of the Information Society Co-ordination Group (ISCG) to the Federal Council 2004. Also available at: www.infosociety.ch

17　See Parliamentary initiatives 00.3714 Motion Pfisterer Thomas. *Cybercriminalité. Modification des dispositions légales.* 01.3196 Motion Aeppli Wartmann Regine *Améliorer la procédure de lutte contre la cybercriminalité.*

18　See p. 37 of the 6th Report of the Information Society Co-ordination Group (ISCG) to the Federal Council 2004. Also available at: www.infosociety.ch

19　See p. 37 of the 6th Report of the Information Society Co-ordination Group (ISCG) to the Federal Council 2004. Also available at: www.infosociety.ch

20　Interview with European Commission official 23/05/04 at the Joint Research Centre.

21　Directive 2001/29/EC of 22 May 2001on the harmonization of certain aspects of copyright and related rights in the information society.

22　Directive 2004/48/EC of the European Parliament and of the Council of 29 April 2004 on the enforcement of intellectual property rights.

23　See COM (2003) 46(01) Proposal for a Directive on measures and procedures to ensure the enforcement of intellectual property rights.

24　European Commission Communication. 'Creating a Safer Information Society by Improving the Security of Information Infrastructures and Combating Computer Related Crime', 26 January 2001; COM(2000) 890.

25　See Council Framework Decision 2004/68/JHA on combating the sexual exploitation of children and child pornography.

26　See the Explanatory Memorandum of the Proposal for a Council Framework Decision on Combating Racism and Xenophobia, COM(2001) 664 final.

27　Directive 2002/58/EC of the European Parliament and of the Council of 12 July 2002 concerning the processing of personal data and the protection of privacy in the electronic communications sector (Directive on Privacy and Electronic Communications).

28　Draft Council Framework Decision on the Retention of Data Processed and Stored in Connection with the Provision of Publicly Available Electronic Communication Services (document 8958/04 CRIMORG 49, Telecom 82). Also available at: http://rregister.consilium.eu.int/pdf/en04/st08/st08958.en04.pdf

29  See the European Commission. Proposal for a Council Framework Decision on attacks against information systems. 19 April 2002; COM (2002) 173.
30  Among the most relevant federal criminal codes are: 18 USC S 2252 Certain activities relating to material involving the sexual exploitation of minors; 18 USC S 2252A Child Pornography Prevention Act.
31  The two main units are the Justice Department's, the Criminal Division's Computer Crime and Intellectual Property Section and the Computer Hacking and Intellectual Property. For statistics on the number of investigations, see the 'Report of the Department of Justice's Task Force on Intellectual Property', US Department of Justice, Office of the Attorney General, October 2004.

## REFERENCES

American Bar Association (1998) 'The Federalization of Criminal Law, Task Force on the Federalization of Criminal Law'. Available at http://www.abanet.org/crimjust/fedreport.html

Bendrath, R. (2001) 'Cyberwar debate: perception and politics in US critical infrastructure protection', *Information and Security* 7: 80–103.

Bermann, G. and Nicolaidis, K. (2001) 'Basic principles for the allocation of competence in the United States and the European Union', in K. Nicolaidis and R. Howse (eds), *The Federal Vision: Legitimacy and Levels of Governance in the United States and the European Union*, Oxford: Oxford University Press.

Börzel, T. and Hosli, M. (2003) 'Brussels between Berlin and Bern: comparative federalism meets the European Union', *Governance* 16(2): 179–202.

Brenner, S.W. (2004) 'US cybercrime law: defining offences', *Information Systems Frontiers* 6(2): 115–32.

Cappelletti, M., Seccombe, M. and Weiler, J. (1986) *Integration through Law: Europe and the American Federal Experience*, New York: W. de Gruyter.

Charlesworth, A. (2000) 'Clash of the data titans? US and EU data privacy regulation', *European Public Law* 6(2): 253–74.

Coglianese, C. and Nicolaidis, K. (2001) 'Securing subsidiarity: the institutional design of federalism in the United States and Europe', in K. Nicolaidis and R. Howse (eds), *The Federal Vision: Legitimacy and Levels of Governance in the United States and the European Union*, Oxford: Oxford University Press.

Donahue, J.D. and Pollack, M.A. (2001) 'Centralization and its discontents: the rhythms of federalism in the United States and the European Union', in K. Nicolaidis and R. Howse (eds), *The Federal Vision: Legitimacy and Levels of Governance in the United States and the European Union*, Oxford: Oxford University Press.

Dunn, M. and Wigert, I. (2004) *International CIIP Handbook: An Inventory and Analysis of Protection Policies in Fourteen Countries*, Swiss Federal Institute of Technology. Available at: http://www.isn.ethz.ch/crn/publications/publications_crn.cfm?pubid=224

Dye, T.R. (1990) *American Federalism: Competition among Governments*, Lexington, MA: Lexington Books.

Easton, D. (1957) 'An approach to the analysis of political systems', *World Politics* 9(3): 383–400.

Elazar, D.J. (1991) *Federal Systems of the World: A Handbook of Federations, Confederations and Autonomy Arrangement*, London: Longman.

Fabbrini, S. and Sicurelli, D. (2004) 'The federalization of the EU, the US and compound republic theory: the Convention's debate', *Regional and Federal Studies* 14(2): 232–54.

Filippov, M. Ordeshook, P.C. and Shvetsova, O. (2004) *Designing Federalism: A Theory of Self-Sustainable Federal Institutions*, Cambridge: Cambridge University Press.

Follesdal, A. (2003) 'Federalism', in *The Stanford Encyclopedia of Philosophy* (Winter 2003 edn), Edward N. Zalta (ed.), URL http://plato.stanford.edu/archives/win2003/entries/federalism/

Gilmore, B. (2003) 'Twin towers and the third pillar: some security agenda developments', *EUI Working Paper Law No. 2003/7*, European University Institute: Florence.

Goldsmith, J. (2000a) 'Unilateral regulation of the internet: a modest defence', *European Journal of International Law* 11(1): 135–48.

Goldsmith, J. (2000b) 'Yahoo! Brought to earth', *Financial Times*, 27 November.

Halberstam, D. (2001) 'Comparative federalism and the issue of commandeering', in K. Nicolaidis and R. Howse (eds), *The Federal Vision: Legitimacy and Levels of Governance in the United States and the European Union*, Oxford: Oxford University Press.

Hargreaves, D. (2001) 'EU and the space cowboys', *Financial Times*, 4 February.

Kalin, W. (2004) 'The judicial system', in U. Klotti, P. Knoepfel, H. Kriesi, W. Linder and Y. Papadopoulos (eds), *Handbook of Swiss Politics*, Zurich: Neue Zürcher Zeitung Publishing.

Kelemen, D. (2000) 'Regulatory federalism: EU environmental regulation in comparative perspective', *Journal of Public Policy* 20(3): 133–67.

Kelemen, D. (2003) 'The structure and dynamics of EU federalism', *Comparative Political Studies* 36(1/2): 184–208.

Kerr, O.S. (2003) 'Internet surveillance law after the USA Patriot Act: the big brother that isn't', *Northwestern University Law Review* 97: 607–74.

Kincaid, J. (1993) 'From cooperation to coercion in American federalism: housing, fragmentation and preemption 1780–1992', *Journal of Law Politics* 9: 333–430.

Lessig, L. (1999) *Code and Other Laws of Cyberspace*, New York: Basic Books.

Mayer, F. (2000) 'Europe and the internet: the old world and the new medium', *European Journal of International Law* 11(1): 149–69.

McKay, D. (1999) *Federalism and European Union: A Political Economy Perspective*, Oxford: Oxford University Press.

McKay, D. (2001) *Designing Europe: Comparative Lessons from the Federal Experience*, Oxford: Oxford University Press.

Monar, J. (2001) 'Justice and home affairs', *Journal of Common Market Studies* 39: 121–37.

Nicolaidis, K. and Howse, R. (eds) (2001) *The Federal Vision: Legitimacy and Levels of Governance in the United States and the European Union*, Oxford: Oxford University Press.

Papadopoulos, Y. (2005) 'Implementing (and radicalizing) art. I-47.4 of the Constitution: is the addition of some (semi-)direct democracy to the nascent consociational European federation just Swiss folklore?', *Journal of European Public Policy* 12(3): 448–467.

Riker, W.H. (1964) *Federalism: Origins, Operation, Significance*, Boston: Little, Brown.

Riker, W.H. (1993) 'Federalism', in R. Goodin and P. Petit (eds), *A Companion to Contemporary Political Philosophy*, Oxford: Blackwell.

Samuelson, P. (1999) 'Intellectual property rights and the digital economy: why the anti-circumvention regulations need to be revised', *Berkeley Technology and Law Journal* 14(519): 562.

Sbragia, A.M. (ed.) (1992) *Europolitics, Institutions and Policymaking in the New European Community*, Washington, DC: Brookings Institution.

Scharpf, F.W. (1988) 'The joint-decision trap: lessons from German federalism and European integration', *Public Administration* 66: 239–78.

Sieber, U. (1998) 'Legal Aspects of Computer-related Crime in the Information Society', COMCRIME Study prepared for the European Commission. See www.europa.eu.int/ISPO/legal/en/comcrime/sieber

Stuntz, W.J. (2001) 'Terrorism, federalism, and police misconduct', *Harvard Journal of Law and Public Policy* 25: 665–81.

Sutter, G. (2000) 'Nothing new under the sun: old fears and new media', *International Journal of Law and Information Technology* 8(3): 338–78.

Trechsel, S. and Killias, M. (2004a) 'Sources of criminal law', in F. Dessemontet and T. Ansay (eds), *Introduction to Swiss Law*, The Hague: Kluwer.

Trechsel, S. and Killies, M. (2004b) 'Laws of criminal procedure', in F. Dessemontet and T. Ansay (eds), *Introduction to Swiss Law*, The Hague: Kluwer.

Walker, N. (2003) 'The pattern of transnational policing', in T. Neburn (ed.), *A Handbook of Policing*, London: Willan Publishing.

# Economic logic or political logic? Economic theory, federal theory and EMU[1]

David McKay

Constitutions are chains with which men bind themselves in their sane moments that they may not die by a suicidal hand in the day of their frenzy.
(John Potter Stockton)[2]

## INTRODUCTION

Five years into the project, there is a growing consensus among economists that certain aspects of the ways in which European monetary union (EMU) operates are in need of reform. At the heart of their concerns is the gross asymmetry between a centralized monetary regime and highly decentralized fiscal regimes and the failure of the Stability and Growth Pact (SGP) to broker the conflicts that result from this asymmetry. Most economists are agreed that the need for reform is urgent and should involve new ways of establishing fiscal discipline among member states. Except in terms of providing a historical record of these events, non-economists have contributed relatively little to this debate (but see the volumes by Dyson 2002 and Verdun 2002 and the essay by Boyer 2000). Either explicitly or by implication, most argue that the *sui generis* nature of the European Union (EU), not to mention EMU and the SGP, renders systematic comparison with other political units inappropriate. Yet the parallels between economic governance in the EU and that in other states, and especially federal states, are striking. So much so, in fact, that applied economists assume *ipso facto* that such comparisons apply. The European Central Bank (ECB) is a central bank with a clear constitutional status. The SGP is a federal level institution designed to limit the fiscal discretion of member state governments. Both have adopted decision rules that bear clear comparison with parallel institutions in federal systems (and indeed in unitary states).[3] And as with these other states, the EU faces difficult trade-offs between what is politically expedient and possible and what is economically desirable.

The purpose of this paper is to place the findings and the implications of the economists' recommendations in the context of federal theory and in particular to establish a link between policy choices deemed to be *economically* sustainable and those that may be *politically* sustainable. To assist me in this (very difficult) task I will apply the nascent rational choice and comparative politics literature on the self-sustainability of federal systems to EMU. The paper will proceed in four parts. In Part 1 I will make the (increasingly uncontroversial) claim that EMU effectively established the federal credentials of the EU. In Part 2 I will summarize the findings and political implications of recent economics research on EMU. Part 3 places EMU in the context of federal theory and Part 4 draws conclusions for the sustainability of the EMU federal project.

## 1. WHY THE EU IS A SPECIES OF FEDERAL STATE

Few observers could – or indeed did – see the utility of categorizing the EU as a federation before the adoption of the Treaty on European Union in 1991. For although the EU displayed all the institutional architecture of a federation, it lacked the policy scope of even the most peripheralized historical example of a federal system. Since Maastricht, however, at first a small trickle and then a gathering flood of scholars have begun to borrow the language and methods of comparative federalism and apply them to the EU (see, for example, Bednar *et al.* 1996; Burgess 2000; McKay 2001a; Nicolaidis and Howse 2001). Maastricht was important both symbolically (the creation of European citizenship and the change in nomenclature from community to union) and substantively. Transferring monetary policy (and later some controls over fiscal policy) to the federal level fulfilled nicely what is broadly agreed to be one of the defining conditions of federalism, namely that it is a 'political organization in which the activities of government are divided between regional governments and a central government in such a way that each kind of government has some activities in which it makes final decisions'

(Riker 1975: 101; see also the discussion in McKay 1999a: ch. 2). Of course, this condition was fulfilled – or was scheduled to be fulfilled – before Maastricht in a number of areas – competition rules, customs union, common commercial policy, fishing policy. But the transfer of these responsibilities to the supranational level hardly qualified the EU as a federation. International organizations and treaties have long undermined sovereign control over most of these policy domains, and in any case the exit cost of reneging in any one of them was relatively low. Put another way, until Maastricht the EU was what Riker calls a 'peripheralized' federation because the powers of the central government were temporally or functionally limited in such a way that the costs of exit – in effect secession – were low (Riker 1975: part 1). In such situations, federations often fail (see Franck 1968) or struggle to maintain themselves and persist only because of the presence of an external threat (the early Swiss confederation or the USA under the Articles of Confederation).

Since the adoption of EMU, however, the economic and political exit costs have increased substantially. Indeed, as time passes it becomes increasingly difficult to claim that because EMU was essentially a technical regulatory matter it has few implications for the broader society and polity (see, for example, Moravcsik 2001: 165–85), If, as is increasingly the case, monetary discipline is linked to fiscal discipline then monetary union impinges on the whole range of distributional functions performed by modern governments. It would appear, then, that the EU is moving inexorably towards the sort of political agenda that typically dominates discourse in other federations – the balance of state power in relation to federal power in fiscal and economic matters.

None of this is to claim that the EU is in any sense a fully developed federation. Clearly it is not. But it shares with other federations enough institutional and policy features to justify the use of common analytical categories. As heuristic devices the language and methods of federalism become increasingly useful. By way of contrast, the concepts and approaches borrowed from international relations and its subdisciplines look less and less appropriate.

As with other federations, then, the most important question for the development of the EU is the balance of central power in relation to state power.[4] More specifically, how does the process of constant intergovernmental renegotiation facilitate the continuing loyalty of both states and federal authorities to the federal project? In effect these are the questions that underpin the economic and the political debate on the operation of EMU and the SGP. What, first, are the conclusions of the economists on this subject?

## 2. ECONOMIC LOGIC AND EMU: ECONOMIC THEORY

Economists have long been sensitive to the fact that EMU has important political repercussions. The first wave of work used the American states and regions as comparators for the EU and applied optimum currency area (OCA) theory to show how conjectural convergence in business cycles and the flexibility and mobility of labour markets might qualify or disqualify the

EU or regions within the EU as optimal currency areas (see, for example, Bayoumi and Masson 1995; Bayoumi and Eichengreen 1993; Krugman 1993; Sachs and Sala-I-Martin 1992; Von Hagen 1993). Although not always stated explicitly, these studies do conflate the economic with the political because in existing federations such as the United States, federal government fiscal policy plays a major equalization and stabilization role. In other words, in the absence of intra-regional freedom to devalue or alter interest rates, federal authorities are obliged to use a wide range of policy instruments ranging from social security and unemployment benefits to regional aid and federal procurement programmes, to compensate individuals and areas for the consequences of economic shocks (see Tondl 2000: 231–5 and sources cited). Many of these studies were criticized for failing to take account of the endogeneity problem (comparing a longstanding currency area with a prospective one) and for failing to note that many external shocks have inter-regional rather than inter-country effects (see the discussions in Masson and Taylor 1993).

Whatever, few now expect that the EU can, or indeed should, play a major redistributive role in bailing out distressed member states. Neither Structural nor common agricultural policy (CAP) funds were designed for this purpose and the political obstacles in the way of expanding 'central' spending to anything approaching the average of federal aid in what prevails in existing federations are legion (see the discussion in McKay 1999b).[5] Instead, most recent economic thinking has dwelt on the shorter-term functioning of EMU and in particular the ways in which the ECB and the SGP operate in the context of the very different economic and budget performances that have characterized the Euroland states. Since 2001, six countries have breached the SGP 3 per cent budget deficit rule with relative impunity, so challenging the integrity of existing arrangements. As a result a number of economists have proposed reform of the SGP with some proposing a loosening of the rules and others a tightening, or even replacing the SGP with a more effective set of institutions (for a review of some of these alternatives and an analysis of the flaws in the SGP, see Buiter 2003). What precisely is proposed depends on the value assumptions and scholars involved. Some believe that because, as at present constituted, the SGP works as a pro-cyclical rather than counter-cyclical influence it is an economic nonsense and should be either abandoned or fundamentally changed (see, for example, Buiter 1999; de Grauwe 2002; and the discussion in Allsop and Artis 2003). These same economists are also critical of the closed, restricted way in which the ECB operates. Others broadly accept the existing ECB constitution and its performance to date but decry the failure of the SGP to control the fiscal irresponsibility of those member state governments that have been unable to limit spending and/or raise taxes (Calmfors *et al.* 2003; McKinnon 1997). Their preferred solution is to control the fiscal discretion of the member states in ways that are broadly equivalent to the restrictions that apply in monetary policy. In particular, a growing movement exists in support of the creation of national Fiscal Policy Committees (FPCs) who, much like the boards of central banks, would decide the detail of policy within broad limits established by national governments. Crucially, all national FPCs would in turn operate according to EU-wide guidelines provided by the Commission and the Council (Calmfors *et al.* 2003; Wyplosz 2002). In other words a 'tight' fiscal regime brokered between national government and the EU would replace the 'loose' fiscal regime represented by the SGP. Crucially, these experts see these policy changes in terms of removing the politically motivated special pleading of member state governments. As Calmfors *et al.* put it: '[The main need is] to depoliticise the decision making process that establishes whether or not individual countries have violated the rules' (Calmfors *et al.* 2003: 60).

A less Utopian (Draconian?) reform, also premised on the assumption that at present the SGP operates imperfectly because it cannot resist the lobbying of national governments, would involve changing Council voting on SGP rules. At present qualified majority voting (QMV) applies both to Commission compliance recommendations and to the imposition of sanctions. But if the rules were changed so that Commission sanctions could only be overturned by a unanimous Council vote, they would acquire more bite. Hence any one member state could veto an attempt to reject the enforcement of SGP sanctions. Because it would force individual fiscal recidivists to toe the EU line, proponents of this view see it also as a 'depoliticization' of the implementation of SGP rules (Buti *et al.* 2003: 107–10). Of course, the Commission has itself proposed changes to the Pact 'to strengthen the co-ordination of monetary policy'. While these proposals imply extra flexibility, they also involve a greater monitoring role for the Commission and could therefore be used to increase rather than reduce the use of fiscal rules (EU Commission 2002).

Notwithstanding the important differences between these reforms – and indeed their respective economic merits – almost all of them involve the removal of important aspects of fiscal policy from the political sphere and its transfer to the domain of the technocrat. Beetsma's comment sums up the consensus view well: 'Excessive deficits or large debt build-ups in the future cannot be ruled out if the [member state] governments' hands are not in some way bound' (Beetsma 2001: 49). In this and other ways the economists make a number of assumptions (explicitly or by implication) that are of particular interest to political scientists in general and federal theorists in particular. Namely:

1 First, and perhaps obviously, they assume some sort of parallelism between monetary and fiscal policy. They point to the fact that at one time central bank independence was considered a politically impossible objective, whereas today it is almost universally accepted as desirable (Calmfors *et al.* 2003: 71–3). Why shouldn't fiscal policy follow in the same direction? After all, the intellectual driving force behind central bank autonomy (price stability) has a clear parallel in fiscal policy (long-term sustainable government debt). There are two problems with this reasoning. First, as Dyson has noted, 'the deeply embedded historical association between taxation and structures of representative government' (Dyson 2002: 349)

suggests that FPCs and the like would help to break the link between elected representatives and the voters. In other words, they would undermine the complex and sensitive arrangements forged out of generations of political struggle that determine the distribution of government largesse in individual member states. Second, claims that FPCs would merely maintain government balances within prescribed limits rather than determine the overall level of taxation and spending assume that the new system would operate in the context of a fiscal *tabula rasa*. But the longer-term (inter-generational) fiscal problems of most Euroland states are such that FPCs would function effectively only *after* these problems were solved (through hefty tax hikes, expenditure cuts or structural reforms of labour and other markets; see Ferguson and Kotlikoff 2000), or if they were to be used as a *means* to fiscal sustainability. True, advocates of FPCs propose that those member states below a consolidated debt level of (say) 55 per cent would have much more short-term budget flexibility than at present. But they would enjoy these only after reducing their debt to that level (Calmfors and Corsetti 2002). Either way, the introduction of FPCs would be fraught with possibly insurmountable political difficulties.

2  While sensitive to the political implications of their recommendations, most economists employ what might be called a simplistic pluralist view of the political world. Economic policies must be perceived as legitimate by *voters*; economic authorities are, through the democratic process, held accountable by *mass publics*. Hence Buiter notes that 'monetary union involves a transfer of national sovereignty to the central or federal level. Unless this transfer of power is perceived as legitimate by the residents of Euroland, the authority of the institutions of the ECB . . . will be questioned and challenged by those who perceive themselves to be adversely affected by it' (Buiter 1998: 6; see also Buiter 1999). And Calmfors notes that 'To ensure the legitimacy of delegation of fiscal policy, an FPC would, of course, have to be subject to democratic oversight and accountability' (Calmfors *et al.* 2003: 71). The broad assumption here is that a seamless web of accountability between voters (or possibly organized interests) and elected representatives exists. In reality, of course, the representative link between political élites and voters is always imperfect and is perhaps particularly so in complex federal and intergovernmental contexts. Indeed, it is élites rather than mass publics who usually drive change in political systems. In the EU, of course, this claim has assumed the status of a truism. We will return to this point later.

3  Related to this is the assumption that fiscal sustainability has to be achieved in the context of EU policy and EMU membership. In other words, a system of EU 'economic governance' should prevail. As such 'federal level' institutions including the Council of Ministers, Ecofin and the Commission should either be charged with driving through reforms, or themselves should be subject to reform. This is necessary to ensure fiscal sustainability. But what about political sustainability? For it could be argued that if reforms are put in place in ways that give member state leaders incentives to renege on their obligations

to the EU in general and EMU in particular, then they may be unsustainable. Of course, this is precisely the criticism that is levelled at current operating procedures of the SGP. But if the alternatives lock member state political actors into decision-making contexts that are even more restrictive, or are restrictive in temporally and/or conceptually different ways (for example, the creation of FPCs), it may be a case of out of the frying pan and into the fire. What some of the economic reforms imply, then, is a fundamental change in the relationship between the member states and the federal authority. As we will see, federal theory suggests that any reform of this magnitude should be conducted in an institutional and policy context that provides incentives both for the federal and the state players to play by the rules of the game. At present incentives are shaped by a constitutional imperative – the Maastricht Treaty and Council amendments to it – which in the form of the SGP provides incentives for many of the participants to renege on the federal bargain. By implication, therefore, any future constitutional change should remove rather than reinforce these perverse incentives.

## 3. POLITICAL LOGIC AND EMU: FEDERAL THEORY

Among the many approaches to the study of federalism the one that is of most concern here is the question of sustainability, or what it is that holds federations together. Unlike work on the classification of federal systems or on the origins of federalism, specifying the conditions under which federal states are likely to succeed or fail is beset with difficulties. This is especially true when, as in the case of the EU, there are no meaningful external threats to provide a *raison d'être* for a close association of the member states (on external threats, see the discussion in Riker 1964: part 1, and for a critique, see McKay 2001b).

However, some sensible inferences on the sustainability of the EU monetary system can be made by drawing on recent rational choice and comparative politics federalist studies.

In contrast to the pluralists who assume that mass opinion will drive the policy agenda, rational choice theorists argue that what matters is the incentives available to individual level élites in the context of particular institutional arrangements. The logic here is quite simple. It is élites, even in democracies, that enable societies to move from one equilibrium to another, and societies remain in equilibrium because there is no winning (élite) coalition able to challenge the existing order. The dominant coalition may be quite diverse in terms of party affiliation, economic interest and territorial identity, but crucially all members of the coalition will abide by the constitutional and other rules of the game because even if they are losers in the short term they know that in the longer term they will be net gainers. Gains and losses can be expressed in a number of ways – votes, economic efficiency, or even ideas (what Schofield (2000) calls 'core beliefs'), although in democracies the first priority of politicians will be re-election. None of this is to imply that the mass citizenry are mere bystanders in this process. In modern democracies, élites will continue to abide by the rules of the game if they know that, if removed from office by the voters, they have a chance of being returned at a later date. Their chances of doing so are, in turn, informed by the myopic self-interest of the voters on such issues as employment, quality of public services, taxation, and so on.

In federal systems, however, this dynamic takes on a different shape, for federalism must *ipso facto* involve both (federal) national interests making concessions to state interests and state interests to national interests. Politicians at both levels, therefore, have to persuade (or act in a way likely to persuade) voters that their immediate territorial interests must be compromised in favour of the federal interest. What a workable federal system requires, therefore, is a constitutional/institutional context that facilitates this dynamic. State level politicians have to persuade their voters to make sacrifices for the federal good. Federal level politicians have to persuade their constituents to make concessions to state interests. If either consistently fails in this project, a crisis of the regime could occur, which might result in constitutional change, secession or even civil war (see the discussion in Ordeshook and Shvetsova 1997).

In the EU all the major political parties and economic interests in each of the Euroland states form winning coalitions in support of euro membership. They do so either because they believe membership is economically beneficial and/or because they see monetary union as a major part of the core belief system underpinning the European 'idea'. It is important to stress that almost all of these coalitions are territorially based. Political and fiscal decentralization is so pronounced and the system of élite representation in EU monetary policy decision-making so territorially defined (via such institutions as the Council of Ministers) that this has to be the case. Two important inferences can be drawn from this conclusion:

1 While winning coalitions exist at present in each of the euro states, the exact nature and strength of each of these will vary from country to country. Supportive coalitions in Germany, for example, may be less well established – and potentially be more fragile – than in Italy (see Dyson 2002: chapters on Italy and Germany).
2 National (member state) support for the euro is essentially analogous to the support for federal political arrangements among the constituent states of established federations. It therefore follows that we can use federal theory as a heuristic device to aid our understanding of member states' support for the euro. It is important to stress that the application of federal theory specifically to the exercise of monetary policy is more relevant in the EU case than in other federations. In the latter, monetary policy is usually 'depoliticized' through a broad acceptance of central bank independence. Federal/state disputes more typically dwell on such issues as fiscal federalism (grants in aid, tax sharing, and so on), and linguistic, ethnic and religious divisions, none of which are (as yet) particularly relevant in the EU context. And as noted earlier, it is because monetary union impinges so

directly on highly decentralized fiscal regimes that this special status of EMU in the nascent EU federation justifies the use of the federal analogy.

If we view the accumulation of EU treaties and regulations, and especially the Maastricht Treaty as a 'monetary constitution' binding Euroland states together in a federal monetary regime, what are the theoretical conditions that will facilitate the self-sustainability of this regime?

The most interesting work in this area is by Bednar *et al.* (2001) and also by Filippov *et al.* (2004). Both attempt to generate general theories on the self-sustainability of federal systems of government (Bednar *et al.* 2001; Ordeshook and Shvetsova 1997; Filippov *et al.* 2004). Although space limitations do not permit a full elaboration here, the most salient points for our purposes are:

1 All parties to the federal bargain must subscribe to what Filippov *et al.* (2004) call Level 1 rules, or an acceptance of the provisions of the constitutional settlement. In our example this means Maastricht and its aftermath. They must also agree to abide by Level 2 rules or the rules of the game inherent in the constitutional settlement that govern the institutions that facilitate day-to-day bargaining and negotiation (Filippov *et al.* 2004: 71–7). In Euroland this would mean accepting the ways in which the ECB operates as well as the working of the SGP (see McKay 2004).

2 The constitution should provide for 'effective co-ordination devices [that] must give local and regional political élites an incentive to uphold federative constraints even when their constituents prefer otherwise' (Filippov *et al.* 2004: 163). The operation of the ECB actually allows for very little in the way of co-ordination between regional (member state) and federal officials. Even national central banks are largely excluded from ECB decision-making. State politicians do, of course, have better recourse to influence federative constraints through Ecofin and the SGP. However, the SGP rules are unambiguous and allow for little in the way of negotiated compromise. The alternative to full compliance is therefore either a loose interpretation by the Commission and Ecofin or simple defiance, in much the way that the German government flouted the rules in the autumn of 2002, soon to be followed by a number of other member states. Either way, the rules are brought into disrepute. This was amply demonstrated when, faced with a refusal by both France and Germany to abide by the Pact, the Council of Ministers decided to suspend the SGP in 2003. The Commission duly took the Council to Court and in July 2004 the Court of Justice found in the Commission's favour.

3 A further theoretical condition for self-sustaining federation is that the federal constitution 'must create (office related) rewards for national [federal] élites that dissuade them from overstepping their constitutionally prescribed authority and to acquiesce in the legitimate authority of the regional governments' (Filippov *et al.* 2004: 163–4). Bednar *et al.* (2001) make the same point when they argue that in a successful federation 'national [federal] forces must be structurally constrained from infringing on the federal bargain'

(Bednar *et al.* 2001: 226). Even in the absence of a fully codified EU constitution, the 'constitutionally prescribed' authority of the EU is constrained by the 'hard' decision rules of the Council of Ministers in a wide range of areas from enlargement to foreign policy to taxing and spending. With EMU, however, few such constraints exist. The rules under which the ECB operates are constitutionally enshrined in the Maastricht Treaty. SGP rules are also legally enforceable, can be appealed to the Court of Justice[6] and can only be changed by a unanimous vote in the Council. It is true that QMV Council voting on Commission recommendations and sanctions leaves some room for bargaining and coalition-building, but the cold clarity of the rules is such that any rejection of them would be seen as a political fudge. In other words, 'federal level' politicians in the Council and Commission have little incentive to compromise and acquiesce in the authority of regional governments. To do so would be to break the rules and make them look foolish. Which is, of course, precisely what inspired Romano Prodi to label the pact 'stupid' (*Financial Times* 2002).

4 The insulated, autonomous nature of EMU decision-making may be rendered irrelevant by the requirement that 'regional and national élites maintain some (possibly evolving) consensus over the constitutionally prescribed and legitimate authority' (Filippov *et al.* 2004: 164). In other words, EMU relies to an inordinate extent on élite consensus. Given the absence of mechanisms available to mediate central/state disputes under EMU, the whole system relies on the affected parties – notably member state politicians and officials – accepting the legitimacy of the ECB, the SGP and its decisions. The failure to make EMU decision-making transparent (even post-hoc) and the rigidity of the SGP rules put further premium on élite consensus. In effect, a precondition for the sustainability of the present system is a high degree of *trust* in the judgements made by EMU decision-makers.

What we have in the operation of EMU, therefore, is a federal authority whose extensive policy scope has powerful effects on the domestic economies and polities of the member states. The constitutional design that informs the day-to-day operations of the ECB was based on a highly centralized decision-making system involving almost no mechanisms for the brokering of member state/federal government differences. As such, EMU violates the constitutional ground rules that federal theory tells us are necessary for a self-sustaining federation. The system will work only if (a) the scope of EMU powers is limited, which is patently not the case; or if (b) an inordinately high degree of élite consensus on its operations exists.

There are two other important sets of conditions that a self-sustaining federation needs to meet. The first of these concerns the *modes of representation* constitutionally mandated for a federal system that can help to facilitate or hinder sustainability. Very broadly 'appropriate' modes of representation optimize the institutional environment in which political actors will have an incentive to abide by the rules of the game. These include a preference for 'within' rather than 'without' representation and for delegated rather than direct representation. 'Within' representation simply means such institutions as chambers of the states (upper houses), which are directly incorporated into federal level decision-making and thus provide a formal setting for the brokering of state interests. 'Without' representation, such as first ministers' conferences, although more flexible, is more likely to provide state interests with the opportunity to challenge not just individual policies but the basic ground rules on the legitimate scope of federal and state power. Similarly, delegated representation, as (to a limited extent) in the German Bundesrat, requires elected officials to stay loyal to state interests, while direct representation, as in the German Bundestag, encourages officials to articulate national or federal level interests (see the discussion in Filippov *et al.* 2004: ch. 4). While there is insufficient space to elaborate on these points here, it is obvious that the Council of Ministers is the apotheosis of within representation, at least when operating in its QMV mode, and that its members act as delegates of national governments.

It is also clear that these categories cannot easily be applied to either the Commission or the ECB which have legislative/policy powers but because they are unelected lack representative status. In monetary policy, therefore, the Council would appear to meet the conditions for federal/state bargaining, while the ECB and the Commission (in its SGP role) do not.

The second important condition for a sustainable federation is 'a properly configured party system' or one that is territorially (or ethnically/linguistically/religiously) inclusive rather than exclusive (Filippov *et al.* 2004: 179 and ch. 6). Exclusive parties will champion the interests of individual territories in an uncompromising fashion and are more likely to *reinforce* territorial (or ethnic) differences as they have done in Belgium and Canada. Institutional devices such as within and delegated representation generally encourage the growth of inclusive parties, as do familiar consociational institutions such as the separation of powers, supermajoritarian voting and proportional representation. The Swiss party system broadly conforms to this model.[7] Classifying the European party 'system' in this context is problematical, because within the EU national parties rather than Europe-wide parties dominate. A further feature of the European system is that national parties are remarkably *unmobilized* on the European issue in general and EMU in particular. Indeed, one of the most remarkable features of the failure of many of the leading Euroland economies to meet the SGP rules is that élite consensus on EMU among almost all the main political parties and their leaders has prevented direct links being made between fiscal retrenchment and EMU *per se*. Hence, in the 2002 German state elections political leaders appeared eager to please voter demands to limit the tax hikes and spending cuts required to restructure the German economy, but made no direct connection between the pressures for structural reform and EMU. Instead, they, along with the Portuguese and the French, have called for the relaxation of SGP rules. Strictly enforced SGP rules, never mind even tougher measures such as the strengthening of the Commission's fiscal hand or the institution of FPCs, might force on to the political agenda a clear link between monetary union and unpalatable policies. It would give political entrepreneurs in one or more Euroland states an incentive to 'go local' by adapting party programmes to an anti-EMU stance.[8] Even worse, political entrepreneurs may have an incentive to form new, and possibly extremist, populist anti-EU parties with secessionist and nativist agendas (on the role of political entrepreneurs in moving the policy agenda to a more extreme populist position, see Rabushka and Shepsle 1972).

Put another way, although EMU was the product of a remarkable élite consensus, its constitutional architecture fails to provide political élites with sufficient incentive to abide by the rules of the game in the longer term. There is little in ECB and SGP operating procedures that allows for the sort of compromise and coalition-building necessary to fuse federal and state officials into mutually reinforcing positions. At the heart of this problem is the fact that consensus on monetary policy is not paralleled by consensus on fiscal policy. The original federal bargain at Maastricht established the 'legitimate authority' of the federal government in monetary affairs, but failed to address the inevitable spillovers from EMU to fiscal policy. Of course, a changing balance of federal and state power is the very stuff of federal systems. But in most federal systems the states work hard to protect those activities that are rooted in unique state histories and cultures. Hence, in Switzerland and India, federal governments do not (and indeed dare not) impose common religious standards on the states. Language uniformity is taboo in some instances (Belgium, Canada). In other instances again, the states protect fiscal autonomy (Switzerland, the USA), although admittedly in the context of fiscally powerful federal governments. In most of these cases, state prerogatives are constitutionally protected. We also know that, as with the EU, the more peripheralized the federation, the greater the number of these protected areas will be. The problems arise when constitutional/institutional arrangements fail to give the states sufficient protection from incursions by the federal government into areas not legitimately their own (see the discussion in McKay 2001a: ch. 8). In the EU, fiscal policy is widely perceived both by existing and by prospective members as a 'state' prerogative, but one in which the federal authorities have expressed an understandable interest. Unfortunately, existing institutional arrangements have facilitated a shift in this interest beyond that which is considered legitimate.

## 4. CONCLUSIONS: FEDERALISM, EMU AND CONSTITUTIONAL CHANGE

Sometimes, politicians and experts invoke technocratic rationales for the extension of federal power, which are later shown to be misguided either in technical or political terms. In the US pleas for the creation of a national bank were present at the inception of the republic, but the subsequent Bank of the United States proved politically unacceptable to the states and its charter lapsed in 1832. It was not until 1913 that a national banking system was created. In India it was once argued that an economically dominant federal government was necessary for the country's survival. Yet over the last fifteen years the federal government has systematically ceded power to the private sector and to the states. Swiss federalism has long been derided as responsible for a 'tax jungle' yet the economy seems to operate adequately nonetheless (see the discussion in Bird 1986: 242–3). Notwithstanding the discussion in Part 1 (above) some economists argue that EU controls over member state fiscal policies are technically unnecessary. Hence Paul de Grauwe notes that the only real danger to EMU that might result from member state fiscal autonomy is the possibility of a member government default on debts. Given that the national finances in all the leading Euroland states are, by global standards, essentially sound, this is extremely unlikely (de Grauwe 2002, 2003).

But even if the consensus opinion is objectively correct, i.e. that the success of EMU requires some central direction to control both annual deficits and consolidated gross debt, it does not mean to say that the trade-off between the imposition of controls and the political costs of doing so falls the right way. As has been argued, the potential political costs of the SGP almost certainly outweigh any possible gains. And it is almost certain that the imposition of tougher rules, whether policed by the Commission or by FPCs, would increase rather than reduce these political costs. In the worst possible scenario, these might be sufficient to produce calls for secession from EMU.

This discussion obviously begs the question of what reform is needed – if any – of the current system of economic governance in the EU. Providing a blueprint for economic policy is hardly the subject of this paper, but two important points need to be made. There is, first, a strong case for leaving what in many cases is urgently needed fiscal and economic restructuring to the member states themselves. As many commentators have noted, most Euroland countries have already made significant progress in the direction of increased fiscal discipline and less use of discretion (see, for example, Fatas and Mihov 2003). Some will do better than others but, Ireland apart, all will have eventually to face the hard reality of how to solve the problem of intergenerational debt (Ferguson and Kotlikoff 2000: table1). How this is done will depend on the unique institutional, political and cultural contexts that prevail in individual countries.[9] In this endeavour we are not dealing with undeveloped polities but with sophisticated, mature and extraordinarily stable democracies. As de Grauwe puts it:

> Seen from [the] political perspective the Stability Pact is a vote of no confidence by the European authorities in the strength of the democratic institutions in the member countries. It is quite surprising that EU countries have allowed this to happen, and that they have agreed to be subjected to control by the European institutions that even the International Monetary Fund does not impose on banana republics.
>
> (de Grauwe 2002: 2)

Second, constitutional (treaty) change is required to change the status of the SGP and also to make the operations of the ECB more transparent. The fiscal independence of member states should be enshrined in a new constitutional settlement with the EU role confined to intelligence and advice. Of course, establishing the primacy of national governments in fiscal matters carries with it some economic risk including free riding and the continuation of an untidy and fragmented pattern of fiscal and budgetary policy across the member states. No doubt this is less than economically optimal. But the most commonly proposed alternative – centralizing policy through the imposition of harder EMU fiscal rules – carries with it the grave political risk of stirring populist sentiment that might manifest itself in the form of nativist and extremist political movements.

Changing the constitutional status of fiscal policy in this way should have a constraining or binding effect on the status of fiscal policy in the EU, especially if, as at present, any subsequent amendment to the constitution (or treaties) can only be achieved by a hard decision rule (unanimity or possibly a double QMV rule by the Council and by member state parliaments and/or voters) (on the constraining effect of constitutions, see Elster 2000). Once enshrined in law, the temptation for technocrats to propose incursions by the federal authorities into the legitimate domain of the member states will be greatly reduced. In sum, it is not just the policy scope of the federal government that needs more careful elaboration, it is also the nature of the federal decision-making institutions and the ways in which states are represented at the federal level. Unfortunately, there are few signs that a clear codification of the law is imminent. The EU draft constitution is largely silent on the subject and when, in July 2004, the Court of Justice overruled the Council of Ministers' decision to suspend enforcement of SGP rules, it was clearly a victory for the Commission and its role as arbiter of EU rules. However, the Court gave no guidance as to how the rules should be changed, although by September 2004 the Commission agreed that a more relaxed enforcement regime was required. But there was no consensus on what this might be, thus leaving the way open to a long period of lobbying by member states and continuing uncertainty over the legal and political status of the SGP.

**Address for correspondence:** David McKay, Department of Government, University of Essex, Wivenhoe Park, Colchester, Essex CO4 3SQ, UK. Tel: (+44) 1206 872741. Fax: (+44) 1206 873234. email: mckad@essex.ac.uk

## NOTES

1 This is a greatly revised version of a paper given to the Swedish Political Science Network for European Research Conference, 'EMU: Who Will Make the Decisions?', University of Gothenburg, 6 March 2003. I am grateful to the discussants on my paper for comments provided.
2 In debate on the 1871 Ku Klux Klan Act, cited in Finn 1991: 5.
3 The central bank comparison is obvious. Exact parallels with the SGP are more difficult to find. The Australian Loan Council has played a similar role in containing spending in the Australian states and a number of Third World states have formal

mechanisms to control state/provincial spending (see Ter-Minassian 1997). Of course, national controls on local spending are commonplace in unitary states, as the example of the British Treasury exemplifies.

4 State and member state will be used interchangeably to describe national governments in the EU.

5 This is not to say that in the longer term pressures for a system of fiscal federalism will not emerge, as they have in all other mature federations. However, a precondition will almost certainly be a more developed sense of European identity.

6 It derives from the Excessive Deficit Procedure (Article 104) of the Maastricht Treaty as amended by Council regulations and resolutions. For a discussion, see Costello 2001.

7 On Switzerland, see the discussion in Lane 2001. The US is also usually classified as having an inclusive party system that results in the main from federalism and the separation of powers. It is, however, clear that institutional tinkering never guarantees that an 'appropriate' party system develops. Sometimes, inclusive parties emerge in the 'wrong' institutional environment (India) while exclusive parties do so in spite of institutional innovation (Northern Ireland). Put simply, history and culture sometimes trump intuitional design.

8 On the relative absence of anti-EU parties, see Mair 2000.

9 Interestingly, many American states find themselves in dramatically worse fiscal shape than any of the Euroland countries. New York's deficit for the fiscal year 2004 is predicted to be 24 per cent of state spending and California's 20.6 per cent. The fiscal year 2005 looks even worse with a projected deficit for all the states of $80 billion. All states bar Vermont have (self-imposed) bans on state deficits so these have to be corrected. Much pain will be endured by the citizens of these states in this process and the federal government will play virtually no role in assisting them. Of course, the American situation is different from that in the EU mainly because federal spending dwarfs state spending. Figures from the *Economist* (2003).

## REFERENCES

Allsop, C. and Artis, M.J. (2003) 'The assessment: EMU four years on', *Oxford Review of Economic Policy* 19(1): 1–29.

Bayoumi, T. and Eichengreen, B. (1993) 'Shocking aspects of European monetary integration', in F. Torres and F. Giavazzi (eds), *Adjustment and Growth in the European Monetary Union*, Cambridge: Cambridge University Press.

Bayoumi, T. and Masson, P.R. (1995) 'Fiscal flows in the United States and Canada: lessons for monetary union in Europe', *European Economic Review* 39: 253–74.

Bednar, J., Eskridge, W.N. and Ferejohn, J. (2001) 'A political theory of federalism', in J. Ferejohn, J.N. Rakove and R. Riley (eds), *Constitutional Culture and Democratic Rule*, Cambridge and New York: Cambridge University Press.

Bednar, J., Ferejohn, J. and Garrett, G. (1996) 'The politics of European federalism', *International Review of Law and Economics* 16: 279–94.

Beetsma, R. (2001) 'Does EMU need a Stability Pact?', in A. Brunila, M. Buti and D. Franco (eds), *The Stability and Growth Pact: The Architecture of Fiscal Policy in EMU*, London: Palgrave, pp. 32–52.

Bird, R.M. (1986) *Federal Finances in Comparative Perspective*, Toronto: Canadian Tax Foundation.

Boyer, R. (2000) 'The unanticipated fallout of European monetary union: the political and institutional deficits of the euro', in C. Crouch (ed.), *After the Euro: Shaping Institutions for Governance in the Wake of European Monetary Union*, Oxford: Oxford University Press.

Buiter, W.H. (1998) 'Alice in Euroland'. Speech before the South Bank University, 1–6 November.

Buiter, W.H. (1999) 'Alice in Euroland', *Journal of Common Market Studies* 37: 181–209.

Buiter, W.H. (2003) 'Ten commandments for a fiscal rule in the EMU', *Oxford Review of Economic Policy* 19(1): 84–99.

Burgess, M. (2000) *Federalism and European Union*, London: Routledge.

*Business Week* (2003) 'Germany's budget gap sets a bad example', 25 November, p. 2.

Buti, M., Eijffinger, S. and Franco, D. (2003) 'Revisiting EMU's Stability Pact: a pragmatic way forward', *Oxford Review of Economic Policy* 19(1): 100–11.

Calmfors, L. and Corsetti, G. (2002) 'A better plan for loosening the Pact', *Financial Times*, 25 November.

Calmfors, L. *et al.* (2003) 'Fiscal policy', *European Economy 2003*, European Advisory Group at CES, Institute for Economic Research, Munich.

Costello, D. (2001) 'The SGP: how did we get there?', in A. Brunila, M. Buti and D. Franco (eds), *The Stability and Growth Pact: The Architecture of Fiscal Policy in EMU*, London: Palgrave, pp. 106–38.

de Grauwe, P. (2002) 'Europe's instability pact', *Financial Times*, 25 July.

de Grauwe, P. (2003) 'The Stability and Growth Pact in need of reform', CEPS Discussion Paper, London.

Dyson, K. (ed.) (2002) *European States and the Euro: Europeanization, Variation and Convergence*, Oxford: Oxford University Press.

*Economist* (2003) 'The head ignores the feet', 24 May, pp. 45–6.

Eichengreen, B. and Wyplosz, C. (1998) 'The Stability Pact: more than a minor nuisance?', in D. Egg, J. Von Hagen, C. Wyplosz and K.F. Zimmerman (eds), *EMU: Prospects and Challenges for the Euro*, Oxford: Blackwell.

Elster, J. (2000) *Ulysses Unbound*, Cambridge and New York: Cambridge University Press.

EU Commission (2002) *Strengthening the Coordination of Budgetary Policies*, Communication from the Commission to the Council and the Parliament, COM (2002) 668 Final, Brussels.

EU (2003) Draft Constitution at www.fedtrust.co.uk/const_draftconstitutions

Fatas, A. (1998) 'Does EMU need a fiscal federalism?', in D. Begg *et al.* (eds), *EMU: Prospects and Challenges for the Euro*, London: Blackwell, CEPR.

Fatas, A. and Mihov, I. (2003) 'On constraining fiscal policy discretion in EMU', *Oxford Review of Economic Policy* 19(1): 112–28.

Ferguson, N. and Kotlikoff, L.J. (2000) 'The degeneration of EMU', *Foreign Affairs* 79(2): 110–21.

Filippov, M., Ordeshook, P.C. and Shvetsova, O. (2004) *Designing Federalism: A Theory of Self-Sustainable Federal Institutions*, Cambridge and New York: Cambridge University Press.

*Financial Times* (2002) 'Commission chief hints that Pact is on last legs', 17 October.

Finn, J.E. (1991) *Constitutions in Crisis*, Oxford and New York: Oxford University Press.

Franck, T.M. (1968) *Why Federations Fail*, New York: New York University Press.

Krugman, P. (1993) 'Lessons from Massachusetts for EMU', in P.R. Masson and P. Taylor (eds) (1993) *Policy Issues in the Operation of Currency Unions*, Cambridge and New York: Cambridge University Press.

Lane, J.E. (ed.) (2001) *The Swiss Labyrinth: Institutions, Outcomes and Redesign*, London: Frank Cass.

Mair, P. (2000) 'The limited impact of Europe on national party systems', *West European Politics* 23(4): 23–51.

Masson, P.R. and Taylor, P. (1993) *Policy Issues in the Operation of Currency Unions*, Cambridge and New York: Cambridge University Press.

McKay, D. (1999a) 'The political sustainability of European monetary union', *British Journal of Political Science* 29: 519–41.

McKay, D. (1999b) *Federalism and European Union: A Political Economy Perspective*, Oxford and New York: Oxford University Press.

McKay, D. (2001a) *Designing Europe: Comparative Lessons from the Federal Experience*, Oxford: Oxford University Press.

McKay, D. (2001b) 'William Riker on federalism: sometimes wrong but more right than anyone else'. Paper before the Riker Conference, Center for Political Economy, University of Washington, St Louis, December.

McKay, D. (2004) 'The EU as a self-sustaining federation: specifying the constitutional conditions', in L. Dobson and A. Follesdal (eds), *Political Theory and the European Constitution*, London: Routledge, pp. 23–39.

McKinnon, R.I. (1997) 'EMU as a device for collective fiscal responsibility', *American Economic Review* 87: 227–9.

Moravcsik, A. (2001) 'Federalism in the European Union: myth and reality', in K. Nicolaidis and R. Howse (eds), *The Federal Vision: Legitimacy and Levels of Governance in the European Union*, Oxford and New York: Oxford University Press, pp. 161–90.

Nicolaidis, K. and Howse, R. (eds) (2001) *The Federal Vision: Legitimacy and Levels of Governance in the European Union*, Oxford and New York: Oxford University Press.

Ordeshook, P.C. and Shvetsova, O. (1997) 'Federalism and constitutional design', *Journal of Democracy* 8: 27–42.

Rabushka, A. and Shepsle, K.A. (1972) *Politics in Plural Societies: A Theory of Democratic Instability*, Columbus, Ohio: Bobbs-Merrill.

Riker, W. (1964) *Federalism: Origins, Operation, Significance*, Boston: Little, Brown.

Riker, W. (1975) 'Federalism', in F.I. Greenstein and N. Polsby (eds), *The Handbook of Political Science. Volume V: Government Institutions and Processes*, Reading, MA: Addison-Wesley.

Sachs, J.D. and Sala-I-Martin, X. (1992) 'Fiscal federalism and optimum currency areas: evidence for Europe from the United States', in M.B. Canzoneri.

Schofield, N. (2000) 'Constitutional political economy: on the possibility of combining rational choice theory and comparative politics', *Annual Review of Political Science* 3: 277–303.

Ter-Minassian, M.T. (ed.) (1997) 'Intergovernmental fiscal relations in a macro economic perspective', in M.T. Ter-Minassian, *Fiscal Federalism in Theory and Practice*, Washington, DC: International Monetary Fund, pp. 3–24.

Tondl, G. (2000) 'Fiscal federalism and the reality of the EU budget', in C. Crouch (ed.), *After the Euro*, Oxford: Oxford University Press.

Verdun, A. (ed.) (2002) *The Euro: European Integration Theory and Economic and Monetary Union*, Boulder and Oxford: Rowman & Littlefield.

Von Hagen J. (1993) 'Monetary union and fiscal union: a perspective from fiscal federalism', in P.R. Masson and M.P. Taylor (eds), *Policy Issues in the Operation of Currency Unions*, Cambridge and New York: Cambridge University Press, pp. 264–96.

Wyplosz, C. (2002) 'A better way to balanced budgets', *Financial Times*, 3 December.

# Bypasses to a social Europe?
# Lessons from federal experience

Herbert Obinger, Stephan Leibfried
and Francis G. Castles

> The twentieth century will herald the age of federations, or humanity will
> resume its thousand years of purgatory.
> Le vingtième siècle ouvira l'ère de fédérations ou l'humanité recommençera
> un purgatoire de mille ans.
>
> Pierre-Joseph Proudhon (1863: 108)

## INTRODUCTION

Arguably, the welfare state is the most important source of output legitimation
in the modern state and a powerful device for promoting social integration in
divided societies (Leibfried and Zürn 2005: 9f.). The welfare state is not only
recognized as an instrument for mediating class conflict but also as a mechanism
of nation- and state-building capable of containing centrifugal forces in ethni-
cally and politically divided nations (Banting 1995, 2004).

All these functions are of immediate relevance to the situation of the European Union (EU). Given the EU's frequently lamented lack of input legitimation and its multi-cultural and multi-ethnic make-up, the emergence of a European welfare state might not only help in overcoming the numerous societal and economic cleavages in Europe, but also strengthen European identity and the legitimacy of EU authorities. Moreover, the deepening of EU economic integration in recent decades has increased the pressure for a strengthening of the social dimension of Europe in order to level out the asymmetry of economic and political integration (Scharpf 2002).

This paper evaluates the prospects for the emergence of a European welfare state based on the past experience of welfare state consolidation in six affluent Organization for Economic Co-operation and Development (OECD) federations: Australia, Austria, Canada, Germany, Switzerland and the United States of America (Obinger *et al.* 2005). Applying these findings to the European multi-level system, we argue that Europe is caught in a *development trap*, arising from a joint-decision trap and deep political and economic cleavages. We analyse the mechanisms that make it difficult for Europe to overcome its built-in institutional rigidities and launch major social transfer programmes at the European tier with a view to enhancing output legitimation and deepening social cohesion. Moreover, we suggest that the experiences of European and New World federations provide powerful insights for understanding prevailing modes of European social policy development, including 'bypass strategies' such as the open method of co-ordination (OMC), and regulatory strategies of policy development.

First, we provide a brief survey of theoretical accounts of the ways in which multi-level systems impact on the dynamics of welfare state development and patterns of welfare provision. We then report core findings of a recently completed collaborative project in which we examined the impact of federalism on welfare state development in the six classic federations in the OECD world (Obinger *et al.* 2005). Finally, we use these findings to analyse the patterns of and the prospects for social policy development at the European level.

## 1. WELFARE STATE DEVELOPMENT IN MULTI-LEVEL SYSTEMS: THEORETICAL APPROACHES

Typically, the EU is described as a multi-level or quasi-federal system that allocates policy jurisdiction across several tiers of government, involving actors from the different levels in the decision-making process at the central tier. We may describe such a system as

- a set of institutional arrangements and decision rules at the central level for incorporating territorially based interests; these arrangements vary in the degree to which they provide veto powers to subordinate branches of government;

- a set of territorially based actors with ideas and interests that vary greatly in number and heterogeneity;
- a set of jurisdictional arrangements for allocating policy responsibilities between different levels of government; this refers to policy-making and implementation;
- a set of intergovernmental fiscal transfer arrangements; and
- a set of informal arrangements – both vertical and horizontal – between governments.

What are the repercussions of such an institutional arrangement for welfare state development? More specifically, what are the chances for deepening the positive integration of social affairs in Europe under circumstances of quasi-federal decision-making? Previous systematic comparative research and most theoretical accounts of the field suggest that the prospects for such an endeavour are not favourable. Econometric research depicts federalism and decentralization as stumbling blocks for the emergence of big government and, especially, a generous welfare state (cf. Cameron 1978; Hicks and Swank 1992; Schmidt 1997; Castles 1999; Huber and Stephens 2001; Swank 2002; Cusack and Fuchs 2003; Ravishankar 2004).

The two main explanatory paradigms focusing on public policy outcomes in territorially fragmented polities are theories of fiscal federalism and various strands of political institutionalism. The first group of theories derives from economic reasoning and argues that federalism is a significant institutional constraint on government growth. The size of government declines as taxes and expenditures are decentralized (Hayek 1976; Brennan and Buchanan 1980). The absence of interstate tariffs, the presence of the free movement of persons and capital between political units, and fiscal competition between constituent units are seen as having significant consequences for social policy development. In particular, competition between the constituent units makes it difficult for sub-state units to introduce benefits that will transform them into 'welfare magnets' or to increase taxes that will lead to the flight of capital and tax-payers.

Political institutionalism also provides powerful arguments that vertical power separation is inimical to comprehensive social policies. A *first* argument emphasizes indirect and long-term effects of federalism on the political economy and its actors. Federalism indirectly influences welfare states by affecting a broad array of other socio-economic and political variables that, in turn, affect trajectories of welfare state development. Federalism is founded on and generates diversity, encouraging the emergence of territorially diverse political economies, each with its own set of deeply rooted political interests and values. Swank (2002), for example, notes that dispersion of policy-making authority diminishes the size of political interests, undermines their unity and the coherence of their strategies, and reduces the availability of conventional political resources. Federalism thus modifies the political capacities and power resources of key actors such as parties, unions and business organizations, undercuts the formation of national policy strategies and makes the formation of powerful welfare state alliances more difficult.

A *second* line of institutional reasoning maintains that the institutional safeguards of the federal settlement, including bicameralism, referendum procedures and constitutional courts, involve an inherent and highly pronounced vertical separation of powers (Lijphart 1999: 186). However, such separation of powers necessarily creates a proliferation of veto players and, hence, is a barrier to policy change (Tsebelis 2002).

A *third* kind of argument stems from the fact that federal systems are necessarily, to some extent, joint-decision systems, i.e. 'constellations in which parties are either physically or legally unable to reach their purposes through unilateral action and in which joint action depends on the (nearly) unanimous agreement of all parties involved' (Scharpf 1997: 143). Thus, from a procedural perspective, altering the status quo in territorially fragmented political systems requires the co-ordination of fragmented resources of action. Since federal systems inflate the number of actors involved in the policy-making process (Pierson 1995: 455), and because sub-governments frequently pursue their own strategies in a given policy field, any major policy change requires the co-ordination of multilayered interests and the approval of a host of actors who have to bargain until they agree on a joint course of action and – especially important for social policy – on the requisite cost-sharing. A joint course of action is particularly difficult to realize if the number of constituent units is high and if deep ethnic, political and socio-economic cleavages exist. If decisions in intertwined systems of decision-making require the consent of sub-governments by means of super-majority or even unanimity requirements, it is likely that a joint-decision trap will occur, resulting in policy stalemate, sub-optimal policy outcomes and lowest-common-denominator policies (Scharpf 1988).

Finally, a *fourth* institutional line of reasoning focuses on the ways in which path dependency and policy pre-emption limit the scope for subsequent policy change (Pierson 2004). Taking theories of path dependence seriously requires us to turn back to history and examine forms and patterns of early policy pre-emption. It is not only important to identify when such initiatives occurred, but also which tier of government took them first. Hence, the initial jurisdictional arrangements of federal states in social and fiscal policy may be seen as having structured and channelled the trajectories of their subsequent welfare state development. It is, for instance, very likely that policy pre-emption by lower tiers of government may hamper the centralization of social policy in subsequent years.

Although the main thrust of the theoretical speculation in this area has strongly reinforced the view that federalism is inimical to welfare state development, an institutional approach does not predetermine such an outcome. Given certain institutional configurations and actor constellations, federalism also may function as a welfare state catalyst or be policy-neutral. With respect to fiscal competition, for example, much depends on the design of the tax system, the taxing powers conferred on sub-governments and the system of fiscal equalization between different tiers of government (Oates 1999). If sub-state governments' budgets are funded by revenue-sharing or by intergovernmental grants, they have a strong incentive to 'overfish' common pool resources, since horizontal tax competition is undermined and sub-governments can exploit resources collected at other tiers of government (Rodden 2003). Under these circumstances, decentralization may even stimulate the size of the public sector. Another source for such an effect might be policy experiments undertaken by lower tiers of governments associated with spill-over effects to the federal tier or to tiers at the same level ('races toward the top or the middle ground') and with competitive innovation by different tiers of government. Finally, federalism is much less likely to have a braking effect in settings where the central state has pre-empted the policy field from an early date.

Hence, from a theoretical vantage point, the potential effects of federalism on welfare state development are indeterminate. There is, moreover, strong evidence that such effects vary across space and time. Different federal setups operate in different ways and they operate differently at different stages of welfare state development. Like other institutional effects, they are contingent on institutional configurations, actor constellations, actor orientations and on a broad range of contextual parameters. In particular, they may depend on specific

- jurisdictional splits and fiscal transfer arrangements,
- veto points, i.e. the secondary institutions of federalism,
- characteristics of the welfare clientele, e.g. whether beneficiaries are viewed as deserving and whether they are well organized and geographically concentrated,
- policy feedbacks, including effects on clientele organization and power resources,
- the government's budgetary situation, and
- partisan configurations, the nature of the party system, the power of the interest organizations of labour and capital and the institutionalized interaction between them.

Given this contingency of outcomes, the impact of federalism on social policy has to be analysed empirically. As already mentioned, the econometric evidence is compelling and strongly backs the hypothesis that vertical fragmentation of powers reins in big government. However, macro-quantitative cross-unit studies report average effects, but do not tell us much about the causal mechanisms by which such effects are generated in specific cases (Gerring 2004). Moreover, the role of sequencing, complex interactions between independent variables, critical junctures and contextual parameters cannot be identified by such an approach. However, this is precisely where case studies and small-N comparisons have a real value in revealing the complexity of particular chains of causation and what they do and do not have in common. This then was the impetus and rationale for a major collaborative research endeavour designed to produce a qualitative and historically nuanced account of welfare state development in six European and New World federations. Relying on case studies, written by leading scholars from each of these nations, our intention was to locate the mechanisms by which vertical power separation has influenced the dynamics of social programme development over a period of more than 120 years and to identify how, in turn, the development of the welfare state has impacted back on the institutions of federal government in these nations. We will now summarize core findings of this comparative analysis (Obinger *et al.* 2005) and then apply these findings to the contemporary circumstances of the EU.

## 2. THE DEVELOPMENTAL DYNAMICS OF SOCIAL POLICY EVOLUTION IN SIX FEDERAL STATES: TOP-DOWN VS. BOTTOM-UP

Our findings suggest that during the early consolidation stage of the welfare state the type of federalism and the political regime type influence its developmental trajectory. In all those federations which were *democratic* throughout the course of the twentieth century and where the type of federal arrangement was initially based on a policy-related separation of powers (interstate or dual federalism), welfare state consolidation took place later and the pace of social expenditure growth was slower than in the majority of unitary states at a comparable level of economic development. Austrian and German development was quite different. These countries were welfare state pioneers, but their early social policy consolidation occurred under non-democratic auspices. They were, moreover, nations whose federal arrangements showed a strong leaning toward intra-state or co-operative federalism from the outset.

By identifying democratic federalism as a major impediment at the formative phase of welfare state development, our main findings dovetail neatly with the evidence from comparative statistical research. It was democratic federations that were in the majority, and it is their retarding effect on programme adoption, and, hence, on the initial stages of programme expenditure growth, that has been picked up in the statistical studies. However, in contradistinction to the necessarily undifferentiated conclusions of such studies, our historical, ideographic approach allows us to locate precisely where federalism matters and to identify the underlying mechanisms explaining why federalism has been an impediment only in some contexts.

A key consideration in these differential dynamics of federal welfare states is the question of which tier of government first occupied the welfare state terrain. Of central importance, therefore, is the original distribution of jurisdictions among government levels. The programme-impeding and expenditure-restraining effects of federalism can be seen most clearly in democratic federations with interstate federal arrangements, where the federal level of government originally had little or no power to take up social policy concerns and the scope for federal fiscal manoeuvre was relatively limited. In such instances, welfare state take-off was delayed until the necessary powers had been acquired. Because they either lacked or shared social and fiscal policy competencies, federal authorities could not act unilaterally but only in collaboration with the constituent units.

This meant that social policy frequently got stuck in a jurisdictional game of hide-and-seek: while the federal level lacked the power to launch national social programmes, constituent units often hesitated to establish welfare programmes unilaterally as they feared the competitive disadvantage of pioneer status. Such considerations were of particular relevance in North America just before the Great Depression and were further strengthened by the complete absence or weak development of systems of fiscal equalization. Although fiscal equalization was a stronger theme in Australian institutional development, the inter-war failure to initiate a scheme of child endowment was a classical instance of jurisdictional hide-and-seek. But there were also instances where constituent units and municipalities established social programmes at the local and regional level. Swiss federalism with its emphasis on local autonomy rather than horizontal competition is a clear case in point. Here, local policy pre-emption not only delayed programme adoption at the federal level, but also reduced the degrees of freedom available for future federal social policy initiatives by reducing the capacity of the federal government to penetrate locally grown social programmes.

As a consequence of limited federal powers and local policy pre-emption, welfare state consolidation took place from the bottom up in all the democratic federations. Prompt upward redistribution of competencies was blocked through a series of institutional veto-points, with the multi-tiered negotiations required to remove such obstacles necessarily involving a considerable number of actors with often conflicting interests. Rigid procedures of constitutional amendment and judicial review have repeatedly struck down federal intrusions in social affairs. In cases where a reallocation of jurisdictions was unsuccessful, the federal government could only launch social policy initiatives through federal grants to the constituent units.

Processes of these kinds were largely absent in Germany and Austria. Neither country was a fully developed democracy until 1918 and judicial review was unknown. Moreover, the constitutional system of the Habsburg Empire was, at best, proto-federal in character. Early and comprehensive policy pre-emption of the welfare state at the central level in both countries was the major reason for unhindered and speedy social policy expansion in later years. A variety of contextual factors accelerated welfare state consolidation under both monarchies. An important stimulus to action was the need for legitimacy of a conservative élite finding itself confronted with a growing working-class movement demanding more extensive political participation. Equally important for subsequent sustained development was an élitist political culture of state-centred reform embedded in an 'enlightened' absolutism. At the same time, contribution-based funding of programmes provided a mechanism for continued welfare state growth, given that fiscal conflicts between different levels of government could be sidestepped by externalizing costs to employers and employees through the para-fiscal mechanisms of the social insurance system. Finally, these early welfare state building initiatives were aspects of state- and nation-building processes, making social policy a catalyst for the reinforcement of unitary trends in political and administrative development. In Germany, after 1871, social insurance policy became an important instrument for the consolidation of the new Reich. Nation-building was also important in the Habsburg Empire, since the emergence of welfare institutions was seen as a means of countering the strong centrifugal forces in a multi-ethnic empire.

In consequence, a great gulf already separated Germany and Austria from the democratic federalist welfare state laggards by the late 1920s. In the former, welfare state consolidation was largely accomplished, while, in the latter, it had, in respect of the vast majority of programmes, yet to begin. Over the next two decades, external shocks – economic depression and total war – influenced social policy development in both types of federal setting, but in ways that reflected their prior contexts of development. In the long-time democratic federations, these shocks provided the necessary leverage for dispersing the logjams of entrenched veto-point opposition to centralized fiscal and expenditure control, especially where the party in office was one favouring reform. In the United States, economic crisis was the major catalyst of change. In Australia, the wartime crisis provided the occasion for centralization of the tax system and an extension of the social services role of the Commonwealth, with the longest Labour administration since Federation as its agent. In Canada, despite the lack of a left party impetus, wartime conditions had very similar effects. Even in neutral Switzerland, the Second World War was a major catalyst for expanding the social and fiscal powers of the federal government. Thus, by the mid-1940s, basic competencies for a major federal role in social policy were substantially developed in democratic as well as in authoritarian federal systems.

After the war, once a full array of programmes was in place, and with democratic institutions now everywhere victorious, the welfare state became an important source of credit claiming and partisan competition. Naturally, this meant that the partisan complexion of government now became a vital factor shaping the trajectory of social expenditure growth in the post-war period. However, the way in which party politics was played out continued to be strongly influenced by the character of governmental (and federal) institutions. Canada is a case in point because the country's social programmes are embedded in and governed by different forms of intergovernmental relations (Banting 2004). Political gridlock was most pronounced in the field of contributory pensions where policy-making is based on joint-decision federalism and framed by a vertically incongruent party system. It was almost completely absent where a classical division of powers prevailed as was, for instance, the case in respect of unemployment benefits. Moreover, given that different policy instruments – social insurance, means-testing and universalism – have diverse potentials for expenditure growth, particular policy strategies chosen in the past continued to have a path-dependent impact on the policy options favoured in the here and now.

Post-war governments also found ways to cope with the inbuilt complexity of federal arrangements and increasingly relied on strategies bypassing the policy blockages inherent in federal arrangements. The emergence of such *bypass mechanisms* results from a functional problem of all evolving democratic federal systems in the modern era: how to get around inbuilt constitutional rigidities to institute and deliver the welfare programmes and reforms demanded by democratic electorates. Federal constitutions are designed to inhibit change or, at least, to slow down changes which alter the balance of power and responsibility between state and federal jurisdictions. Those who seek to affect change must find a way around existing institutional barriers. Our analysis identifies three bypass strategies, which are identified and summarized in Table 1. These bypass strategies have not only influenced patterns of benefits provision but have also channelled and shaped the public-private mix in social policy over the long term.

To sum up, a comparative analysis of Western federal states shows that two dimensions of distributional conflict interact when federalism meets the welfare state, namely (1) the (re)distribution of (mostly) money between social classes (and regions), and (2) the distribution of power between tiers of government. The consolidation of the welfare state in these six federations was mainly determined by the extent to which the distribution of power allowed social policy to unfold and that, in turn, was driven by how conflictual these politics were. Two aspects seem crucial here: on the one hand, the level of democratic development at the time the welfare state emerged and, on the other, the type of federalism dictated by constitutional arrangements. *Intra*-state (co-operative) federalism allows federal level social policy to flourish early on, whereas *inter*-state (dual) federalism tends to protect the political status quo, and, thus, to retard welfare state growth. These institutional factors have been overlaid by social interest patterns: where there were fewer regional cleavages – in party systems and the economy – it was much easier to nationalize power than where regionalism was strong or where there was substantial ethnic or economic fragmentation. We now draw on these conclusions to identify the dynamics of European social policy development and to evaluate the prospects for a European welfare dimension, or, in many people's view, for a 'European welfare state'.

## 3. LESSONS FOR THE EU

Politically, the situation in the EU has some resemblances to conditions in Germany and Austria in the late nineteenth century. Though the EU is clearly not an autocratic regime,[1] most scholars agree that Europe suffers from a democratic deficit. As in the early years of the Germanic federations, improving internal cohesion and creating a common identity are core contemporary issues in the EU. Moreover, and with parallels to the Habsburg monarchy, the Union is highly fragmented in both national and economic terms and

*Table 1* Bypass structures in six OECD federations

| Bypass | Description | Exemplary countries |
|---|---|---|
| Patchwork quilt | An array of discrete agreements between federal and state authorities gives lower tiers of government control over aspects of social policy initiation and implementation, while compelling them to carry out national programmes. One important route to overcome lacking federal social policy competencies was to rely on the federal spending power for providing grants to subordinate governments but increasingly also to employers and employees. Going beyond some conceptions of federalism, where each programme is run and financed by a single level of government, the patchwork quilt may be based on *joint decisions*, whereby agreements require approval by both levels of government, or be run on a *shared-costs basis*, with the federal government providing financial support for multi-tier programmes. | Canada, USA |
| Regulatory | The state mandates *private* parties to pay for and provide certain benefits, such as pensions, health care, etc. Most regulation concerns *employers'* provisions to employees. Mandates may be hard (*binding*) or soft (*optional*). In the latter case, the effectiveness of regulation is dependent on the largesse of tax deductions or subsidies. In Australia the federal arbitration system used its power to control wages in order to provide a social policy minimum, and, thus, in principle, removed the need for specific poverty alleviation measures. It also served as the legal authority for providing mandated benefits such as sickness expenditure and, initially, second-tier pensions and in the process not merely bypassed the states and federation as providers of benefits, but also the federal executive and legislature as social policy decision-makers. | Australia, Switzerland |

(*Table continued*)

*Table 1* Continued

| Bypass | Description | Exemplary countries |
|---|---|---|
| Para-fiscal (or, when fully developed, para-state) | Multi-level governance problems were avoided by creating a new sublevel (the para-fiscus), regularly also spun off organizationally, creating new exit options for offloading costs from the state or federal level to the para-fiscal level. Hence institutionalized *independent* public agencies, mandated by the state but with their own tax base (contributions) *outside* of the state's general budget (*para-fiscus*), manage the delivery of benefits. These agencies, in addition, often have an *independent power base* of employer associations and unions, with state representatives from various levels of federalism serving as arbiters between and amongst the 'social partners'. In its fully developed form, with almost half of public finances dedicated to the *para-fiscus*, independent agencies are so pervasive they form an effective para-state. | Austria, Germany [Switzerland] |

therefore in need of a strengthening of integrative and centripetal forces. Hence, expanding common social policy beyond the level already achieved (cf. for an overview Leibfried and Pierson 1995; Leibfried 2005; Falkner 1998, 2005) might, amongst other things, be considered a strategy for reinforcing a European identity and improving the output-legitimation of EU institutions. A common social policy would also assist in overcoming the 'constitutional asymmetry' between policies promoting market efficiencies and endorsing social protection and equality (Scharpf 2002). Without such policies, it seems probable that the forces unleashed by negative integration will induce a competitive downward spiral in benefit provision at the member state level, in turn, weakening the cohesion of the Union in the long run.

However, while Germany and Austria found it relatively easy to launch social policy from the top down, the situation of contemporary Europe is unique in several respects, making a federal European welfare state a rather unlikely prospect. In order to develop the logic of this argument, we apply our findings with respect to welfare state formation in six federations to the contemporary circumstances of the EU. Specifically, we discuss the explanatory factors we have identified as influencing social policy development in federal states, showing how they help us to explain previous and contemporary patterns of EU social policy.

## 3.1 Policy pre-emption

In contrast to the six federations examined in our study, the social policy terrain in Europe is comprehensively pre-empted by the member states. Historically, the development of the welfare state in Europe was intimately connected with the emergence of the modern nation state (Flora 1986). From the outset, solidarity and legitimation issues were strongly related to the concept of the nation. One, perhaps overly cynical, view of the welfare state is to see it as a device for redistributing money between people sharing a common language and similar cultural norms. In the context of heterogeneous societies, however, it has been argued that ethnicity and territorial differences have constituted more limited and spatially separated entities of solidarity, potentially impeding the emergence of a comprehensive and redistributive welfare state at the national level. It can also be argued that contemporary Europe is characterized by territorially fragmented spaces of solidarity with default lines running along the borders between the member states, thereby limiting the chances of supplementing much less replacing national social programmes with uniform community-wide schemes. Moreover, within Europe, the nation-based welfare state remains a powerful source of legitimation for national governments. Since we know from many surveys that the welfare state is extremely popular amongst European mass electorates, both citizens and the governments of the member states will resist any transfer of social policy related powers. For instance, Eurobarometer data, mapping the preferences of citizens in the EU15 with regard to their preferred locus of social policy-making, suggest that only about one-third of the population supports a shift of social policy jurisdiction to the Union (Mau 2003: 311).

Welfare state building in Europe is, therefore, subject to intrinsically similar constraints as those governing competitive state-building in Canada (Banting 1995). As the dispute between Ottawa and Quebec over the authority in social policy-making reveals, legitimation issues can lead to severe tensions over the locus of benefit provision. However, the popularity of national welfare states creates a powerful status quo bias. In terms of welfare regime patterns, social policy pre-emption at the national level has created a patchwork quilt that has become increasingly Byzantine after waves of European enlargement (Scharpf 2002). Since Eastern enlargement, no less than five different welfare regimes can be distinguished in Europe, which differ in funding principles, forms and levels of benefit supplied and degrees of inclusiveness, thereby reflecting the different political power constellations and national policy legacies from which they have emerged. With the benefit of hindsight, we may conclude that the window of opportunity for the supersession of national social programmes by European schemes has diminished with each enlargement, because each increase in membership has multiplied the number of constituent units and thereby increased the number of possible veto players potentially opposed to greater uniformity of provision.

Apart from the interests of the member states in retaining their own powers and in enhancing their own legitimacy, a broad array of private interests have crystallized around the existing social programmes in the member states. As a result, the policy status quo is generally defended not only by national governments but also by entrenched interests, such as the medical profession. 'German doctors and patients would unite in protest against any moves toward a British-style National Health Service' (Scharpf 2002: 651). Again, important lessons can be learnt from welfare state development in federal nation states. In particular, the Swiss experience demonstrates the mechanisms through which local policy pre-emption and the vested interests surrounding these programmes constrain the ability of the central government to enact uniform and redistributive social policy. Given the Swiss federation's initial lack of powers in the latter half of the nineteenth century, the impact of industrialization was first encountered at municipal and cantonal level, giving an impetus to local schemes and the emergence of a heterogeneous web of local social security arrangements. Using the numerous veto-points enshrined in the Swiss constitution, local programme carriers, business and regional interests were able, in the short to medium term, to fend off the intrusion of the federal government in social affairs. As a consequence, federal social programmes were either delayed or structurally pre-configured by locally adopted solutions or the federal government had to limit its role to the provision of subsidies to these programmes. Frequently, moreover, the federal government was only capable of enacting framework legislation stipulating minimum social standards. Sometimes, it was constrained from action of any sort.

The lesson to be drawn is that the interplay between policy pre-emption, entrenched interests and institutional veto-points is an important key to understanding the dynamics of welfare state building in multi-level systems. The more comprehensive is the policy space pre-empted by lower tiers of government and the more veto-points are available, the less likely it is that jurisdictional competencies will be reallocated between different levels of government or that uniform policy solutions will be adopted. These are the circumstances currently prevalent within the EU. Not only are social policies fully developed in member states, but vested interests and national governments also face extraordinarily favourable opportunities to defend the status quo. As we will now point out, the institutional rigidities and high thresholds of consensus necessary to alter the status quo built into the European multi-level system provide powerful leverage for countering moves towards European welfare-state-like development.

## 3.2 Policy jurisdiction and institutional rigidities

The comparison of OECD federations has revealed that the initial distribution of powers between different levels of government and the institutional checks and balances enshrined in their constitutions have substantially impeded policy reform. This was particularly true for interstate federal arrangements based on a policy-related separation of powers. In order to ascertain the prospects for a European welfare state one obvious step is to examine the social policy related powers as they are spelled out by the European Treaties. This analysis is to be found in Table 2, which identifies the assignment of explicit social policy mandates in EU treaty documents from the Treaty of Rome to the Rome (II) Constitutional Treaty of 2004.

Note the crucial difference between the structuring of interstate federalism and the present framework of European institutions. With respect to social policy, the EU is a unique multi-tiered system, with three distinctive character-istics: a propensity towards 'joint-decision traps' and policy immobilism; a pro-minent role for courts in policy development; and an unusually tight coupling to market-conforming processes (Leibfried 2005). Similar to the democratic federal states, the European Community (EC) initially had no social policy mandate of any kind. However, it has acquired a considerable range of social policy related competencies over the past two decades. Moreover, barriers to social policy decision-making have been relaxed as qualified majority voting (QMV) has been extended to an increasing number of jurisdictions. What still distinguishes the EU from the situation of the federal nation states is that decision-making at the central level nonetheless requires supermajorities and thus an unusually high level of consensus among member states. Political dead-lock therefore does not primarily emerge from a lack of policy authority, but rather from the rigid and vertically intertwined decision-making rules built into Europe's system of multi-level governance (Scharpf 1988).

This fundamental barrier to progress has not been substantially altered by the recent enhancement of QMV, since changes to core branches of social policy such as social security still require unanimity. Moreover, a new provision adopted by the Treaty of Nice rules out any harmonization of the laws and regu-lations of the member states (Art. 137 [2] (a)). Instead, the Council may, by means of directives, adopt 'minimum requirements for gradual implementation' but shall avoid imposing administrative, financial and legal constraints that may impede the creation and development of small and medium-sized undertakings. Also, directives intended to enact minimum standards in the realm of social security still require unanimity.

Also related to the allocation of powers is the question of whether the centre is fiscally and administratively capable of formulating positive social policy and building a redistributive welfare state. Compared with other 'multi-tiered' systems, the EU's social policy-making apparatus is extremely bottom-heavy (Leibfried and Pierson 1995; Kleinman 2001). Moreover, the centre is extra-ordinarily weak in fiscal matters, as it lacks the power to levy taxes and therefore entirely depends on the transfer payments of the national governments. Seen from a historical perspective, however, the administrative and fiscal weakness of the European centre has analogies with the situation of the US and Switzerland in the nineteenth century.

A second distinctive characteristic of the EU is that the role of courts differs from that in the six federal states featuring in our research. Whereas in the latter, the general trend of early court judgments was to limit federal social policy

Table 2 The assignment of explicit[a] social policy mandates to the EU, 1957–2004

| Field of mandate | European Economic Community EEC 1957 (1958) | Single European Act (SEA) EEC 1986 (1987) | Maastricht Treaty EC-MT 1992 (1993) | Social Protocol SP 1992 (1993) | Amsterdam Treaty EC-AT 1997 (1999) | Nice Treaty EC-NT 2000 (2003) | Rome (II) Constitutional Treaty EC-CT 2004 (?) |
|---|---|---|---|---|---|---|---|
| Discrimination on grounds of nationality | Unan 7 | No ref | QMV 6 | No ref | QMV 12 | QMV 12 | QMV III-123 |
| Other anti-discrimination measures, harmonization excluded | No ref | No ref | No ref | No ref | QMV 13 (2) | QMV 13 (2) | QMV III-124 (2) |
| Free labour movement | Unan 48–50 | QMV 48–50 | QMV 48–50 | No impact | QMV 39–40 | QMV 39–40 | QMV III-133–134 |
| Gender equality in pay[b] | Unan 119 | Unan 119 | Unan 119 | Unan 6 | QMV 141 | QMV 141 | QMV III-214 |
| Gender equality for labour force[b] | No ref | No ref | No ref | QMV 2 (1) v | QMV 137 (1) v | QMV 137 (1) i | QMV III-210 (1) i |
| Working environment | No ref | QMV 118a | QMV 118a | QMV 2 (1) i | QMV 137 (1) i | QMV 137 (1) a | QMV III-210 (1) a |
| Working conditions (outside former Art. 118a, line 6) | No ref | No ref | No ref | QMV 2 (1) ii | QMV 137 (1) ii | QMV 137 (1) b | QMV III-210 (1) b |
| Worker information and consultation | No ref | No ref | No ref | QMV 2 (1) iii | QMV 137 (1) iii | QMV 137 (1) e | QMV III-210 (1) e |
| Integration of persons excluded from labour market[c] | No ref | No ref | No ref | QMV 2 (1) iv | QMV 137 (1) iv | QMV 137 (1) h | QMV III-210 (1) h |

(Table continued)

Table 2 Continued

| Field of mandate | European Economic Community EEC 1957 (1958) | Single European Act (SEA) EEC 1986 (1987) | Maastricht Treaty EC-MT 1992 (1993) | Social Protocol SP 1992 (1993) | Amsterdam Treaty EC-AT 1997 (1999) | Nice Treaty EC-NT 2000 (2003) | Rome (II) Constitutional Treaty EC-CT 2004 (?) |
|---|---|---|---|---|---|---|---|
| Combating of social exclusion | No ref | No ref | No ref | No ref | No ref | QMV 137 (1) j | QMV III-210 (1) j |
| Modernization of social protection systems | No ref | No ref | No ref | No ref | No ref | QMV 137 (1) k | QMV III-210 (1) k |
| Public health | No ref | No ref | QMV 129 | No ref | QMV 152 | QMV 152 | QMV III-278 |
| Social security co-ordination | Unan 51 | Unan 51 | Unan 51 | n. a. | Unan 42 | Unan 42 | QMV III-136 (but see III-136 (2)) |
| Harmonization of other anti-discrimination measures (see line 2)[d] | No ref | No ref | No ref | No ref | Unan 13 (1) | Unan 13 (1) | Unan III-124 (1) |
| Social security and protection of workers | No ref | No ref | No ref | Unan 2 (3) i | Unan 137 (3) i | Unan 137 (1) c | Unan III-210 (1) c |
| Protection of workers (employment contract termination) | No ref | No ref | No ref | Unan 2 (3) ii | Unan 137 (3) ii | Unan 137 (1) d | Unan III-210 (1) d |
| Collective interest representation, codetermination | No ref | No ref | No ref | Unan 2 (3) iii | Unan 137 (3) iii | Unan 137 (1) f | Unan III-210 (1) f |
| Employment of third-country nationals | No ref | No ref | No ref | Unan 2 (3) iv | Unan 137 (3) iv | Unan 137 (1) g | Unan III-210 (1) g |
| Funding for employment policy[c] | No ref | No ref | No ref | Unan 2 (3) v | Unan 137 (3) v | No ref | No ref |

| | No ref | No ref [e] | No ref in 100a (2) [e] | Excl in 2 (6) | Excl 137 (6) | Excl 137 (5) | Excl III-210 (6) |
|---|---|---|---|---|---|---|---|
| Pay | No ref | No ref [e] | No ref in 100a (2) [e] | Excl in 2 (6) | Excl 137 (6) | Excl 137 (5) | Excl III-210 (6) |
| Right of association | No ref | No ref [e] | No ref in 100a (2) [e] | Excl in 2 (6) | Excl 137 (6) | Excl 137 (5) | Excl III-210 (6) |
| Right to strike and to impose lock-outs | No ref | No ref [e] | No ref in 100a (2) [e] | Excl in 2 (6) | Excl 137 (6) | Excl 137 (5) | Excl III-210 (6) |
| Mandates for the open method of co-ordination[g] (OMC) | | | | | | | |
| Employment | | | | | (128) 140[f] | (128) 140[f] | III-213 a |
| Labour market and working conditions | | | | | | 140 | III-213 b |
| Professional education and training | | | | | | 140 | III-213 c |
| Social security | | | | | | 140 | III-213 d |
| Prevention of occupational accidents and diseases | | | | | | 140 | III-213 e |
| Protection of health at work | | | | | | 140 | III-213 f |
| Law of coalitions and collective agreements between employers and employees | | | | | | 140 | III-213 g |

*Source:* Leibfried (2005).
*Notes:*
Years given for treaties refer to the signing and (in parentheses) the ratification of the treaty. Numbers listed in the table refer to articles in each treaty. Abbreviations used: Unan = unanimity required; QMV = qualified majority voting; No ref = no reference to mandate; n. a. = not applicable; Excl = mandate explicitly excluded.
Shading denotes weaker mandate. Heavier shading shows explicit denial of mandates, anchored in the treaties only since 1992 in these areas.
[a] As a rule the table refers to explicit powers mentioned in the treaties, in contrast to unspecified general powers, as under Articles 100 and 235 EEC (since AT 95 and 308 EC) or to non-enabling norms (on an exception, see note [b] and note [d], under Art. 21).
For notes [b] to [g], see Leibfried (2005: 250–253, 253). We are grateful to Josef Falke, Centre for European Law and Politics (ZERP) at the University of Bremen, for his continuous support in compiling this table.

initiatives and thus protect the policy autonomy of the constituent units at the expense of nation-wide social programmes, European Court of Justice (ECJ) activism related to economic integration has undercut the sovereignty and policy autonomy of sub-governments. It is widely acknowledged that the ECJ has been a key actor in unleashing the forces of negative integration. In other words, the process of market-building and its backing by the ECJ has put national welfare states under heavy strain, but these pressures have not been forcefully addressed by efforts to re-regulate through the further development of policy at the centre.

Why has the centre remained so inactive with respect to redistributive social programmes? We have pointed to the status quo bias resulting from policy pre-emption at the national level, to fiscal and administrative shortcomings and to rigid decision-making rules providing member states with strong veto powers. Now we turn to why the supermajorities required for changing the status quo are most unlikely to occur. To this end, it is necessary to examine the political and economic cleavages characterizing contemporary Europe and to map out associated patterns of interest formation.

## 3.3 Political and economic cleavages

Tsebelis's veto player theory suggests that it is not sufficient to focus on the number of veto players alone. His core axioms for explaining policy change also refer to the importance of the ideological distance between veto players and their internal cohesion. This suggests a focus on the partisan complexion of member states' governments and their cohesion if we wish to understand political cleavages in the European Council. Manow *et al.* (2004: 13–14) have recently shown that Europe has become increasingly politically heterogeneous over time, and have also convincingly argued that a knowledge of partisan complexion of national governments is crucial for understanding the dynamics of EU social policy. As with the increasing pluralism of welfare regime patterns over the past forty years, increasing political fragmentation occurred in the wake of the enlargements. Today, the European political landscape reflects the full spectrum of ideological positions, ranging from Swedish-style social democracy to secular conservative and right-wing nationalist parties. Although different party families converged with respect to attitudes toward the welfare state and the market economy, differences remain that are likely to create tensions over social policy-making at the national and European level. The parties programmatically most inclined to pro-welfare state attitudes are not those most forcefully backing the integration process given that 'support for integration quite strongly varies inversely with the "leftness" of EU member-state governments' (Manow *et al.* 2004: 13). There is some evidence that this trend is changing, as Eurosceptic leftist parties have recently 'become distinctly more pro-integration as regulated capitalism has come on the European agenda' (Hooghe *et al.* 2004: 129). But rightist parties have also begun to selectively oppose European integration in order to avert re-regulation at the European level. As a result, European issues related to redistribution have become more closely aligned to traditional conflicts between left and right. Nevertheless, Europe's national governments are now comprised of such a wide, and still diverging, array of political parties and coalitions from across the left-right spectrum that cohesive policy initiatives at the European level are most unlikely to emerge.

With respect to internal cohesion, Tsebelis argues that policy stability increases with the internal homogeneity of collective veto players. Increasing cohesion is most likely to occur where national interests and territorially bounded values are at stake. A recent study of political conflict in Europe concludes that EU policies with strong distributional impacts across countries give rise to national coalitions (Marks 2004). Where legitimation issues, national values and topics related to financial obligations and the competitive position of the economy are to the forefront of debate, it seems probable that cohesive forces will become much stronger. Under such circumstances, territorial (i.e. national) interests may even outweigh ideology. We noted that the welfare state is a powerful source of output legitimation that is closely connected to the nation state and which, therefore, pre-configures strong national interests.

This is clearly true of economic interests, where the basis for interest cleavages has increased markedly with enlargement. Indeed, 2003 data (Eurostat 27/2004) show that most of the former communist countries enjoy only 50–60 per cent of EU average income and that countries like Romania, Bulgaria and Turkey, which are seeking to join the EU in the near future, are even poorer, with current income levels of around 30 per cent of the European average.

These huge differences in economic wealth are closely associated with conflicting economic interest patterns that differ systematically as between rich and poor member states, making tensions over social policy-making and, in particular, welfare state funding more likely. According to neoclassical growth theory, poor nations have a natural competitive advantage deriving from their status as economic laggards. Given capital shortage, low non-wage labour costs, free trade and capital movement, they benefit from the influx of investment and jobs outsourced by the rich countries. Wishing to sustain this competitive advantage, governments and especially business organizations in the poorer countries obviously have no major interest in raising social standards. The rich member states are quite differently placed. Facing the competition of low-wage economies with a well-educated labour force, they clearly have an interest in championing the uniform social standards imposed by the Union. However, they also have an interest in avoiding the financial burden necessary to fund such efforts. Moreover, this burden has increased markedly in the wake of the most recent enlargement when only relatively poor countries joined the EU. Nor is there any prospect of the situation improving. Europe's wealthiest countries, including Norway, Switzerland and Iceland, with gross domestic product (GDP) per capita exceeding mean income levels by 20–50 per cent, hesitate to join and, in any case, are too small to make much difference.

But this is not the only reason why no common denominator policy is available. Things are made worse by the fact that national populations and their governments are often in disagreement. Using Eurobarometer data, Mau (2003) has examined whether the populations of the fifteen EU member states support a transfer of social policy responsibilities from the national to the European level. Attitudes towards European social policies seem crucially influenced by welfare regime type and the level of social security hitherto achieved nationally. Whereas citizens in the Nordic countries are opposed to an enlargement of EU social competencies, because they fear that uniform European social schemes will undercut the high standards of their advanced welfare states, citizens in southern Europe show a greater proclivity to expand the role of the European level in social affairs for precisely the opposite reason. Moreover, existing welfare regimes also structure partisan dispositions toward European integration. Brinegar *et al.* (2004) find that, in redistributive welfare states, the left opposes further EU integration, whereas, in residual welfare states, it is the right that resists enhanced integration. Political polarization over EU integration is less pronounced in conservative welfare regimes.

In sum, Europe is facing a fundamental social policy dilemma. Though Europe initially lacked powers to establish social programmes of its own that could compete with those of member states, it undermined the policy autonomy and sovereignty of member states in social affairs in the process of developing a supranational supremacy in policies related to the establishment of a single market, a process also catalysed and protected by ECJ activism. To cope effectively with direct and indirect spill-over effects on national welfare states imposed by economic integration would require concerted European-wide action on the positive integration front. However, given a fiscally and administratively weak centre and a set of veto players characterized by substantial ideological distance and strong internal cohesion makes it rather unlikely that the high degree of consensus required for altering the status quo can be achieved. Europe, in other words, is caught in a joint-decision trap.

But this is not necessarily the end of the story. In this context, it may be illuminating to examine the ways in which our six federations managed to overcome the institutional rigidities that stymied their early steps towards welfare state consolidation. Recall that bypass strategies played an important role in facilitating welfare consolidation and that major breakthroughs in the reallocation of powers were only achieved through severe external shocks. The Great Depression and the Second World War were important critical junctures, which led to a centralization of social and fiscal powers and fuelled a wave of solidarity among the population that paved the way for welfare state take-off in the post-war period. War and depression are not, of course, eventualities to be welcomed under any circumstances. Indeed, avoiding them has supplied much for the rationale for post-war EU development. This being so, it becomes clear that Europe's most promising way to deepen social integration is to rely on bypass strategies.

## 3.4 Bypass strategies

Having shown that the European joint-decision system is unable to overcome its institutional rigidities, we now explore whether the institutional development in our six federal welfare states suggests ways in which bypass strategies could assist in circumventing these blockages.

The experience in the North American federations shows that whenever the federal government was denied the power to legislate on social matters, it could rely on its spending power in order to stimulate programme development at the subordinate level. Moreover, the power to provide grants gave the central government leverage to influence basic principles of programme design. At the same time, the federation's taxing powers opened an avenue for achieving social policy objectives by other means such as tax expenditures and subsidies for privately and occupationally run programmes. However, in light of Europe's present fiscal constitution, it should be clear that this bypass route is blocked. The EU lacks an autonomous financial basis for social policy development since it has no genuine fiscal powers. The Community's budget is fed by payments from the member states, which are related to their capacity to pay. Again, a deep asymmetry between the interests of rich and poor member states, along with the high barriers of consensus required for altering the status quo, precludes any major policy shift in fiscal matters. Moreover, as is well known, the bulk of such revenues is devoted to the common agricultural policy, therefore crowding out public expenditure devoted to other public policy objectives.

However, semi-sovereignty in fiscal affairs was also the starting point for the majority of federations. The fiscal powers of the central state were then significantly extended in wartime and in the aftermath of war. However, some of the European federations discovered ways to cope with fiscal shortcomings prior to the Second World War. Taking the para-fiscal bypass route of creating autonomous social insurance agencies, major social programmes were funded through contributions. Political gridlock was avoided by externalizing costs to third parties, i.e. employers and employees, not involved in the bargaining game between different branches of government. However, the para-fiscal route is no more available in the current EU context than is financial leverage through grants from the centre. Though corporatism has gained importance in recent years (Falkner 1998), the main roadblock is the variety of welfare regime patterns. Adopting the para-fiscal route would automatically imply a structural shift towards the Bismarckian social security model that would not have any appeal to countries with alternative welfare regime patterns. Indeed, given that, in many quarters, the contributory model is blamed for the contemporary economic malaise of the countries of continental Western Europe, it might also not be enthusiastically welcomed by all the countries in the Bismarckian tradition.

Thus, the only bypass route remaining is the regulatory one (cf. Majone 1997, 2005). Here, the Swiss and also the Australian experience is intriguing and shows some parallels with the situation of contemporary Europe. Initially, after the Swiss constitution was revised in 1874, labour protection was the only social policy jurisdiction on which the federal government could rely. Although this realm was pre-empted by some industrially advanced cantons, the federal government was able to enact a federal factory law in 1877 which regulated working conditions in factories and made Switzerland a European leader in terms of labour protection. A major reason for this early programme adoption was the purely regulatory nature of this policy field that did not require major public expenditure. In contrast, redistributive programmes were substantially postponed because of the federation's lack of fiscal and social security powers. Severe struggles between different branches of government and constitutional rigidities associated with the reallocation of fiscal powers protracted or even impeded the reallocation of fiscal responsibilities. Only by adopting a para-fiscal approach could the federal government initiate redistributive pro-grammes.[2] As a consequence, Switzerland's welfare state trajectory is marked by a strong asymmetry in terms of the temporal sequence of labour protection legislation and the enactment of social transfer programmes: while Switzerland was pioneer in regulating working conditions in comparative perspective, the country was in the rearguard regarding the enactment of redistributive social programmes. The Australian experience illustrates the same dualistic develop-ment. The use of the power to arbitrate industrial disputes made it possible to establish minimum wages and compulsory sick pay by requirements imposed on employers, but standard social programmes were initiated late and were miserly in their expenditure levels (see Castles 1985).

Similar patterns can be observed in Europe. Regulatory social policy – with 'new' pan-European and cross-societal anti-discrimination legislation possibly slowly overlaying the 'old' employment-centred regulation (Leibfried 2005; on similar post-1960s US developments, see Kochan *et al.* 2001) – has been the realm in which social policy progress has been made lasting in recent decades for several reasons. *First* of all, no major fiscal resources are required to launch such initiatives. *Secondly*, decision-making in this field is based on QMV and is thus less prone to political deadlock. *Thirdly*, and with a strong resonance to Australia, where the impetus for regulation were judgements of the Court of Arbitration, social policy initiatives from the centre are unusually court-driven in character. It is as much a series of rulings from the ECJ as the process of Com-mission and Council initiatives that has been the source of new social policy. While the Council and Commission are prone to stasis, the ECJ's institutional design fosters activism – a situation emphasized even more in the Draft Consti-tutional Treaty signed in Rome in October 2004. The Court relies on simple majority votes, taken in secret, sheltering it from the political immobility typical of the EU. Only a unanimous vote of the Council or a Treaty revision can undo ECJ decisions when they relate to primary European law. Legal strat-egies have had the advantage of leaving taxing, spending, and administrative powers at the national level – and this is even more so where the substantive policy content of those strategies is regulatory in character. It is important, however, to emphasize that such a court-led process of social policy development has its own logic. Decisions are likely to reflect demands for doctrinal coherence as much as, or more than, substantive debates as to the desirability of various social policy outcomes. The capacity of reforms built around a judicial logic to achieve substantive goals may be limited. Furthermore, courts may have less need to consider political constraints in prescribing solutions. One danger is that court initiatives may exceed the tolerance of important political actors within the system. After all, centralized policy-making was made difficult in the EU for a reason, and ECJ activism may generate resentment. This is, of course, one aspect of the current disquiet over the 'democratic deficit'.

The most recent bypass strategy adopted, however, is the attempt to increase policy co-ordination between the member states by means of, at least initially, soft forms of governance. The prime example is the OMC. In its ideal-typical form, the OMC is a new type of governance (Radaelli 2003: 8; Mosher and Trubek 2003: 64) that can be traced back to the difficulty of achieving uniform policies by means of the classic binding instruments of hierarchical governance. Instead, the route taken strongly emphasizes (semi-)voluntary co-ordination of policies across different levels of government. The main idea is to promote the exchange of information, experience and best practice between the member states and the Commission. More specifically, Art. 140 ECT stipulates that the 'Commission shall encourage cooperation between Member States and facilitate the coordination of their action in all social policy fields;' this co-ordination should be achieved by 'making studies, delivering opinions and arranging consultations both on problems arising at national level and on those of concern to international organisations'. Initially, this is a route which is not legally binding since it is mainly concerned with monitoring, consulting and recommending, and therefore focuses mainly on the diffusion of knowledge. Policy change is thus expected to result from policy learning and from mechanisms of blaming and shaming connected to benchmarking. But as we know from the federal experience and from EU practices – e.g. the trajectory of European currency development from 1957 to the present – nothing prevents a *selective hardening* of soft forms of government, when the political need arises. This could conceivably come about by defining European 'reform corridors' for pensions policy, where in an ageing Europe most member states have found it difficult to effect a timely recalibration of policy, or by a supranational delineation of 'privatization corridors' in health policy, building on breakthroughs in the areas of freedom of services *cum* competition policy since the mid-1980s.

## CONCLUSION: THE LONG TERM

Are there lessons to be learnt from welfare state development in the established federal states that can help us to understand contemporary patterns and future trajectories of EU social policy? In general, multi-level systems based on strong separation of policy jurisdictions are prone to stasis and political gridlock.

However, compared to the six federal nation states analysed here (and in Obinger *et al.* 2005), the European multi-level system is peculiar in many respects. Its unique system of joint decision-making inhibits social policy change, with contemporary institutional and actor constellations conforming closely to all the axioms of veto player theory. The proliferation of veto-points gives member states powerful levers to defend the status quo. Thus, and in a similar way to the institutional development of the six federations featuring in our analysis, the policy route taken has been based on strategies seeking to bypass the in-built institutional rigidities and limited fiscal and administrative capacities of the EU. Specifically, we have identified two genuine bypass routes that play a key role in contemporary EU social policy-making. The first is strongly regulatory in nature, while the second is principally based on voluntary action, but simultaneously embedded in a common framework of monitoring and consultation and potentially open to subsequent 'hardening'. As a result, social policy evolution and harmonization is likely, at first, to be more the result of mutual adjustment and incremental accommodation than of central guidance. This means that EU social policy development, if it is to happen on any major scale, is a project for the very long term. The opportunity for a European 'age of federations' as prophesied by Proudhon still remains a project for the new century.

**Addresses for correspondence:** Herbert Obinger, Principal Investigator, Tran-State Research Centre and Centre for Social Policy Research (CeS), University of Bremen, POB 330 440, D 28335 Bremen, Germany. email: hobinger@zes.uni-bremen.de and Center for European Studies, Harvard University, 27 Kirkland Street, Cambridge, MA 02138, USA/Stephan Leibfried, Director, TranState Research Centre and Co-Director, Centre for Social Policy Research (CeS), University of Bremen, POB 330 440, D 28335 Bremen, Germany. email: stephan.leibfried@sfb597.uni-bremen.de/ Francis G. Castles, Department of Social Policy, University of Edinburgh, Adam Ferguson Building, George Square, Edinburgh EH8 9LL, UK. email: F.Castles@ed.ac.uk

## NOTES

1 Late nineteenth-century Germany had some proto-democratic features, notably universal manhood suffrage for the lower house of parliament. Austria, with a franchise restricted to 9 per cent of the adult population, did not.
2 This route, however, attracted the fierce opposition of business interest organizations. In contrast to Germany and Austria, Swiss business could launch a referendum to obstruct an increase in non-wage labour costs. Indeed, health insurance and pension insurance schemes were rejected in referendums held in 1900 and 1931 respectively.

## REFERENCES

Alber, J. (1982) *Vom Armenhaus zum Wohlfahrtsstaat*, Frankfurt/New York: Campus.
Banting, K.G. (1987) *The Welfare State and Canadian Federalism*, Kingston/Montreal: McGill Queen's University Press.

Banting, K.G. (1995) 'The welfare state as statecraft: territorial politics and Canadian social policy', in S. Leibfried and P. Pierson (eds), *European Social Policy. Between Fragmentation and Integration*, Washington, DC, Brookings Institution Press, pp. 269–300.

Banting, K.G. (2004) *Canada: Nation-building in a Federal Welfare State*, ZeS-Arbeitspapier 6/2004, Universität Bremen.

Benz, A. and Lehmbruch, G. (eds) (2002) *Föderalismus. Analysen in entwicklungsgeschichtlicher und vergleichender Perspektive*, Wiesbaden: Westdeutscher Verlag (= *Politische Vierteljahresschrift* special issue 32).

Brennan, G. and Buchanan, J.M. (1980) *The Power to Tax: Analytical Foundations of a Fiscal Constitution*, Cambridge: Cambridge University Press.

Brinegar, A.P., Jolly, S.K. and Kitschelt, H. (2004) 'Varieties of capitalism and political divides over European integration', in G. Marks and M.R. Steenbergen (eds), *European Integration and Political Conflict*, Cambridge: Cambridge University Press, pp. 62–89.

Cameron, D.R. (1978) 'The expansion of the public economy: a comparative analysis', *American Political Science Review* 72(4): 1243–61.

Castles, F.G. (1985) *The Working Class and Welfare*, Sydney: Allen & Unwin.

Castles, F.G. (1999) 'Decentralisation and the post-war political economy', *European Journal of Political Research* 36(1): 27–53.

Castles, F.G. (2004) *The Future of the Welfare State*, Oxford: Oxford University Press.

Cusack, T.R. and Fuchs, S. (2003) 'Institutionen, Parteien und Staatsausgaben', in H. Obinger, U. Wagschal and B. Kittel (eds), *Politische Ökonomie*, Opladen: Westdeutscher Verlag, pp. 321–54.

Esping-Andersen, G. (1990) *The Three Worlds of Welfare Capitalism*, Cambridge, UK: Polity Press/Princeton, NJ: Princeton University Press.

Falkner, G. (1998) *EU Social Policy in the 1990s. Towards a Corporatist Policy Community*, London: Routledge.

Falkner, G., Treib, O., Hartlapp, M. and Leiber, S. (2005) *Complying with Europe. EU Harmonisation and Law in Member States*, Cambridge: Cambridge University Press.

Flora, P. (1986) 'Wachstum zu Grenzen – Stabilisierung durch Wandel. Zur historischen Lage der entwickelten Wohlfahrtsstaaten Westeuropas', in M. Kaase (ed.), *Politische Wissenschaft und politische Ordnung*, Opladen: Westdeutscher Verlag, pp. 27–39.

Gerring, J. (2004) 'What is a case study and what is it good for?', *American Political Science Review* 98(2): 341–54.

Gillingham, J. (2003) *European Integration 1950–2003. Superstate or Market Economy?*, Cambridge: Cambridge University Press.

Hall, P. (2003) 'Aligning ontology and methodology in comparative research', in J. Mahoney and D. Rueschemeyer (eds), *Comparative Historical Analysis in the Social Sciences*, Cambridge: Cambridge University Press, pp. 373–404.

Hayek, F.v. (1976) 'The economic conditions of interstate federalism', in *Individualism and Economic Order*, London: Routledge & Kegan Paul, pp. 255–72.

Hicks, A.M. and Swank, D.H. (1992) 'Politics, institutions, and welfare spending in industrialized democracies, 1960–82', *American Political Science Review* 86(3): 658–74.

Hooghe, L., Marks, G. and Wilson, C.J. (2004) 'Does left/right structure party positions on European integration?', in G. Marks and M.R. Steenbergen (eds), *European Integration and Political Conflict*, Cambridge: Cambridge University Press, pp. 120–40.

Huber, E. and Stephens, J.D. (2001) *Development and Crisis of the Welfare State. Parties and Policies in Global Markets*, Chicago: University of Chicago Press.

Kleinman, M. (2001) *A European Welfare State? European Union Social Policy in Context*, Basingstoke: Macmillan.

Kochan, T., Locke, R., Osterman, P. and Piore, M. (2001) *Working in America: Blueprint for a New Labor Market*, Cambridge, MA: MIT Press.

Leibfried, S. (2005) 'Social policy. Left to judges and the markets?', in H. Wallace, W. Wallace and M. Pollack (eds), *Policy-Making in the EU*, 5th edn, Oxford: Oxford University Press, pp. 243–78.

Leibfried, S. and Pierson, P. (eds) (1995) *European Social Policy: Between Fragmentation and Integration*, Washington, DC: Brookings Institution Press.

Leibfried, S. and Zürn, M. (2005) 'Reconfiguring the national constellation', in S. Leibfried and M. Zürn (eds), *Transformations of the State?*, Cambridge: Cambridge University Press, pp. 1–36.

Lijphart, A. (1999) *Patterns of Democracy. Government Forms and Performance in Thirty-Six Countries*, London/New Haven: Yale University Press.

Majone, G. (1997) 'From the positive to the regulatory state: causes and consequences of changes in the mode of governance', *Journal of Public Policy* 17: 139–67.

Majone, G. (2005) *Dilemmas of European Integration. The Ambiguities and Pitfalls of Integration by Stealth*, Oxford: Oxford University Press.

Manow, P. (2004) *Federalism and the Welfare State. The German Case*, ZeS-Arbeitspapier 8/2004, Universität Bremen.

Manow, P., Schäfer, A. and Zorn, H. (2004) *European Social Policy and Europe's Party-Political Center of Gravity, 1957–2003*, Discussion Paper 04/6, Max Planck Institute for the Studies of Societies, Cologne.

Marks, G. (2004) 'Conclusion: European integration and political conflict', in G. Marks and M.R. Steenbergen (eds), *European Integration and Political Conflict*, Cambridge: Cambridge University Press, pp. 235–59.

Mau, S. (2003) 'Wohlfahrtspolitischer Verantwortungtransfer nach Europa? Präferenzstrukturen und ihre Determinanten in europäischen Ländern', *Zeitschrift für Soziologie* 32(4): 302–24.

Mosher, J.S. and Trubek, D. (2003) 'Alternative approaches to governance in the EU: EU social policy and the European Employment Strategy', *Journal of Common Market Studies* 41(1): 63–88.

Oates, W.E. (1999) 'An essay on fiscal federalism', *Journal of Economic Literature* 37(3): 1120–49.

Obinger, H., Leibfried, S. and Castles, F.G. (eds) (2005) *Federalism and the Welfare State. New World and European Experiences*, Cambridge: Cambridge University Press.

OECD (2002) *Social Expenditure Database*, CD-ROM. Paris.

Pierson, P. (1995) 'Fragmented welfare states: federal institutions and the development of social policy', *Governance* 8(4): 449–78.

Pierson, P. (2004) *Politics in Time. History, Institutions, and Social Analysis*, Princeton, NJ: Princeton University Press.

Proudhon, P.-J. (1863) *Du principe fédératif et la nécessité de reconstituer le parti de la revolution*, Paris: Dentu.

Radaelli, C.M. (2003) *The Open Method of Coordination: A New Governance Architecture for the European Union?*, Swedish Institute for European Policy Studies, Rapport nr. 1, March 2003.

Ravishankar, N. (2004) 'Decentralization and the welfare state', Unpublished manuscript, Department of Government, Harvard University, 11 October 2004.

Rodden, J. (2003) 'Reviving Leviathan: fiscal federalism and the growth of government', *International Organization* 57(4): 695–729.

Scharpf, F.W. (1988) 'The joint-decision trap: lessons from German federalism and European integration', *Public Administration* 66(3): 239–78 (first published 1985).

Scharpf, F.W. (1997) *Games Real Actors Play. Actor-Centered Institutionalism in Policy Research*, Boulder, CO: Westview Press.

Scharpf, F.W. (1999) *Governing in Europe. Effective and Democratic?*, Oxford: Oxford University Press.

Scharpf, F.W. (2002) 'The European social model: coping with the challenges of diversity', *Journal of Common Market Studies* 40(2): 645–70.

Schmidt, M.G. (1997) 'Determinants of social expenditure in liberal democracies: the post World War II experience', *Acta Politica* 32(2): 153–73.

Swank, D.H. (2002) *Global Capital, Political Institutions, and Policy Change in Developed Welfare States*, Cambridge, UK: Cambridge University Press.

Tiebout, C.M. (1956) 'A pure theory of local expenditures', *Journal of Political Economy* 65(5): 416–24.

Tsebelis, G. (2002) *Veto Players. How Political Institutions Work*, Princeton, NJ: Princeton University Press.

Wilensky, H.L. (1975) *The Welfare State and Equality. Structural and Ideological Roots of Public Expenditures*, Berkeley/Los Angeles: University of California Press.

# Towards a stable *finalité* with federal features? The balancing acts of the Constitutional Treaty for Europe[1]

Andreas Follesdal

## INTRODUCTION

The 'institutional balance' of the European Union has been a recurrent concern among politicians and scholars.[2] The federal features of the Constitutional Treaty for Europe (CTE) add to the challenges of balancing, but may also contribute to their resolution.

The Union must achieve and maintain four quite different forms of balancing or stability:

- between the member states and the Union institutions;
- among Union institutions;
- among member states *within* Union institutions;
- institutions must also foster citizens' and officials' 'dual loyalty' toward their own member state and to the union as a whole.

These balances must themselves be 'balanced' against each other, without loss of problem-solving capacity.

The federal features of the CTE also increase the salience of insights and solutions familiar from the political theory of federalism. This old tradition has much to contribute, even though it has received less recent attention than theories of justice for unitary states. For instance, in the liberal, Kantian tradition, John Rawls addressed 'sovereign states with central administration'. Jürgen Habermas's contributions understandably focus on the preconditions and possibilities of a common European public sphere and political culture, rather than on the future political role of member states and their governments in an EU with federal features.[3] The federal tradition addresses several of the challenges of stability which the EU must address.

I shall argue that the CTE improves several of the four forms of stability in a legitimate manner. In particular, it bolsters institutional mechanisms that merit and facilitate trust and trustworthiness in institutions and in fellow citizens. This is crucial to citizens' long-term support for any political order, and for authorities' ability to govern. The challenges are even greater in federal arrangements in 'plural societies', characterized by population groups 'sharply divided along religious, ideological, linguistic, cultural, ethnic, or racial lines into virtually separate subsocieties' (Lijphart 1999: 32, 195).

The collapse of the 'permissive consensus' toward further European integration may reflect precisely this challenge.[4] Examples of trust-building features of the EU include interlocking federal arrangements, more visible human rights obligations, and added scope for contestation among political parties, aided by increased transparency. These measures may foster preference formation toward an 'overarching loyalty' among all Europeans – which may be worth some apparent efficiency losses, or so I shall argue.[5]

Section 1 highlights some relevant elements from federal thought. Section 2 explores the need for a trustworthy political order that promotes compliance by resolving problems of assurance. The next sections address aspects of the CTE's contribution to the four forms of balance.

## 1. FEDERALISM

For our purposes, a federation is a political order where competences are constitutionally split between sub-units and central authorities.[6] The CTE enhances these features of the EU. The treaty specifies more carefully the exclusive competences of the Union institutions and of member states. The EU also has features at variance with a 'confederation' in the standard senses. Central legislation has *direct effect*, so the Union's subjects are not only member states but also citizens.[7] Decisions by *qualified majority voting* (QMV) in central bodies can be binding over the objections and votes of some member states.

This does not mean that the EU's *finalité* is or should be a centralized federation, nor that its confederal elements will or should wither away. Many competences remain shared between sub-units and central authorities, and the

EU remains decentralized, and should perhaps remain so.[8] The federal features will coexist with several confederal elements for the foreseeable future (Meehan 2001): treaty changes must still be unanimous (Art IV-443), and the CTE confirms states' right to withdraw (Art I-60).

The federal features of the European political order mean that at least four 'balances' must be achieved and maintained. Each raises important normative issues, as does the second-order balancing between them.

### Between the member states and the Union institutions

Central to federations is the split of authority between sub-units and central authorities. The distribution and redistribution of competences is likely to remain a contested issue where normative arguments are commonplace. James Madison eloquently observed about the US Constitution: 'The federal and state governments are in fact but different agents and trustees of the people, constituted with different powers, and designed for different purposes' (Madison 1961). Madison's plausible normative description has important implications for framing the debates. In particular, when EU member states refuse to pool sovereignty, or when they vote against Commission proposals, critics cannot plausibly use this as the sole basis to accuse them of 'egoism' in pursuit of their 'national interests'. The question is rather whether common or member state action in one particular issue-area best secures and promotes the important interests of individual Europeans. Arenas and institutions must facilitate deliberations and negotiations on how member states and Union institutions, acting separately and jointly, best pursue and protect these interests (McKay 2005).

### Among Union institutions

The second form of balance concerns how to allocate and exercise powers and checks among Union institutions, including the powers of member state representatives to nominate and select office holders. This institutional balance is familiar to scholars of federalism and harkenss back to the ratification debates of the US Constitution. The challenge was clearly stated regarding the EU: 'the treaties set up a system for the distribution of powers among the different European Community institutions, assigning to each institution its own role. Observance of institutional balance means that each of the institutions must exercise its powers with due regard for the powers of the other institutions.'[9]

### Among member states within the Union institutions

The third need for balance occurs when federal political orders have sub-units with different population size. Small populations typically enjoy more powers than warranted by the principle of 'one person one vote' when sovereign states bargain to become a 'coming together' federation (Stepan 1999). Small units want overrepresentation in common decisions to avoid domination by more populous sub-units. In hindsight such safeguards are often challenged on empirical or normative grounds (Dahl 2001). Lines of political contestation may seldom follow territorial borders. Ideals of political equality may come to replace mistrust. The CTE reflects this bias in two ways. Unanimity continues to be required for future revisions of the Constitutional Treaty (Art IV-443). Qualified majority is defined by the CTE so as to favour small member states. Several governments objected to the formula, both during the Convention and afterwards (Art I-24).

## Fostering dual assurance and loyalty

Scholars at least since James Madison insist that federal institutions must address the peculiar assurance problems among sub-units and citizens in these circumstances of complex mutual dependence.[10] If mutually beneficial and just arrangements are not to unravel, citizens and officials must have the 'confidence of the future regularity of their conduct'.[11] Union citizens and officials must create and maintain political loyalty to the complex regime. They must be officials and citizens *both* of their own member state and of the EU at large.[12] The task is certainly not to create 'post-national' citizens without particularist ties or special duties to compatriots, but rather to fashion institutions that maintain dual loyalties.

Such trustworthiness is especially hard in federations, for at least two reasons. They tend to have a higher level of ongoing *constitutional contestation* than unitary states concerning the interpretation of the constitution, its objectives, and the allocation and reallocation of competences (Linz 1999). Yet citizens' mutual trust and support for the polity are weaker in many federations than in unitary states. After all, politicians often created federal arrangements explicitly to accommodate territorially based cultural or economic tensions.

Federal institutions have sometimes emerged explicitly to reduce mistrust among 'contingent compliers', who will not comply in fair arrangements unless assured that others do likewise. Institutions play crucial roles to create and maintain this form of self-sustaining stability (Filippov *et al.* 2004).

## 2. TRUST AMONG CONTINGENT COMPLIERS

With increased interdependence, the need for trust and trustworthiness increases among Europeans. Consider the shift to QMV, wrought by a shared sense that too many veto points had proved collectively irrational. Under QMV governments can no longer protect their citizens against disadvantageous arrangements. Stable popular support for QMV requires well-developed trust among Europeans and their officials (Nicolaidis 2001). Politicians and their voters must adjust or even sacrifice for the sake of other Europeans, while trusting others to do likewise. No wonder that QMV does not apply in areas where national differences and identity seem at stake.

A central challenge is what we now label the assurance problem among contingent compliers. Arguing for federal solutions rather than confederal arrangements, James Madison noted that

> a distrust of the voluntary compliance of each other may prevent the compliance of any, although it should be the latent disposition of all . . . If the laws of the States were merely recommendatory to their citizens, or if they were to be rejudged by County authorities, what security, what probability would exist, that they would be carried into execution?
>
> Madison (1787)

A contingent complier[13] decides to co-operate with government demands because she

(a) perceives government as trustworthy in making and enforcing normatively legitimate policies; and
(b) she has confidence in other citizens, that they do their part.

To illustrate, one motivation may be what John Rawls called a *duty of justice*,[14] a commitment

> that they will comply with fair practices that exist and apply to them when they believe that the relevant others likewise do their part; and to further just arrangements not yet established, at least when this can be done without too much cost to ourselves.

Compliance among contingent compliers raises challenges of assurance long recognized by political theorists, now informed by game theory.[15] Institutions can provide crucial assurance through positive laws, transparency, shared practices, and socialization.[16] Institutions thereby reduce the risks or suspicion of others' defection, and socialize citizens to certain preferences. The CTE provides several institutional mechanisms that should promote trustworthiness among such contingent compliers.

Consider the conditions for when I will comply with rules, institutions and officials' decisions:

*(a) I must believe that they are normatively legitimate*
In situations of doubt this requires public knowledge of several kinds:

1 of a plausible *public political theory* regarding democracy, solidarity, and the other objectives of the political order. The European political order seems to lack this, as evidenced by the heated debates in the Convention on the Future of Europe on the grounds, objectives and means of the EU (Olsen 2004).
2 that the institutions are *simple and transparent* so that citizens can comprehend and assess them. Public media may assist citizens and authorities to determine sufficient match between institutions and decisions and such normative requirements. Federations are more difficult to assess because of the complexity of constitutional rules that establish, check, divide and disperse

authority. The CTE improves the situation: it simplifies the institutions and processes, and provides public access to legislative processes in the Council of Ministers and elsewhere – possibly with some efficiency loss (Naurin 2004).

3 a general, public knowledge that institutions are sufficiently *effective* and *efficient*: when generally complied with, they actually achieve their objectives without much waste. The CTE may contribute to such knowledge since it increases transparency, the salience of human rights and the domain of majority rule. Yet it is insufficient. Whether the efficiency gains are an overall improvement depends on a normative assessment of the objectives of the Union. But the wide-ranging objectives of Art. I-3 are vague and unranked. Free and undistorted competition, full employment, social inclusion and solidarity between generations and member states must be specified and weighed, and the roles of the EU and of member states in these aspects must be resolved. Democracies address these vexing challenges by deliberation and decision by accountable politicians, but the EU has yet to develop these mechanisms.

*(b) I believe that most other actors will comply*
In addition to the belief that the system is normatively legitimate, contingent compliers must also believe that other citizens and officials comply with the practices.

## The contributions of institutions: pay-offs and preference formation

Institutions create and maintain such confidence in the compliance of others in at least three interacting ways.

They can monitor compliance, or provide transparency and access to information for monitoring agents such as the media and the political opposition.[17] The CTE facilitates monitoring: it increases opportunities for public scrutiny and political contestation at European and national levels, for both member state governments and national parliaments (e.g. Art. I-50, Art. III-163).

Institutions can also affect agents' pay-offs by adjusting sanctions and rewards (cf. Papadopoulos 2005). Trustworthy centralized sanctioning authority can boost trust in general compliance.[18] An authority can even establish sanctions to enhance its own trustworthiness, to convince citizens that its self-interested option also provides collective benefits (Levi 1998b). This may explain why political élites have sought to democratize EU institutions. The CTE adjusts such pay-offs when it increases the powers of the European Parliament, highlights human rights, and increases transparency of the legislative process. A trustworthy European Court of Justice seems essential for the trustworthiness of other authorities, to reduce suspicion that powerful states do as they will while weak member states do as they must. Two important test cases were the 'Reactions against Austria' when the Freedom Party was put in government. Some thought the protests exposed the vulnerability of smaller member states. Such suspicions are at stake in EU treatment of the German and French unilateral rejections of the Stability and Growth Pact (McKay 2005). The CTE could have further reduced fears of others' non-compliance, by taking over implementation and enforcement of Union decisions which largely remain member state responsibility.

To modify pay-offs by sanctions is insufficient to secure long-term stable support. Institutions may also *socialize* citizens, 'transform obedience into duty' – for instance, into a sense of justice.[19] To trust a majoritarian system, the minority must be assured that the majority will consider their plight.[20] Authors differ in their views about the necessity of such socialization – whether incentives for self-interested actors are likely to engender sufficient trustworthiness that citizens generally comply with legitimate rules. Institutions may facilitate endogenous preference formation in the public political forum (Rawls 1999: 134) and the broader public sphere (Habermas 1994). The CTE enhances such mechanisms by increasing the scope and arenas of political contestation at the Union and national levels.

## 3. BALANCE BETWEEN MEMBER STATES AND UNION INSTITUTIONS

All federations suffer pressures toward centralization and decentralization.[21] These drifts must be checked whilst securing effectiveness, efficiency, and flexible reassigned competences.

The CTE allocates competences in different forms – exclusive, shared, complementary or with Union co-ordination – leaving the authority distribution clearer but not lucid (Christin *et al.* 2005). These measures may reduce unintended drifts. Yet this fixed distribution of competences requires a strong judiciary, possibly at odds with norms of accountability. On the other hand, centralization is more likely if competences are not constitutionally embedded in a competence catalogue but can be reassigned democratically.[22] This is a risk with a stronger European Parliament. There still remain two ways to stem centralization: to leave the burden of argument with those who wish to centralize in the form of a principle of subsidiarity variously specified;[23] or to give member states permanent powers to check Union authorities. The CTE pursues both of these options, and grants democratic legitimacy for competing views on the issues (von Beyme 2005).

Other institutionalized 'centrifugal' forces may also prevent a transformation into a 'post-national' political order with no constitutional role for sub-units.[24] The CTE provides the member states with several such mechanisms. In particular, treaty changes must be unanimous. Some might cite this and the explicit right to secede as evidence that the constitutionalization process came too early, before sufficient trust had emerged. The European Council remains powerful. Its power to nominate the Commission President for European Parliament approval will check the European Parliament's inclination to centralize. Thirdly, the CTE grants national parliaments access and power to appeal legislative proposals and suggested Treaty reforms (Art. I-18(2), Art. IV-443,

Protocols 1 and 2). National parliaments shall monitor the application of subsidiarity and may give 'yellow cards' for suspected violations (Protocol 2). This mechanism has two important limitations. It only concerns shared competences, not the exclusive competence of the Union (Art. I-11(3)). And the appeals only go to the legislative institutions rather than to the European Court of Justice – whose willingness to prevent centralization has been doubted.[25]

## 4. BALANCE AMONG UNION INSTITUTIONS

The second form of balancing concerns the allocation of powers and immunities among central institutions. The CTE acknowledges the need to 'enhance the role of each of the Union's three institutions' (Preamble). This configuration of authority requires careful craftsmanship. The framework must be 'demos-constraining' so as to prevent usurpation and abuse of power and domination.[26] Yet it must also be 'demos-enabling' to achieve its legitimate objectives.[27] These important issues of balance among Union institutions must be settled partly based on a normatively acceptable account of the objectives of the Union. The proper roles of the Commission and of political parties in furthering 'the European interest' illustrate the challenges.

### The case of the Commission and political contestation

The Commission has near monopoly on legislative proposals, presumably owing to its mandate to 'promote the general European interest and take appropriate initiatives to that end' (Art. I-26).

The CTE holds that the European Parliament must endorse the European Council's proposed Commission President, who will in turn formulate and pursue 'the European interest'. Some worry that this form of parliamentarism *politicizes* the Commission. Its credibility is at stake.[28] What are we to make of such worries?

The CTE skirts crucial issues. Union institutions shall 'serve its interests, those of its citizens and those of the Member States' (Art. I-19); many of the Commission's initiatives in the 'European interest' enjoy legal supremacy: they override Member State legislation in furtherance of the 'national interest'. Yet it is not obvious that the Commission's sense of European interest should always have such a priority.

Some Union regulations concern the need for *concerted action*, for reasons of scale, such as the need to have a unified voice as a world actor in global regime building. These gains may surely sometimes be less important than gains wrought by national policies, in which case the Union should respect national preferences. Other Union policies may be required to avoid co-operation traps such as prisoners' dilemmas. These *collective action preferences* should surely trump the 'egoistic' member state preferences – but it is not obvious that the Union institutions are best situated to discern when they should override national decisions for the sake of 'the European interest'.

Moreover, the CTE does not detail the nature of this political project. Art. I-3 provides a list of laudable objectives: peace, the well-being of its peoples, freedom, security, a single market, sustainable development, a social market economy, aimed at full employment, combating social exclusion, promoting solidarity and respecting cultural diversity, contributing to international free and fair trade, and so on.[29]

The all-important details, weights and limits remain obscure, and are contested among parties and ideologies within member states, in the Council of Ministers and in the European Parliament. Moreover, the appropriate weighting is likely to differ among member states, as well as between these sub-units and the Commission institutions.

Yet Art. I-26 lays down that 'The European Commission shall promote the general European interest and take appropriate initiatives to that end.' How should the Commission handle disagreements? The White Paper on Governance assumed that disagreements were due to the sectoral interests inappropriately pursued by the Council of Ministers (p. 30). Inappropriate deadlocks over treaty reforms may also occur if citizens can use referendums to protest against other domestic policies (Trechsel 2005). However, other reasons for deadlock may be far more legitimate; for instance, if citizens of one member state have very much at stake. There seems no reason to assume that the Commission is best suited to make these judgements. National protests and appeals to national interest, e.g. in legally binding national referendums, cannot always be regarded as illegitimate. Procedures should therefore not always allow an uncontested conception of 'the European interest' to overrule such protests. That the Commission becomes 'politicized' to reflect such contested views does not seem to threaten its credibility. To the contrary, such contestation seems crucial to maintain its trustworthiness. Consider the European Parliament's rejection of Barroso's first slate of Commissioners. The political contestation showed that the rules provide a degree of responsiveness to elected representatives, and did not tarnish but bolstered the institution of the Commission.

This event showed some of the roles of political parties and of human rights standards. They are important agents for citizens' preference formation, especially to promote other-regarding perspectives and consistency. Political contestation increases the political salience of issues; the parties create policy platforms, specify policy objectives, make complex policy trade-offs, and scrutinize competitors' attempts at these tasks (Linz 1999). In particular, federation-wide political parties seem crucial to develop cross-border concern and respect when they co-operate and compete within sub-units and in central institutions. Referendums and other instruments of direct democracy also enhance broader support and a common identity, even when they also create conflict (Papadopoulos 2005).

Parties do not currently serve these functions in the EU institutions. But the CTE acknowledges political parties (Art. I-46(4)), increases transparency about the legislative process (Art. I-50), and increases European Parliament powers

(Art. I-20). The result may well be that elections to the EP stop being 'second order' and become contested among European-level parties.[30]

Optimists may hope that the institutional changes will stimulate parties to further shape Europeans' political preferences toward the requisite overarching loyalty over time. This is more likely to occur under the interlocking arrangements of the EU, where national institutions take part in Union governance.[31] The CTE also promotes public negotiations and preference modification by requiring public proceedings and copies of legislative proposals and Commission consultation documents.[32] Transparency is not always as beneficial as proponents claim: it may reduce the quality of agreements and hinder fair outcomes (Naurin 2004). However, public reasoning about common interests is important for preference formation in the general public. And transparency seems necessary for trustworthy institutions, since it facilitates accountability of politicians. Such long-term benefits in trustworthiness seem worth the possible costs in effectiveness and efficiency.

Pessimists will suspect that EU lack of taxing and spending powers will limit public interest, and that the confederal style of European parties reduces their integrative role.[33] The upshot here is that the proper balance among Union institutions also requires great attention to the roles both of member states and of political parties. 'The European interest' is contested, especially in so far as it overrides all other legitimate political objectives in a political order with federal features. Political contestation is crucial in order to address these topics in ways that maintain trust.

## 5. BALANCE AMONG MEMBER STATES: VOTING WEIGHTS

EU member states with small populations enjoy powers beyond what the principle of 'one person one vote' seems to warrant. This conflict between the ideals of equality of states and of persons is not only one of theoretical relevance, but also a source of political conflict. Overrepresentation of small states is a typical concession when they join a 'coming-together' federation among sovereign states (Stepan 1999). Yet these concessions are often questioned by citizens of populous sub-units when the federations come of age (Pinder 1993: 101). The EU is no exception. Indeed, the skewed voting weights caused the CTE to fail at the Intergovernmental Conference (IGC), where the populous countries Spain and Poland objected to the distribution of votes.

Whether overrepresentation of small states can be defended remains contested in normative political theory. Some arguments appear to be based on 'communitarian' normative theories that take communities rather than individuals as their fundamental objects of concern. This fits poorly with liberal egalitarian thought, which holds that it is only the interests of individuals that should be of ultimate and equal concern.

Other defences of disproportionate voting say that majority rule is inappropriate for populations divided along cultural, ethnic or other deep cleavages. In these societies individuals of large and small groups face different risks of being in the minority.[34] Skewed voting weight may be important to secure equal non-interference, non-domination, enhanced capability sets or a combination of these (Dobson 2004). Overrepresentation of small states in coming-together federations may also be justified based on citizens' interests in fulfilling their established, legitimate expectations, which requires representation in common decision-making bodies.[35]

To conclude, it seems premature to criticize Spain and Poland for their refusal to back down from the voting weight agreement of the Treaty of Nice which granted them 'disproportionate' voting weight. 'Proportional' voting is not simply a matter of finding the obvious mathematical solution, but a choice among mathematical formulae from normative premises addressing issues such as trust and risks. For instance, what matters for individuals may be a weighing of the opportunity to be part of a 'winning' coalition, against the opportunity to be part of a 'blocking' coalition to prevent severe harm. A decision rule may therefore seek to combine the two, and, for instance, equalize citizens' net opportunity expressed as the probability of ending up in a winning coalition minus the (weighted) probability of ending up in a losing coalition.[36] This explication of 'proportional' voting weight should underscore the need for careful normative reflection concerning the objectives of democratic decision-making and institutions' roles in facilitating sufficient trust among citizens marked by different cleavages and institutional bonds.

## CONCLUSION

The federal tradition of political thought sheds some light on the various challenges of balance and stability needed in a stable and legitimate EU, and the solutions offered by the CTE. Many of the changes in the CTE improve the present balances between the member states and the Union institutions, among the Union institutions, and among member states within the Union institutions. The document confirms and strengthens four mechanisms and opportunity structures that may build support for the institutions and facilitate trust and trustworthiness among Europeans: the increased visibility of human rights, the role of national parliaments, European Parliament control over the Commission, and political parties. All of these will operate under greater transparency. The gains in trust and trustworthiness may be worth some apparent efficiency losses in promotion of 'the European interest', for several reasons. 'The European interest' is contested and can most legitimately be tracked, specified and pursued by democratically accountable officials against a background of political and public scrutiny. Effectiveness and efficiency can only be assessed according to specified objectives that are complex mixes of legitimate 'European' as well as 'national' interests. Furthermore, these mechanisms foster a reliable pursuit of these objectives, and a general trust in officials in this regard.

The challenge of creeping centralization could have been addressed even more fully if national parliaments were given broader and stronger power to halt what they would regard as Union violations of the principle of subsidiarity.

This could hamper the Union's ability to reach optimal common decisions, and such arrangements could fuel undue decentralization. But we must remember that blocking certain common decisions need not be ineffective. Appeals to 'national interests' may be normatively legitimate, and they should not always be overruled by 'the European interest'.

The CTE changes the balance among Union institutions, partly by the method for selecting the Commission President. The greater role of the European Parliament enhances the opportunities for political contestation. Such parliamentarism threatens the conception of the Commission as an unbiased and effective guarantor of an uncontroversial 'European interest', but I have argued that this conception is flawed and unlikely to engender the requisite trust.

The balance among member states within Union institutions raises unresolved fundamental normative issues concerning the best distribution of voting weights on which issues. The IGC made clear that the CTE did not succeed in bringing closure to this important topic. Some progress toward reasoned agreement may be gained by considering the reasons for the various interests at stake – non-interference, non-domination or enhanced capability sets.

The CTE also confirms and strengthens several mechanisms that may induce citizens' willing compliance and support for the institutions. These mechanisms include the somewhat public nature of the Convention debates themselves and their aftermath, 'interlocking' federal arrangements, more salient human rights standards, and the increased opportunities for contestation among political parties of issues concerning European level policies.

All in all, these changes indicate that the CTE goes some way toward creating a federal European political order more likely to facilitate trust and trustworthiness among Europeans with a sense of justice. This is good news for contingent compliers prepared to comply with institutions that are normatively and socially legitimate. Importantly, the federal tradition of political thought also suggests that such a revised European political order may also merit such increased trust.

**Address for correspondence:** Andreas Follesdal, Norwegian Centre for Human Rights, University of Oslo, PO Box 6706, St Olavs plass, N-0130 Oslo, Norway. email: andreas.follesdal@nchr.uio.no

## NOTES

1 This research was funded by the University of Oslo and the Fulbright 'New Century Scholar' Program 2003. I am particularly grateful for constructive comments at the Federal Trust, 16 December 2003, and from Erin Delaney, Mel Marquis, Tore Olsen, Jo Shaw, Alexander Trechsel and Anna Verges.
2 Nentwich and Falkner 1997; Sbragia and Cram 2002.
3 Rawls 1993: xxii; Habermas 1998 [1995]; Habermas 1992.
4 Easton 1965: 161; Lindberg and Scheingold 1970.

5 These contributions of the CTE add to any legitimizing impact of the Convention on the Future of Europe itself (cf. Dobson and Follesdal 2004; Olsen 2004; Follesdal 2005; Shaw 2003).

6 This is not the only useful definition. Cf. others, who seem to regard federal structures as fully centralized (Moravcsik 1998: 6). This definition allows that sub-unit governments participate in central institutions (*pace* King 1982). See McKay 2005; Auer 2005; Sbragia 1992; Follesdal 2003.

7 *Van Gend en Loos* v. *Nederlandse administratie*, Case 26/62 [1963] ECR 1. Cf. Weiler 1996. Hamilton and J.S. Mill regarded this as incompatible with confederations (Hamilton 1961; Mill 1958 [1861]).

8 Auer 2005; Schmitter 2004; Moravcsik 2001.

9 Case 70/88 *Parliament* v. *Council* [1990] ECR I-2041 ('Chernobyl'). I owe this reference to Smismans 2004.

10 Madison 1787.

11 Hume 1960 [1739]: 490.

12 McKay 2005; Follesdal 2001. Cf. the related study by Filippov *et al.* 2004 on 'self-enforcing' federal institutions.

13 I here modify Margaret Levi's model of 'conditional consent' (Levi 1998a: ch. 2).

14 Rawls 1971: 336 and cf. Scanlon 1998: 339.

15 Before Madison, Rousseau 1978 [1762]: 2.4.5.

16 Sen 1967; Taylor 1987; Elster 1989: 187; Ostrom 1991; Scharpf 1997; Rothstein 1998; Levi 1998a. Recent normative contributions addressing the standards of normative legitimacy on the explicit assumption of such conditional compliance include Rawls 1971; Thompson and Gutmann 1996; 72–3; Miller 2000.

17 Dehousse 1999: Héritier 1999.

18 Cf. Mendez 2005 on the weak federal powers in Switzerland.

19 Rousseau 1978 [1762]: Book 1, ch 3; cf. Rothstein 1998; Rawls 1971; Bellamy and Warleigh 1999, etc.

20 On conditions for expecting minorities to obey, cf. Papadopoulos 2005.

21 Weiler 1999: 318; Dehousse 1994; Tushnet 1996; Donahue and Pollock 2001; McKay 2004; Filippov *et al.* 2004; McKay 2005; Mendez 2005.

22 Swenden 2004; Trechsel 2005.

23 On theories of subsidiarity, cf. Follesdal 1998b.

24 Nicolaidis 2001; Craig 2003.

25 Weiler 1999: 318. The annulment of the Tobacco Advertising Directive in 2000 reduced the suspicion of Community competence expansion (Follesdal 2003b). Case C-376/98 *Germany* v. *Parliament and Council* and C-74/94 *R* v. *Secretary of State for Health, ex parte Imperial Tobacco Ltd and Others* [2000] ECR I-8419. I am grateful to Agustin José Menéndez for this reference.

26 Stepan 1999; Pettit 1997; Bellamy 1999.

27 The legitimacy of institutionalized vetoes or checks on majorities is contested: some are sceptical (Goodin 1996; Waldron 2000; Cohen 1997: 79), others hold it to be an open question, partly for reasons of balance, trust and trustworthiness (Scharpf 1999: 20–2; Shapiro 1996: 231; v. Sunstein 2001: 9). Others argue that non-elected or non-majoritarian institutions best secure the legitimate interests of citizens (Majone 1998; Moravcsik 2002).

28 Majone 2001: 261–2; Craig 2003: 3; Follesdal and Hix 2005.

29 The White Paper on Governance (European Commission 2001) contains a similar list, p. 28, and suffers from the same lack of precision – cf. Follesdal 2003b.

30 Reif and Schmitt 1980; Hix 1999; Hix and Lord 1997; Magnette 2001; McKay 2001.

31 McKay 2000; Simeon and Conway 2001; McKay 2004.

32 Art. 50, Protocols 1 and 2.

33 Thorlakson 2005.

34  Barry 1991; Follesdal 1998a; Lijphart 1999; McKay 2001: 146–7.
35  Follesdal 1997.
36  On this measure and its relation to Banzhaf's Power Index, cf. Midgaard 1998.

## REFERENCES

Auer, A. (2005) 'The constitutional scheme of federalism', *Journal of European Public Policy* 12(3): 419–431.

Barry, B. (1991) 'Is democracy special?', *Democracy and Power*, Oxford: Oxford University Press, pp. 24–60.

Bellamy, R. (1999) *Liberalism and Pluralism*, London: Routledge.

Bellamy, R. and Warleigh, A. (1999) 'From an ethics of integration to an ethics of participation: citizenship and the future of the European Union', *Millennium: Journal of International Studies* 27(3): 447–70.

von Beyme, K. (2005) 'Asymmetric federalism between globalization and regionalization', *Journal of European Public Policy* 12(3): 432–447.

Christin, T., Hug, S. and Schulz, T. (2005) 'Federalism in the European Union: the view from below (if there is such a thing)', *Journal of European Public Policy* 12(3): 488–508.

Cohen, J. (1997) 'Deliberation and democratic legitimacy', in J. Boham and W. Rehg (eds), *Deliberative Democracy: Essays on Reason and Politics*, Cambridge, MA: MIT Press, pp. 67–91.

Craig, P. (2003) 'What constitution does Europe need? The house that Giscard built: constitutional rooms with a view', The Federal Trust. http://www.fedtrust.co.uk/uploads/constitution/26_03.pdf.

Dahl, R.A. (2001) *How Democratic is the American Constitution?*, New Haven: Yale University Press.

Dehousse, R. (ed.) (1994) *Europe After Maastricht: An Ever Closer Union?*, Munchen: Law Books in Europe.

Dehousse, R. (1999) 'Towards a regulation of transitional governance? Citizens' rights and the reform of comitology procedures', in C. Joerges and E. Vos (eds), *EU Committees: Social Regulation, Law and Politics*, Oxford: Hart, pp. 109–27.

Dobson, L. (2004) 'Conceptions of freedom and the European Constitution', in L. Dobson and A. Follesdal (eds), *Political Theory and the European Constitution*, London: Routledge.

Dobson, L. and Follesdal, A. (eds) (2004) *Political Theory and the European Constitution*, London: Routledge.

Donahue, J.D. and Pollock, M.A. (2001) 'Centralization and its discontents: the rhythms of federalism in the United States and the European Union', in K. Nicolaidis and R. Howse (eds), *The Federal Vision: Legitimacy and Levels of Governance in the United States and the European Union*, Oxford: Oxford University Press, pp. 73–118.

Easton, D. (1965) *A Systems Analysis of Political Life*, New York: Wiley.

Elster, J. (1989) *The Cement of Society*, Studies in Rationality and Social Change, Cambridge: Cambridge University Press.

European Commission (2001) [25.7.2001] *European Governance: A White Paper*. Com (2001) 428. Brussels.

Filippov, M., Ordeshook, P.C. and Shvetsova, O. (2004) *Designing Federalism: A Theory of Self-sustainable Federal Institutions*, Cambridge: Cambridge University Press.

Follesdal, A. (1997) 'Democracy and federalism in the EU: a liberal contractualist perspective', in A. Follesdal and P. Koslowski (eds), *Democracy and the European*

*Union: Studies in Economic Ethics and Philosophy,* ARENA Reprint 98/9, Berlin: Springer, pp. 231–53.

Follesdal, A. (1998a) 'Democracy, legitimacy and majority rule in the EU', in A. Weale and M. Nentwich (eds), *Political Theory and the European Union: Legitimacy, Constitutional Choice and Citizenship,* London: Routledge, pp. 34–48.

Follesdal, A. (1998b) 'Subsidiarity', *Journal of Political Philosophy* 6(2): 231–59.

Follesdal, A. (2001) 'Union citizenship: unpacking the beast of burden', *Law and Philosophy* 20(3): 313–43.

Follesdal, A. (2003a) 'Federalism'. Edward N. Zalta Stanford Encyclopedia of Philosophy. http://plato.stanford.edu/entries/federalism/.

Follesdal, A. (2003b) 'The political theory of the White Paper on Governance: hidden and fascinating'. *European Public Law* 9(1): 73–86.

Follesdal, A. (2005) 'Looking for deliberative democracy', *Acta Politica – Special Issue on Empirical Approaches to Deliberative Politics.* Forthcoming.

Follesdal, A. and Hix, S. (2005) 'Why there is a democratic deficit in the EU: a response to Majone and Moravcsik', *European Governance Papers (EUROGOV) No. C-05-02.* http://www.connex-network.org/eurogov/pdf/egp-connex-C-05-02.pdf.

Goodin, R.E. (1996) 'Institutionalizing the public interest: the defense of deadlock and beyond', *American Political Science Review* 90(2): 331–43.

Habermas, J. (1992) 'Citizenship and national identity: some reflections on the future of Europe', *Praxis International* 12(1): 1–19.

Habermas, J. (1994) 'Further reflections on the public sphere', in C. Calhoun (ed.), *Habermas and the Public Sphere,* Cambridge, MA: MIT Press, pp. 421–61.

Habermas, J. (1998) [1995] 'Does Europe need a constitution? Remarks on Dieter Grimm', *The Inclusion of the Other: Studies in Political Theory.* First printed as 'Remarks on Dieter Grimm's "Does Europe need a constitution?"', *European Law Journal* 1995 (1): 303–7, Cambridge, MA: MIT Press.

Hamilton, A. (1961) 'The Federalist No. 23', New York: Mentor.

Héritier, A. (1999) 'Elements of democratic legitimation in Europe: an alternative perspective', *Journal of European Public Policy* 6(2): 269–82.

Hix, S. (1999) *The Political System of the European Union,* London: Macmillan.

Hix, S. and Lord, C. (1997) *Political Parties in the European Union,* London: Macmillan.

Hume, D. (1960) [1739] *A Treatise of Human Nature,* L.A. Selby-Bigge and P.H. Nidditch (eds), Oxford: Clarendon.

King, P. (1982) *Federalism and Federation,* Baltimore: Johns Hopkins/London: Croom Helm.

Levi, M. (1998a) *Consent, Dissent and Patriotism,* New York: Cambridge University Press.

Levi, M. (1998b) 'A state of trust', in V. Braithwaite and M. Levi (eds), *Trust and Governance,* New York: Russell Sage.

Lijphart, A. (1999) *Patterns of Democracy: Government Forms and Performance in Thirty-Six Countries,* New Haven: Yale University Press.

Lindberg, L.N. and Scheingold, S.A. (1970) *Europe's Would-Be Polity: Patterns of Change in the European Community,* Englewood Cliffs, NJ: Prentice-Hall.

Linz, J.J. (1999) 'Democracy, multinationalism and federalism'. in W. Busch and A. Merkel (eds), *Demokratie in Ost Und West,* Frankfurt am Main: Suhrkamp, pp. 382–401.

Madison, J. (1787) 'Vices of the political system of the United States', *The Papers of James Madison,* Chicago, pp. 348–57.

Madison, J. (1961) 'The Federalist No. 46.' New York: Mentor.

Magnette, P. (2001) 'European governance and civic participation: can the European Union be politicised?', in C. Joerges, Y. Mény and J.H.H. Weiler (eds), *Symposium: Responses to the European Commission's White Paper on Governance,* Florence:

European University Institute. http://www.iue.it/RSCAS/Research/OnlineSymposia/Magnette.pdf.

Majone, G. (1998) 'Europe's "democratic deficit": the question of standards', *European Law Journal* 4(1): 5–28.

Majone, G. (2001) 'Regulatory legitimacy in the United States and the European Union', in K. Nicolaidis and R. Howse (eds), *The Federal Vision: Legitimacy and Levels of Governance in the United States and the European Union*, Oxford: Oxford University Press, pp. 252–74.

McKay, D. (2000) 'Policy legitimacy and institutional design: comparative lessons for the European Union', *Journal of Common Market Studies* 38: 25–44.

McKay, D. (2001) *Designing Europe – Comparative Lessons from the Federal Experience*, Oxford: Oxford University Press.

McKay, D. (2004) 'The EU as a self-sustaining federation: specifying the constitutional conditions', in L. Dobson and A. Follesdal (eds), *Political Theory and the European Constitution*, London: Routledge, pp. 23–39.

McKay, D. (2005) 'Economic logic or political logic? Economic theory, federal theory and EMU', *Journal of European Public Policy* 12(3): 528–544.

Meehan, E. (2001) 'The constitution of institutions', in K. Nicolaidis and R. Howse (eds), *The Federal Vision: Legitimacy and Levels of Governance in the United States and the European Union*, Oxford: Oxford University Press, pp. 403–12.

Mendez, F. (2005) 'The European Union and cybercrime: insights from comparative federalism', *Journal of European Public Policy* 12(3): 509–527.

Midgaard, K. (1998) 'Consensus, majority decisions, power and autonomy: fragments related to the European Union', *ARENA Working Paper*, 10.

Mill, J.S. (1958) [1861] *Considerations on Representative Government*, New York: Liberal Arts Press.

Miller, D. (2000) *Citizenship and National Identity*, London: Blackwell.

Moravcsik, A. (ed.) (1998) *Centralization or Fragmentation? Europe Facing the Challenges of Deepening Diversity, and Democracy*, New York: Council on Foreign Relations.

Moravcsik, A. (2001) 'Federalism in the European Union: rhetoric and reality', in K. Nicolaidis and R. Howse (eds), *The Federal Vision: Legitimacy and Levels of Governance in the United States and the European Union*, Oxford: Oxford University Press, pp. 161–87.

Moravcsik, A. (2002) 'In defence of the "democratic deficit": reassessing legitimacy in the European Union', *Journal of Common Market Studies* 40(4): 603–24.

Naurin, D. (2004) 'Transparency and legitimacy', in L. Dobson and A. Follesdal (eds), *Political Theory and the European Constitution*, London: Routledge, pp. 139–50.

Nentwich, M. and Falkner, G. (1997) 'The Treaty of Amsterdam: towards a new institutional balance', *European Integration Online Papers (EIOP)* 1(15). http://eiop. or.at/eiop/pdf/1997-015.pdf.

Nicolaidis, K. (2001) 'Conclusion: The federal vision beyond the nation state', in K. Nicolaidis and R. Howse (eds), *The Federal Vision: Legitimacy and Levels of Governance in the United States and the European Union*, Oxford: Oxford University Press, pp. 439–81.

Olsen, T.V. (2004) 'United under God? Or not?', in L. Dobson and A. Follesdal (eds), *Political Theory and the European Constitution*, London: Routledge.

Ostrom, E. (1991) *Governing the Commons: The Evolution of Institutions for Collective Action*, Cambridge: Cambridge University Press.

Papadopoulos, Y. (2005) 'Implementing (and radicalizing) art. I-47.4 of the Constitution: is the addition of some (semi-)direct democracy to the nascent consociational European federation just Swiss folklore?', *Journal of European Public Policy* 12(3): 448–467.

Pettit, P. (1997) *Republicanism: A Theory of Freedom and Government*, Oxford: Clarendon Press.

Pinder, J. (1993) 'The new European federalism: the idea and the achievements', in M. Burgess and A.-G. Gagnon (eds), *Comparative Federalism and Federation: Competing Traditions and Future Directions*, New York: Harvester Wheatsheaf, pp. 45–66.

Rawls, J. (1971) *A Theory of Justice*, Cambridge, MA: Harvard University Press.

Rawls, J. (1993) *Political Liberalism*, New York: Columbia University Press.

Rawls, J. (1999) 'The idea of public reason revisited', in *The Law of Peoples*, Cambridge, MA: Harvard University Press, pp. 129–80.

Reif, K. and Schmitt, H. (1980) 'Nine second order national elections: a conceptual framework for the analysis of European election results', *European Journal of Political Research* 8: 3–44.

Rothstein, B. (1998) *Just Institutions Matter: The Moral and Political Logic of the Universal Welfare State*, Theories of Institutional Design, Cambridge: Cambridge University Press.

Rousseau, J.-J. (1978) [1762] *On the Social Contract*, Roger D. Masters (ed.) and Judith R. Masters (trans.), New York: St Martin's Press.

Sbragia, A.M. (1992) 'Thinking about the European future: the uses of comparison', in A.M. Sbragia (ed.), *Euro-Politics: Institutions and Policymaking in the 'New' European Community*, Washington, DC: Brookings Institution, pp. 257–90.

Sbragia, A.M. and Cram, L. (2002) 'Special issue on "The Institutional Balance and the Future of European Union Governance"', *Governance* 15(3): 309–412.

Scanlon, T.M. (1998) *What We Owe to Each Other*, Cambridge, MA: Harvard University Press.

Scharpf, F.W. (1999) *Governing in Europe: Effective and Democratic?*, Oxford: Oxford University Press.

Schmitter, P.C. (2004) 'Is federalism for Europe a solution or a problem: Tocqueville inverted, perverted or subverted?', in L. Dobson and A. Follesdal (eds), *Political Theory and the European Constitution*, London: Routledge, pp. 10–22.

Sen, A.K. (1967) 'Isolation, assurance and the social rate of discount', *Quarterly Journal of Economics* 81: 112–24.

Shapiro, I. (1996) *Democracy's Place*, Ithaca: Cornell University Press.

Shaw, J. (2003) 'What's in a convention', *Reihe Politikwissenschaft*, Institut Für Höhere Studien (IHS), Wien.

Simeon, R. and Conway, D.-P. (2001) 'Federalism and the management of conflict in multinational societies', in A.-G. Gagnon and J. Tully (eds), *Multinational Democracies*, Cambridge: Cambridge University Press, pp. 338–65.

Smismans, S. (2004) 'The constitutional labelling of "the democratic life of the EU": representative and participatory democracy', in L. Dobson and A. Follesdal (eds), *Political Theory and the European Constitution*, London: Routledge.

Stepan, A. (1999) 'Federalism and democracy: beyond the U.S. model', *Journal of Democracy* 10: 19–34.

Sunstein, C.R. (2001) *Designing Democracy. What Constitutions Do*, Oxford: Oxford University Press.

Swenden, W. (2004) 'Is the European Union in need of a competence catalogue? Insights from comparative federalism', *Journal of Common Market Studies* 42(2): 371–92.

Taylor, M. (1987) *The Possibility of Cooperation*, Cambridge: Cambridge University Press.

Thompson, D.F. and Gutmann, A. (1996) *Democracy and Disagreement*, Cambridge, MA: Harvard University Press.

Thorlakson, L. (2005) 'Federalism and the European party system', *Journal of European Public Policy* 12(3): 468–487.

Trechsel, A.H. (2005) 'How to federalize the European Union … and why bother', *Journal of European Public Policy* 12(3): 397–400.

Tushnet, M. (1996) 'Federalism and liberalism', *Cardozo Journal of International and Comparative Law* 4: 329–44.

Waldron, J. (2000) *Law and Disagreement*, Oxford: Oxford University Press.

Weiler, J.H.H. (1996) 'European neo-constitutionalism: in search of foundations for the European constitutional order', in R. Bellamy and D. Castiglione (eds), *Constitutionalism in Transformation: European and Theoretical Perspectives*, Oxford: Blackwell, pp. 105–21.

Weiler, J.H.H. (1999) *The Constitution of Europe*, Cambridge: Cambridge University Press.

# Notes on contributors

**Andreas Auer** is Professor of Constitutional Law in the Law Faculty of the University of Geneva, Switzerland. He is also the director of the Research and Documentation Centre on Direct Democracy (c2d) at the University of Geneva.

**Klaus von Beyme** is Professor of Political Science at the Institute of Political Science, University of Heidelberg, Germany.

**Francis G. Castles** is Professor of Social and Public Policy at the University of Edinburgh, UK.

**Thomas Christin** is a research assistant at the Institute of Political Science, University of Zurich, Switzerland.

**Andreas Follesdal** is Professor of Philosophy at the Norwegian Centre for Human Rights, University of Oslo, Norway.

**Björn Hörl** is a Ph.D. candidate in the Department of Government, Uppsala University, Sweden.

**Simon Hug** is Professor of Political Science at the Institute of Political Science, University of Zurich, Switzerland.

**Stephan Leibfried** is Professor of Public and Social Policy in the Department of Political Science, University of Bremen, Germany, and co-initiator of CeS and of the TranState Research Centre (Sonderforschungsbereich) of the German Research Foundation (DFG), both at the University of Bremen.

**David McKay** is Professor of Political Science in the Department of Government, University of Essex, UK.

**Fernando Mendez** is a researcher in the Department of Political and Social Sciences, European University Institute, Florence, Italy. He is also a research assistant at the Research and Documentation Centre on Direct Democracy (c2d) of the University of Geneva, Switzerland.

**Herbert Obinger** is Assistant Professor at the Centre for Social Policy Research (CeS), and principal investigator at the TranState Research Centre (Sonderforschungsbereich) of the German Research Foundation (DFG), both at the University of Bremen, Germany.

**Yannis Papadopoulos** is Professor of Political Science at the Institute of Political and International Studies, University of Lausanne, Switzerland.

**Tobias Schulz** is a research assistant at the Institute of Political Science, University of Zurich, Switzerland.

**Lori Thorlakson** is Lecturer at the School of Politics, University of Nottingham, UK and 2004/2005 Jean Monnet Fellow at the SPS Department of the European University Institute, Florence, Italy.

**Alexander H. Trechsel** is Professor of Political Science and holder of the Swiss Chair on Federalism and Democracy at the European University Institute, Florence, Italy. He is also co-director of the Research and Documentation Centre on Direct Democracy (c2d) and director of the e-Democracy Centre (e-DC), both located at the University of Geneva, Switzerland.

**Andreas Warntjen** is a Ph.D. candidate in the Department of Government, London School of Economics and Political Science, UK.

**Arndt Wonka** is a Ph.D. candidate at the Mannheim Centre for European Social Research (MZES), Mannheim University, Germany.

# Index

*For Product Safety Concerns and Information please contact
our EU representative GPSR@taylorandfrancis.com Taylor & Francis
Verlag GmbH, Kaufingerstraße 24, 80331 München, Germany*